MOVIES: A PSYCHOLOGICAL STUDY

But when a dream night after night is brought
Throughout a week, and such weeks few or many
Recur each year for several years, can any
Discern the dream from real life in aught?

JAMES THOMSON

Movies

A PSYCHOLOGICAL STUDY

by Martha Wolfenstein
and Nathan Leites

WITH A NEW PREFACE BY THE AUTHORS

ATHENEUM 1970 NEW YORK

Published by Atheneum
Reprinted by arrangement with The Free Press
Copyright © 1950 by The Free Press
Copyright © 1970 by Martha Wolfenstein and Nathan Leites
All rights reserved
Manufactured in the United States of America by
The Murray Printing Company
Forge Village, Massachusetts
Published in Canada by McClelland and Stewart Ltd.
First Atheneum Edition

NOTE

WE OWE very much to the work of Margaret Mead, to our collaboration with her in the Columbia University Research in Contemporary Cultures, to many delightful and illuminating conversations, and to her ideas in connection with this study. We are indebted to Geoffrey Gorer's work on American culture, and to Gregory Bateson's analyses of films. We have been stimulated by discussions with Marjorie and Irving Janis, and Evelyn and David Riesman. We are grateful to the Motion Picture Association of America, Inc. for their generous help in obtaining the stills which we use as illustrations. We wish to thank the editors of *The Annals of the American Academy of Political and Social Science* for permission to use material from our article in their volume on the motion picture industry.

—*The Authors*

Preface to the
Paperback Edition

THIS BOOK was first published in 1950. When the manuscript was shown to publishers at that time, the authors were told: "People who go to the movies can't read, people who can read don't go to the movies, so who's going to read this?" Evidently the climate of opinion has changed in the last twenty years. What was said earlier about movies would be said today about television. In the meantime movies have ascended in the hierarchy of artistic media. This exemplifies a frequent development in the history of taste, in which what was once vulgar may be taken up by the élite, folk songs, for example; or, conversely, what was once avant-garde may become popular, like Van Gogh reproductions in suburban living rooms.

It should be recalled, however, that there had been a small group of film connoisseurs from the 1930's on, as exemplified in the sponsors and devotees of the Museum of Modern Art Film Library in New York and the Cinémathèque in Paris. Then as now the high-brow approach to films has tended to emphasize directors and film technique, an emphasis which may reflect the influence of art criticism.

The focus in this book is on themes and plots, and the approach derives from psychoanalysis and cultural anthropology. Movies are regarded in the sequence of mythology, stories, and drama, as expressions of often obscure fantasies in the people among whom they are produced and diffused. The ways in which the basic impulses of sex and aggression are worked out, the manifest and latent motives in family relations are structured on one level in real life behavior, on another, complementary level in the shared day-dreams of a particular culture at a particular epoch, as embodied in art forms.

We are living in a period in which the recent past, of a quarter century ago, seems to have been long outgrown, while awareness of the phenomena of that time tends to become vague. The films whose basic plot patterns are elucidated here are of American, British, and French cultures of the late 1940's. They may provide the student of films of the seventies with a base-line for assessing changes which have occurred in the years between. Certain attitudes of the forties will seem outmoded: notably the need to prove that one type of heroine of the melodramas, the good-bad girl, was only apparently involved with men other than the hero, or that the young couple in the comedies never made use of their sexual opportunities in the ways suspected by comically misguided onlookers. At the same time, the degraded position of those censors of morals anticipates the subsequent increase in tolerance of sexual relations between the young, in films as in life. The relation between what is permitted in life and what may be shown in public media has also changed: the chastity of mature heroes and heroines in the films of the forties exceeded that of their real life counterparts, while at present more variegated sexual happenings may be appearing in films (and plays) than commonly occur in life.

The value attached to fantasy life has changed too in recent years. The quest for, and cultivation of individual fantasy has become widespread, notably facilitated by the vogue for drugs among the younger generation. In American films of the forties, appearance and reality were pervasively counterpointed to one another. Forbidden wishes, sexual or aggressive, were realized on the level of false appearances. What was then morally unacceptable materialized as a dream within a dream, with the protagonists struggling to establish its unreality. Some of the boundaries between the forbidden and the bidden have changed in the meanwhile. Perhaps not unrelated to this, uncertainties about what is real and what is unreal have increased, and more fluid shifts occur between the commonplace and the bizarre.

In a culture like ours where high value is placed on novelty, it is easier to see differences than continuities. Viewing movies in temporal perspective, however, one may not only observe what new themes have developed, what old ones have become passé, but also trace what persists, sometimes in disguise. For instance, in American films of the late forties, the characteristic way of dealing with oedipal motives was to project and deny them. A mother-figure wanted to seduce the hero, a father-figure attacked him, while he, ridding himself of both, would set off with his own girl. This was typically the plot of melodramas (e.g., *The Strange Love of Martha Ivers*). In a popular film of the late sixties, *The Graduate,* the hero is seduced by the mother of the girl he later falls in love with, and is attacked by the girl's father. Freeing himself of these entanglements with the older generation, he succeeds in carrying off the young girl. The same plot pattern reappears, but the treatment has become comic, fraught with the misunderstandings which plague a comic hero. The sexual relation of the hero with a mother-figure is now more overt; but this is mitigated by the comic mode, in which the hero is child-like, helpless and not to be blamed for what befalls him. If what was serious may now appear comic, reversals in the opposite direction may also be observed. A motif of American films of the forties was that of unused sexual opportunities, say, Bob Hope or Bing Crosby in some exotic locale, surrounded by harem beauties, sucking lollipops. In a serious film of the late sixties, *Faces,* two middle-aged men spend a wearisomely protracted evening with two call-girls, drinking and arguing, postponing the sexual undertaking on which they are ostensibly bent. The situation is similar, but the mood has changed from light to somber; anxious doubts about the desirability of sex are closer to the surface.

Twenty years ago it was easy to discern differences between the films of the three cultures we compared, American, British, and French. (Italian and Scandinavian films were only beginning to be shown in America; Czech, Polish, Indian, and Japanese films had not yet reached us.) Film-making has since tended to become an international mélange, and the question arises to what extent films now express a more inclusive western, or world culture, to what extent traditional cultural styles retain their distinctive qualities. Whether in a cross-cultural frame of reference, or one of merging cultures developing over time, the problem remains of analyzing the variations on the basic human themes.

M. W.
N. L.

May, 1970

CONTENTS

Contents

INTRODUCTION

IN RECENT years we have been learning increasingly what a large number of people think about politics, what they prefer to eat for breakfast, whether they think it advantageous for a girl to have a job before she gets married, what they think about atomic fission, prefabricated houses, and the length of women's skirts, and what if anything they expect in an after-life. As compared with these samplings of opinion, we know relatively less about people's day-dreams. Day-dreams contain clues to deeper-lying, less articulate aspirations, fears and wishes: a revision of that talk with the boss or last night's date, a career as a singer bowing to the applause of thousands, round-the-world tours on luxury-liners or tramp-steamers, sometimes the fulfilment of more sombre wishes in which the angry exclamation, "I could kill him for that," is literally realized, raising the problem of concealment and escape and fear of punishment, sometimes the overstepping of other boundaries, the pursuit of forbidden love, of a life of crime, of living a dangerous and footloose existence, or of feats of daring, rescues and rewards. Everyone has his own character- istic way of patterning his day-dreams, his favorite themes that come up over and over again. These day-dreams are not merely escapes from the routines of daily life. They represent a working-over of emotional problems, conflicts of love and hate which find in these imaginary careers a variety of solu- tions.

Day-dreams provide the starting point for literary and dra- matic productions. The capacity for transforming day-dreams into such productions gets specialized in poets, playwrights, novelists, script-writers. In their works the original day-dream with its naive self-reference and self-glorification, its personal and often painfully private connotations, undergoes a change. The hero ceases to be just the day-dreamer himself, and as- sumes a separate existence; he becomes someone with whom we all can identify. The thinly sketched characters of the day- dream acquire a more full-bodied life, and inarticulate feel- ing tones are elaborated into concrete events and background details. Through the skillful use of the literary or dramatic medium, the author is able to make his transformed day- dreams accessible to large numbers of people.

These ready-made day-dreams come to occupy a larger place in the conscious experience of most individuals than their more fugitive, private, home-made day-dreams. The capacity for rich day-dream production is largely interfered with in most of us. This is partly because certain disturbing impulses tend to break through in day-dreams. Partly it may be because in a culture like our own, day-dreaming itself is apt to be frowned on as impractical, an unproductive use of one's energies, even a mark of failure. We are aware of the resultant impoverishment of our own day-dream production, so that we take up a novel, tune in on the radio or television, or go to the movies, instead of being able to tune in on our own day-dreams for vivid make-believe experience. The story or drama which thus becomes the shared day-dream of thousands or millions has the further advantage over the private day-dream that we know that others share it, and we feel that it is about others rather than about ourselves. In this way, the embarrassments and anxieties which often haunt private day-dreams are removed.

Where a group of people share a common culture, they are likely to have certain day-dreams in common. We talk for example of the American dream, of which success in the sense of continually rising to better jobs and higher income, and the acquisition of gleaming cars and ice-boxes are components. The common day-dreams of a culture are in part the sources, in part the products of its popular myths, stories, plays and films. Where these productions gain the sympathetic response of a wide audience, it is likely that their producers have tapped within themselves the reservoir of common day-dreams. The corresponding day-dreams, imperfectly formed and only partially conscious, are evoked in the audience and given more definite shape. Numerous young men, for instance, may be developing out of experience and fantasy, out of disconnected impressions and feelings, the image of their ideal girl. A new type of movie heroine appears, and the image comes to life; they see how the girl who fits their half-formulated wishes looks and talks and how she behaves with her man.

In this book we have looked at contemporary American films to see what are the recurrent day-dreams which enter into the consciousness of millions of movie-goers. Critics often remark that films are repetitious, but they rarely specify with any exactitude what the pattern is that is repeated. We frequently hear that there is a great deal of violence in American films. But so is there in Greek tragedy, in Shakespeare, in Grimm's fairy tales, and in Dick Tracy. The point is to discern what form the violence takes, into what plot patterns it is woven: who kills whom, under what circumstances, for what reasons; what are the sequels of crime, who is suspected, who investigates; is the criminal pursued by conscience or by the police; through what agencies is justice done, or by what chance does it miscarry. Similarly with love, we want to see how lovers meet and what difficulties they encounter; who is the dream girl, and what is wrong with the one who fails to get her man; how heroes and heroines react to disappointment in love, whether they get enraged and kill someone, or depressed and commit suicide, or whether they find someone else just as attractive; whether a lost opportunity for love-making is comic or tragic; whether a woman becomes more attractive or is renounced when she appears to be connected with another man.

In part, the recurrent patterns which we find in American films may be consciously contrived, in an attempt to reproduce past successes or to conform with code requirements. But both the positive sanctions of the box-office and the negative ones of the code are probably indicative of more or less widely diffused feelings and attitudes in American culture. In part also, the selection of certain themes and omission of others would seem to be less calculated, expressive of deeper and less conscious emotional tendencies. Within the limits of a code or a general plot formula there remains a choice of a considerable range of possibilities. For instance, it is equally in keeping with the maxim "crime does not pay" to show a Raskolnikov type of hero, suffering from feelings of guilt for his crime, as to show the usual American film melodrama hero who is falsely suspected and who succeeds in clearing himself by discovering the real murderer. It would also be equally compatible with this maxim to show the official police discovering the criminal (as they usually do in British films), as to show the police pursuing the wrong track while the main task of crime investigation devolves on the private investigator (the situation which we find most frequently in American films).

We have tried to point up what is characteristic in American films by comparisons with French and British films. In looking at a French film, one is apt to feel that it is pervaded by a distinctive atmosphere and that it evokes quite a different feeling tone from an American film. We have tried to show in detail what produces these contrasting effects. We do not mean to deny the similarities in these three groups of films, American, French, and British. There are common themes running through all three. However, what we have mainly tried to discover is the different ways in which they handle common themes. For instance, in both French and American films the police are apt to be incompetent, and innocent characters are suspected. But the consequences of such a situation are markedly different in the French and American treatments. In American films, for the most part, the falsely accused is intensely energetic on his own behalf, carries on his own investigations, which are much more efficient than those of the police, and succeeds in clearing himself. The atmosphere is one of suspense, pursuit, and mounting tension, in which the hero must ward off violent assaults while trying to find out the facts of the case. Since he is usually quite competent in both these activities, the result is that the danger which has surrounded him throughout the film is suddenly dissipated at the end, and he is ready to start a bright new life. In a French film, the falsely accused may attempt suicide or allow himself to be captured without a struggle. Ironically, the real murderer may attempt in vain to convince the authorities of his guilt. A feeling of disappointment and reproach seems to be expressed against the authorities: how little they understand or care to understand. There is also implicitly the opposite of the American feeling that it is possible to clear oneself completely: who can say that he is altogether innocent? Again, a recurrent situation in both French and American films is that of missing an opportunity for love-making. In French films, this situation tends to be fraught with regret; the opportunity once lost does not come again. In American films, such a missed opportunity usually occurs in a comic setting. It is almost invariably a happy portent for the couple, who will have the same opportunity again when they are ready to take advantage of it.

In this book we shall look systematically at such regularities and variations in the treatment of certain major relationships. The first chapter focuses on the relation between lovers and loved ones, and details how the course of love appears in the films. The second deals with parents and children and other familial relations. It shows how manifest parent figures are depicted and also attempts to uncover some of the latent feelings in relation to parents which are expressed in more disguised form. The third chapter is about violence and analyzes the relations between killers and victims, the interplay between the criminal and the investigator, and the ways in which the agents of justice deal with the guilty and innocent. The fourth chapter deals with a less obvious but pervasive relation, that between those who look and those who are looked at. It has to do with the experience of the excluded onlooker, the role of onlookers who are deceived by misleading appearances, as well as with the particular relation between onlookers and professional public performers. In the concluding chapter we attempt to formulate and to evoke the essential drama of each of the three groups of films which we have considered.

MOVIES: A PSYCHOLOGICAL STUDY

1

LOVERS AND LOVED ONES

THE PROBLEM of love in current American films is
how to make it safe but keep it interesting. The fatal men
and women, vamps and seducers, who, surviving from nine-
teenth century literature, strutted their little hour in the
early films, seem to be quite dead, with stakes of aspen firmly
piercing their vampire hearts. Sexual wickedness has dwin-
dled to become a mere external ornament, a forepleasure
stimulus to wholesome love. Just as we have seen nice girls
assume the make-up formerly associated with painted ladies,
so current film heroines present a façade of wickedness which
is easily shown to be deceptive. The hero is immune to the
blandishments of the vamp since the nice girl has an equal

stimulus value. The vamp has degenerated into a comic figure; she has gone into the lingerie business, providing black lace night-gowns for rosy-cheeked brides (*The Sailor Takes a Wife*).

American films make a heroine exciting by a procedure similar to that of the charm school. They take a sturdy, wholesome girl, fit her into a tight and revealing black gown, and teach her to hold her stomach in and her bosom out and to smile ambiguously. The films further set her in circumstances which make her suspect. She appears to be involved in crime, associated with bad men. She moves in an underworld milieu and sings in a shady night-club. This is essential to her attractiveness; it relieves her of the dullness of the obviously good girl. However, it is equally necessary to her acceptability in the end that these dubious involvements be shown to be merely apparent. The hero takes the beautiful spy whom he has met in the Orient back to his farm in Iowa and she is last seen perched on top of a hay wagon with hay-seeds in her hair (*Rogues' Regiment*). The before and after pictures of the charm school appear in reverse order; the shift in the films is from black satin to gingham. But there is no transformation in the heroine's personality. The potentiality which she reveals in the end was always there, only the hero was in doubt about it, and it is this which has made her interesting.

American films thus provide an eat-your-cake-and-have-it solution to the old conflict between sacred and profane love. The exciting qualities of the bad woman and the comradely loyalty of the good one are all wrapped up in one prize package, which we have called the good-bad girl. It is generally characteristic of American films that badness should be disposed of as mere appearance. Just as the heroine so often appears to be a bad girl but turns out to be good, the hero in melodramas is often accused of crimes, but in the end succeeds in clearing himself. In either case there is no development of character, but rather a process of proof, a breaking down of a deceptive appearance and a demonstration of the facts to all concerned.

The seducer who in early films preyed on trusting young females, leading them into mock marriages and leaving them with illegitimate babies, is equally out. The heroines of current films know their way around too well to be susceptible to such devices. Correspondingly the good man who formerly assumed the role of protector of women has degenerated into a comic figure. Only the comic hero imagines he must rescue the girl who is more competent than he to cope with any emergency. While he tremblingly closes his eyes and shoots not too hopefully, the heroine drops the attacker with her well-aimed six-shooter (*The Paleface*).

The solution of love problems tends to be phrased mainly in terms of female types and functions. Thus two current love requirements, which in part conflict with one another, find satisfaction in various film heroines. There is on the one hand the impact of what we call goodness morality, which leads to high estimation of the charms of wickedness as well as to guilt about pursuing them. The good-bad girl represents a solution to the problem which goodness morality poses to the man. On the other hand, expressing a more recent trend, there are the demands of what we call fun morality: you've got to have fun (whether you like it or not). If you are not having fun, you must ask yourself what is wrong with you. The strength of impulse, which seemed so assured when faced with the barriers of goodness morality, often dwindles before the imperative of fun morality. A relatively new type of heroine has appeared to help the man over this difficulty. She boldly takes the initiative in love relations and assures the man of her confidence in his masculinity even when he is not proving it. She estimates appraisingly the quantity of pleasure produced by a kiss, but does not seem to demand any all-out letting go of emotion, which might be difficult to achieve. Thus she approaches sex with a man's point of view, helps the man who is inhibited when confronted by an excess of femininity, and makes the requisite achievement of fun seem not too much of a strain. We might suppose that some of the most impactful heroines of current films would combine these two functions: that of the good-bad girl who appears attractive through her seeming relations with other men, and that of the girl who takes the initiative towards men, demonstrating a masculine approach, and not making too many demands on the man.

The image of the film heroine seems to be in part conjured up in response to otherwise incompletely satisfied wishes. In part this image seems to develop from attempts to assimilate certain aspects of real life behavior. Numerous film heroines show tendencies to direct the lives of their men. The destructive potentiality of such behavior breaks through only in exceptional cases. Mainly this potentiality is guarded against by making the directional activity of the woman benevolent. She is like the mother who educates her child to use his capacities to best advantage. Women tend to be much more competent than men in American films. However, this is rarely an occasion either for female domination or for male resentment. The competent woman arranges things so that her man can succeed. She correctly assesses his talents and sees that opportunities are provided for him to use them. He is then able to succeed on his merits and she gives him full credit for this. There are few cases where women appear more favorably than in this educational role. However, the woman must be careful not to use her superior competence in a high-brow, independent, non-man-orientated way; if she tries this, she will be severely penalized.

Love relations in British and French films often present contrasting pictures to those we find in American films. The issue between good and bad women in French films tends to be more tragic. The bad woman retains the superior charm, and the man is apt to suffer serious disappointment through her. He begins by seeing her in an idealized light, but eventually the painful discovery of her promiscuity or other wickedness is forced upon him. This sequence is the reverse of that in American films, where doubts about the apparently bad woman are evoked first, while the hero in the end can see her as he would wish her to be. Thus French films dramatize the breaking down of the ideal image of the woman, American films, the justification of this image. British films in contrast to both American and French tend to see women more as possible victims of men's violence or betrayal. Correspondingly they give more emphasis to the dual potentialities of men, as attackers or rescuers. The unexciting good man who stands by is a more valued character in British than in American films because he is more needed. The cautionary images of the beautiful girl found strangled in the park, of a girl about to jump off a moonlit bridge because she is driven to distraction by a violent and moody man, or simply of a beautiful blond head bowed in suffering, are recurrent motifs in British films. The tenderness of the hero is given depth since it guards against his potentiality for causing such suffering; gentle as he appears, he may be suspected of the murder in the park, and his image is enhanced by the suggestion of this possibility (*October Man*). In British films the male character bears the interesting ambiguity which in American films is associated with the good-bad girl.

Love never runs down in American films. If it is true love it remains as unaltered through the years as if it had been wrapped in cellophane and kept in the deep-freezer. If feelings ever change in a relationship, this can only be because it was not true love. It was based on a mistaken premise which later gets disproved. Thus again a process of proof is substituted for a transformation of feelings. Love is shown to be an erroneous conclusion from the revised premises, and the man (it is usually a man) who has made the false inference revises the reckoning and finds he has been in love with the right girl all along and never really loved the wrong one. Feelings are thus on the whole easily rectified, and a desperate involvement with the wrong person, someone bad or disappointing, tends to appear as either comic or pathological.

There is little risk of suffering through love in American films. The impulsive, unreasoningly tenacious aspects of love, which have provided material for literary and dramatic plots elsewhere, find little expression here. Partly, as we have just said, attachments are flexible. Once it is demonstrated that a man or woman is not the right one, not entirely satisfactory, the feeling for them is discovered to be not really love, that is, it evaporates. At the same time, or perhaps even before this, the right person has appeared, so that there is rarely a gap of lovelessness or loneliness. The wealth of opportunities remains boundless. Whenever life may look discouraging, a beautiful girl turns up at the next moment. If the hero and heroine pass up an opportunity, or several opportunities, to get together, they will always get another chance. This is in marked contrast to British, and particularly French films where a lost opportunity is not recapturable and becomes an occasion for endless regret. In French films, a reproach seems to be expressed against the malice of fortune which fails to provide the opportunity when it is wanted. British films seem to stress the restraint of the characters, who may not be impulsive enough to overcome obstacles a second time. American films express confidence both in the plenitude of opportunities and in the adequate strength of impulses. However there also seems to be another reason why the lost opportunity is comic rather than tragic in American films. There appears to be a feeling of relief in not having to go through with amorous requirements. Euphoria in escaping from sexual exigencies is frequently illustrated in comedy. The comic hero who sucks a lollypop while surrounded by harem beauties symbolizes this. Thus the absence of danger in sexual impulses is related to the possibility and welcomeness of intermissions from their demands.

In love, as in the expression of other emotions, American films tend to exempt the hero and heroine from responsibility for their impulses. The wishes of the central characters are apt to be carried out by apparently uncontrollable external agencies. The young couple are thrown together by the swaying of the train, or find themselves assigned to the same berth by a whimsical ticket agent. In the same way, as we shall see, trains, cars, boats, wind, water, unpredictable circumstances, or unrelated characters dispose of the hero's rivals or enemies. There is a marked sway of omnipotence fantasies in these plots, in which the outer world, behaving in a seemingly uncontrollable way, acts to fulfil the hero's wishes without his assuming responsibility for them. On behalf of the hero, risks ranging from humiliation for a refused love gesture to inculpation in a crime of violence are thus warded off.

In this chapter we begin with a consideration of the problem of sacred and profane love and its various solutions in recent films, particularly in the images of different types of women. We proceed to the problem of the transformation of feelings: whether it is possible to love more than once. This is followed by observations on the distinctive educational role of the heroine in relation to her man in American films, ...d an analysis of the relatively new style of heroine who assumes the initiative in a love relation. Finally we consider the general attitude towards love expressed in films, the place assigned to it in the range of the pleasures life affords, and. the estimation of its hazards.

§ THE GOOD-BAD GIRL

THE difficulty of choosing between a good and a bad girl is one of the major problems of love-life in western culture. The problem is to fuse two feelings which men have found it hard to have in relation to the same woman. On the one hand, there are sexual impulses, which a man may feel to be bad, and which he may find it hard to associate with a woman whom he considers admirable. The image, and the actuality, of the "bad" woman arises to satisfy sexual impulses which men feel to be degrading. On the other hand, there are affectionate impulses evoked by women who resemble the man's mother or sister, "good" women. A good girl is the sort that a man should marry, but she has the disadvantage of not being sexually stimulating.

There are various possible solutions to this conflict. The attempt may be made to satisfy one of these impulses at the expense of the other, to satisfy them both but in different directions, or to combine the two impulses in a single relationship. Exclusive devotion to a good woman constituted the stock image of Victorian marriage. Oppressed by the sway of the Angel in the House, rebels might go to the opposite extreme of seeking only prostitutes. In the supposedly frequent pattern of various continental European cultures, a man might keep both a wife and a mistress. Satisfaction was thus sought for both sexual and affectionate feelings, but it was not supposed that one woman could satisfy both. Another presumably frequent arrangement has been for a young man to have relations with bad women up to marriage, after which there is a substantial shift of attachment towards the good woman. In the reverse possibility the established husband and father of a family breaks away, or is diverted by a wicked seductress.

Efforts to combine the two components produce a variety of real or imagined feminine types. The image of the bad woman may be transformed so that she becomes the object of more ideal feelings. The prostitute may be redeemed by love, as in the case of Camille. Her prostitution may be compensated for by a saintly character, as in the case of Sonia, in Dostoyevsky's *Crime and Punishment,* who walked the streets only to save her family from starvation. Her involvement in low life may seem irrelevant to the essential nature of the beautiful woman who passes through it detached and unaffected. Or the attempt may be made to glorify the bad woman, to see her as a priestess of a pleasure unspoiled by scruples (Swinburne's Dolores). Proceeding in the other direction, an effort may be made to infuse the image of the good woman with some qualities of her opposite. The good woman may appear for a time to be bad, so that she acquires an exciting aura which is not entirely dissipated when her goodness becomes established. Or the good woman may become transformed—the business-like career girl takes off her glasses. The dull wife may learn a lesson from a lover and return to her husband more pleasurable.

The man may see the beloved woman in different ways. He may mistakenly form an idealized picture of a bad woman, and suffer disillusionment. The good girl may appear to him as bad, and the eventual revelation may be in her favor. The woman also may present herself in various ways. The bad woman may conceal her badness; the good woman may pretend to be bad, or make no effort to conceal what, misleadingly, looks bad. A variety of dramatic possibilities results from combinations of the different feminine types, the ways they present themselves, and the sequence of impressions that the man gets. While Camille was being transformed by love, she deceived her lover into believing that she was still bad. His image of her declined at the same time that her character became ennobled.

Current American films have produced the image of the good-bad girl. She is a good girl who appears to be bad. She does not conceal her apparent badness, and uncertainty about her character may persist through the greater part of the film. The hero suspects that she is bad, but finally discovers this was a mistaken impression. Thus he has a girl who has attracted him by an appearance of wickedness, and whom in the end he can take home and introduce to Mother.

Usually the good-bad girl appears to be promiscuous, or to be involved with a bad man. Occasionally she appears guilty of theft or murder. The title character in *Gilda* (after whom a Bikini bomb was named) appears quite promiscuous through the greater part of the film; in the end she turns out to be a faithful and devoted woman who has never loved anyone but the hero. Gilda and the hero had been lovers before the action of the film begins and had separated because of his jealousy. When they meet again the hero has become the right-hand man of a big gambler and international schemer; Gilda has become the gambler's wife. The hero is tortured not only by seeing Gilda as his boss's wife, but also by her strenuous flirtations with other men. Eventually the boss disappears and is considered dead. Gilda has tried to persuade the hero of her continued love for him and he now agrees to marry her. But he does not believe in her. To punish her for her apparent infidelities to the boss and to himself, he holds her a virtual prisoner. His strong-arm men follow her wherever she goes and forcibly dissuade her admirers. One night Gilda appears at the swank night-club adjoining the gambling casino which the hero now runs. She sings and dances seductively and begins stripping off her clothes (she doesn't get much farther than her long black gloves) while men from the audience rush forward to assist her. The hero, who enters just in time to get a glimpse of the climax of the performance, sends his men to carry her out.

While episodes of this sort present the image of the beautiful promiscuous woman, they are interspersed with occasions when Gilda pleads with the hero to believe that she has never loved anyone but him. In the end it turns out that what the hero saw was a deceptive appearance, and what Gilda told him was quite true. An understanding police official, who interests himself in their affairs, persuades the hero of this. All the carryings-on of Gilda with other men have been motivated by her love for the hero, whom she wished to hold by making him jealous. Once this has been explained to the hero by an impartial observer, everything is cleared up.

The hero's distress when he believed in Gilda's promiscuity did not impel him to look for a more quiet domestic type. In the end he finds that he can eat his cake and have it. He gets the girl with the aura of innumerable men in her life, and the guarantee that she is a good girl and belongs to him alone.

In *Till the End of Time,* the hero has several occasions for suspecting the heroine of promiscuousness, but each time this is successfully explained away. While the image of Gilda seemed intensely bad till the final explanation, the image of this heroine fluctuates back and forth between apparent lapses and virtuous explanations. The figure of the beloved woman who continually allays doubts about her fidelity with plausible explanations is familiar. Only in other versions this woman was deceiving her man. His suspicions were well founded, and her explanations were false. In the case of the good-bad girl this is reversed. What the man sees turns out to be illusory; what the woman tells him is true. Deceptive circumstances have been substituted for the deceiving woman. And the denouement in which the trusting man realizes that his beloved is false has been replaced by the happy outcome in which the suspicious hero learns that the seemingly bad girl is really good.

In *The Big Sleep,* the heroine appears involved with a shady night-club owner, who turns out to be a gangster and murderer. The hero, a private detective, who has been hired by the heroine's father, finds the girl trying to block his investigations. Her efforts seem related to her connection with the night-club owner. The hero appears unexpectedly at the night-club and finds the heroine there singing with the band and apparently very much in her element. Later she wins a lot of money at roulette. The night-club owner seems reluctant to let her leave when she is so much ahead. Under pressure from the hero she leaves, but is immediately held up by the night-club owner's thugs. The hero is convinced that this is all an act put on to conceal from him some guilty partnership between the girl and the night-club owner, to fool him into thinking that their relations are unfriendly. After more

confusion of this sort, it finally comes out that it is not the
night-club owner whom the heroine is trying to shield, but
her unfortunate sister who has committed a murder. Since
the night-club owner knows about this killing he is able to
blackmail the heroine. It was to pay the blackmail that she
had to come to the night-club so often.

In *The Strange Love of Martha Ivers,* the combination of
badness, seeming badness, and goodness in the heroine is
quite complicated. The girl has just come out of jail, to
which she had been sent for stealing a fur coat. She explains
to the hero that the coat was given to her by a boy-friend who
later disappeared. Thus she did not steal the coat, but wasn't
she rather friendly with the thief? In another episode she is
forced by the wicked district attorney, who is still pursuing
her for the crime she didn't commit, to play a rather mean
trick on the hero. She gets the hero to go with her to a café
where, by pre-arrangement, a man appears who claims to be
her husband and demands that the hero come outside and
fight. The hero is then forced into a waiting automobile in
which several thugs beat him up. The heroine later has a
chance to explain the whole thing to the hero; she really has
no husband, and so on. In this series of bad appearances and
explanatory denials, one or two bad things remain that are
not explained. However, since the girl repeatedly turns out
to be so much better than she seemed, there is probably the
feeling that with a few more explanations, for which the film
perhaps didn't have time, she could be shown to be completely good.

The good-bad girl has supplanted the vamp of earlier
American films. The vamp created the illusion of exclusive
passionate attachment to the hero, but was in the end found
out to be untrue. The hero at first believed in her, later became disillusioned. The picture was the reverse of that of the
good-bad girl, whose apparent badness rouses the hero's suspicions but is later explained away. In a Greta Garbo film of
the 20's, *Flesh and the Devil,* the hero fell in love with a

seductive woman who responded passionately to the advances she provoked. He was forced to go away and, during his absence, she married his best friend. On the hero's return a bitter quarrel arose between the two men. They were about to shoot each other in a duel, but, suddenly remembering their old friendship, fell into each other's arms. The wicked woman was, by an appropriate accident, drowned. The dangerousness of the vamp was associated with the man's intolerance for sharing her with other men. Her seductive appearance and readiness for love carried a strong suggestion that there had been and might be other men in her life. But while the hero loved her, he excluded this possibility from his thoughts. When the proof of her infidelity was established, he renounced her. The good-bad girl is associated with a greater tolerance for sharing the woman, although this sharing remains subject to limitations. The hero believes that the woman he loves is involved with other men. While this disturbs him, it does not drive him away. In effect, the woman's attraction is enhanced by her association with other men. All that is needed to eliminate unpleasantness is the assurance that these relations were not serious (only apparent).

The good-bad girl is perhaps a melodramatic reflection of the American popular girl, whose attractiveness is directly proportional to the number of men she goes out with. The American attitude is in contrast to that of cultures where attractive women are secluded, where men feel that the attractiveness of a beautiful woman for other men is a liability. The man who guards the beautiful woman whom he loves from the eyes of others believes that if they only look at her they will start making plans to go to bed with her. American courtship patterns are based on a series of breaks between looking and going to bed. It is possible to look and go no further, to kiss and go no further, to pet and go no further. The attractiveness of the popular girl derives from her association with many men, combined with the assurance that she has not gone too far with them. In the case of her movie counterpart, the good-bad girl, the hero's doubts express uneasy fantasies about the possibly more serious involvement of the girl with these other men. The films express the man's uncertainty about whether the girl has only gone so far and no further, and the difficulty of holding in check his own fantasies about her relations with other men. The happy outcome reassures us that the system works. The girl's relations with other men were only apparent (did not go too far sexually). Her attractiveness for other men then ceases to arouse anxiety and becomes positive. Where the vamp evoked a complete sexual response, and so could not be shared without intense jealousy, the good-bad girl is sexy in a different sense. Her attractiveness is not in her inducement to passion, but in her (harmless) association with other men.

In comedies it may be manifest that the girl's associations with other are harmless. She may, to the knowledge of the audience, construct a pretense of such relations in order to interest the man she wants. The desired man may see through the pretense, and nevertheless be favorably influenced by the appearance of the girl with other men. In *Every Girl Should Be Married,* the hero is mostly aware that the heroine has contrived the semblance of a relationship with a rich playboy in order to make herself attractive to him. Eventually she draws a third man into her scheme, a hillbilly radio comedian who poses as her old sweetheart from back home. Although the hero also recognizes the comedian, he is moved to oust these pseudo-rivals and claim the girl. Her desperate efforts to make herself appear to be associated with other men achieve the desired result. (The hero's positive reaction despite his awareness of what goes on behind the scenes appears related to a larger trend. There seems to be a fairly widespread American tendency not to devalue an effect though one sees how it is achieved—whether it is the technique of a movie trick shot, or the beautiful complexion derived from assiduous application of a certain soap.)

Another film reflection of the popular girl with her many

1. America: Got a match? (*The Strange Love of Martha Ivers*)

2. The American wish: The dominant woman is benevolent. *(The High Wall)*

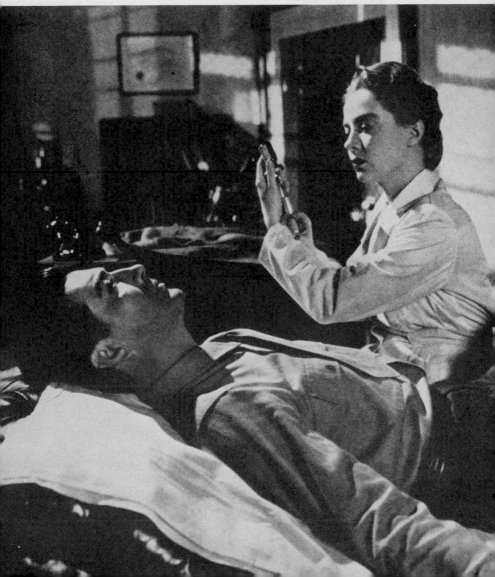

3. The American fear: The dominant woman is destructive. (*The Macomber Affair*)

4. America: The missed opportunity is comic. (*Road to Morocco*)

5. Britain: The missed opportunity is tragic. *(Brief Encounter)*

6. America: The son judges the father. (*All My Sons*)

7. Britain: The father judges the son. (*Notorious Gentleman*)

8. France: The son will become like the father he fights. *(Marius)*

9. America: The hero and his boss—who will kill whom? *(The Big Clock)*

10. America: The Private Eye—hazards of investigation. *(The Big Sleep)*

11. France: Hazards of justice—death of the innocent. *(Panique)*

12. America: Killing with a purpose. (*The Postman Always Rings Twice*)

13. Britain: Killing for revenge. (*The Upturned Glass*)

14. America: There's less than meets the eye. *(Gilda)*

15. France: The hero reenacts his love disappointment. *(Les Enfants du Paradis)*

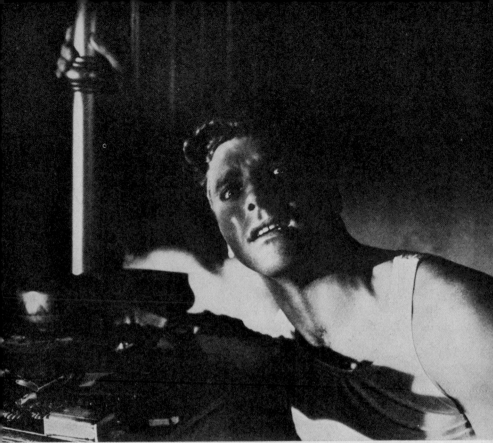

16. The American nightmare: The hero awaits the killers. (*The Killers*)

escorts is a frequent dance pattern in musicals where a girl dancer appears with a chorus of men. Her relation to them is stylized and superficial as she dances with each in rapid succession, not favoring one more than another. The male chorus alternate their attentions to the girl with routines in which they dance together in amicable accord. This parallels a frequent comedy theme of playful woman-sharing which has no negative effect on the friendly relations between the men. The girl's potentiality for bestowing true love on one man alone may be expressed by her singing, while she dances with several dozen men, a song whose sentiment is that of exclusive love: "You do something to me that nobody else can do" (*Night and Day*). Thus in her dance the girl gratifies the wish of the man who will eventually win her to see her associated with other men, while in her song she satisfies his demand for assurance that she is not emotionally involved in these other relations.

The good-bad girl is an American product; the vamp was an import. As sex is no longer associated with the strange woman, it ceases to be admittedly mysterious and dangerous. What was formerly dangerous, but no longer appears so, frequently becomes comic. The foreign vamp now appears mainly as a comic figure. Her charms are revealed as a set of obvious tricks, as we see her dimming the lights and spraying perfume around the room. She seems to be trying too hard, the more so as her tricks prove ineffective. In *She Wouldn't Say Yes,* the heroine, who wants to get rid of the hero, arranges for him to have dinner alone in her apartment with a foreign woman called Allura, who has conceived a passion for him. Allura appears at their rendezvous in a tight satin gown, half-closes her eyes in apparent love-sickness, and expresses her warm feelings with an exuberant foreign accent. Her efforts to envelop the hero lead to his running away from her while she chases him around the table. In *The Sailor Takes a Wife,* the hero similarly finds it easy to resist a too obviously alluring Rumanian with a heavy accent and an exotically furnished apartment.

The degeneration of sexual dangers into comedy is expressed in the changed use of the symbolism of falling. In an early vamp movie, *A Fool There Was,* the hero has been lured away from his family and respectable life by a wicked, seductive woman. As he becomes increasingly debauched, a symbolic passage shows him falling down a flight of stairs. In current films, a fairly frequent comic episode shows the hero and heroine, in an early stage of their courtship, falling together, while skiing or at a dance. This is a favorable portent for the future of their relationship. The man was being made to fall by the dangerous woman. The wholesome young couple are falling for each other.

The disappearance of the vamp, except in the comic version, is illustrated in the change of movie spy types from World War I to World War II. The earlier spy, like Mata Hari, was an irresistible woman who lured men from the opposite side to betray their secrets to her. She was cold and ruthless until the day when she fell in love with one of her victims. At this point her employers had to kill her; she was no longer useful. In contrast to this version of the prostitute ennobled by love, World War II women spies tend to be clean-cut American girls doing a patriotic job. They do not have to be redeemed by love since they are good all along; and they are in love with men on their own side. The enterprising girl from home is thus substituted for the alluring foreign woman. A foreign woman spy may be a forbidding person who goes around most of the time in men's clothes. (*The House on 92nd Street.*)

In *OSS,* the recruiting agent tries to kiss the future woman spy at their first meeting. When she slaps his face he hires her. In the course of her work, she gradually falls in love with a fellow-worker. She is also called upon to dupe a Nazi officer, but a minimum of amorousness is required for this. She chiefly spends her time with him modeling his bust in explosive clay. The Nazi takes the bust on a train with him and it blows him up, together with an important tunnel.

While *Notorious* retains the most vestiges of the spy who uses sex as a lure, its heroine, unlike Mata Hari, is not a professional bad woman. At the beginning of the movie she is temporarily leading a wild life as a reaction to a personal disillusionment. The hero succeeds in recruiting her as a spy because of her patriotism. She immediately concludes her interlude of debauchery and conceives a deep and lasting love for the hero. They would proceed happily as lovers and comrades if she did not get the assignment to marry an important elderly Nazi in order to spy on him. The hero for a while cannot realize that her heart is not in her work. When he finally becomes aware of it, they are happily reunited. The heroine of *Mata Hari* was a professional vamp without any convictions, who seduced the hero and robbed him of secret documents, discovering too late that she loved him. The betrayal of the man by the old type of vamp was symbolized by the scene in which Mata Hari forced her lover to blow out the lamp in front of the ikon his mother gave him; she wanted the apartment in complete darkness so that her accomplices could steal the papers while she was distracting her victim with kisses. Greta Garbo, as Mata Hari, first appeared to the man she was going to betray as she was performing an allegedly Hindu dance before an idol. Ingrid Bergman, the round-cheeked spy in *Notorious,* pursues her acquaintance with her Nazi victim during brisk canters before breakfast.

In the place of the vamp there now appears a new type of bad girl who exactly resembles the good-bad girl, except that she really is all the things the good-bad girl seems to be. (The same actress may play either interchangeably; for instance, Lizbeth Scott in *The Strange Love of Martha Ivers* and *Dead Reckoning.*) The bad girl has no appeal which the good-bad girl does not also have, but she has a considerable disadvantage. The good-bad girl has demonstrated that it is possible to get sex and a square deal at the same time. The man no longer has to pay the current bad girl's price. In the majority of films where the issue about the goodness and badness of women is raised, the good-bad girl is the main female character. Sometimes she has no other woman to compete with. More often she is opposed by a bad girl, over whom she regularly wins out. The cards are stacked. The vamp offered excitement and passion not otherwise available. The man was tempted away from the less stimulating good woman, and concealed from himself the indications of the vamp's wickedness. His progress was from idealization to disillusionment. The current bad girl does not start with any advantage. She looks suspicious, just as the good-bad girl does. In the end, the suspicions about her are confirmed. It is only where the bad girl is opposed to a good girl that she has a chance to win. In *The Killers,* the hero drops his colorless and loyal girl-friend when he meets the glamorous gangster's moll. The bad girl's loss of power over men is frequently indicated by the fact that, while she is unable to get the man she wants, she is pursued by others whom she detests.

Among the bad girls who come to no good is the hero's wife in *The Blue Dahlia.* The hero returns from the war to find her drunk in the midst of a wild party, and on terms of obvious intimacy with an older man who later turns out to be a gangster. After the party has dispersed she tells her husband that their baby was killed in an auto accident caused by her drunken driving. In *The Big Sleep,* the sister of the heroine is a nymphomaniac and has killed a man who repulsed her advances. The title character in *The Strange Love of Martha Ivers* has a long list of crimes to her credit. She has murdered her aunt and let someone else hang for it; she has taken possession of the vast fortune of the murdered aunt; she has married a man she loathes in order to cover up her crimes and has driven him to drink by her contempt. When the hero appears she immediately wants to make love to him, a gesture which, according to an unchecked statement of her husband's, is habitual with her. And she attempts alternately to kill the hero and to get the hero to murder her husband. In each of these cases, the bad girl loses out to a good-bad girl who is equally attractive and less harrowing to have around.

The most forbidding feature of the bad girl, even more than promiscuity or crime, is that she coldly uses men, or at least is willing to sacrifice them for her own advantage. The bad woman in *Johnny Angel* has married a rich ship-owner whom she despises, and forces him to board a ship and kill the whole crew to steal a cargo of gold for her. She shows no regard for his protest that being on a ship makes him sick. In *The Killers*, the bad woman allows the hero to go to jail for a theft she committed, and then dupes him into taking the blame for a grand larceny from which she and her husband get all the benefit.

For the current bad girl love comes second. More brutal than the old-style roué who cast aside the women of whom he tired, she is ready, at any moment, to kill the man she loves if he becomes a threat to the security of her criminal career. The murderess in *Framed* is making coffee for the hero, whom she loves. As he seems to be making some objection to helping her cover up her crimes, she is about to put poison in his coffee. The conversation takes a more reassuring turn and she puts the poison back on the shelf. They proceed to an affectionate breakfast. In *Dead Reckoning*, the girl who has committed murder and grand larceny is secretly married to her partner in crime. She falls in love with the incorruptible hero, but tries to kill him when he uncovers the truth about her. These girls justify their actions by stories of early deprivations. They had to work as waitresses or model beautiful clothes for other women to wear. They have felt these hardships as so cruel and unusual that anything is justified which insures escape from such a life. Where the vamp was a kept woman, the current bad girl uses her lovers as witting or unwitting partners in crime. Coldly self-centered and controlled, she does not run the risk, as the vamp did,

that unanticipated feelings of love will disrupt her exploitative way of life. She is not subject to any conflict; it is quite
clear what comes first. However, she is not a woman with
only one interest. As long as her man is useful to her income
and safety, or at least not dangerous to them, the pleasure
she gets from her relation with him occupies a major place
in her life. The hero, on his side, suffers no conflict in relation to her. The lover of the vamp tended to be drawn into
a guilty abandonment of honor for her sake. The hero who
loves the current bad girl turns her over to the police as soon
as he learns about her crimes. In *Framed,* the hero turns up
with the police just as the girl is taking out of a safety deposit
box her long-dreamed-of fortune, which she had offered to
share with him. In *Dead Reckoning,* the girl tries to persuade
the hero to go away with her instead of turning her over to
the police. He refuses and she tries to shoot him. They struggle, the car in which they are driving is wrecked, and she is
fatally injured. In the hospital, he holds her hand while she
dies. The hero may resist the bad girl even though there is
no one to take her place, as in the two films just mentioned.
In a world where the good-bad girl is an ever-present possibility, he presumably feels no need to accept the unfavorable
terms proposed by the bad girl.

These bad girls, however, are not entirely unsympathizable. The world threatened to withhold from them the luxury
which they felt was their due, and they look very beautiful
in the furs and jewels which they had to commit murder to
obtain. While the hero brings love into their lives for the
first time, and this really matters, they cannot abandon their
previous interests. In this they are unlike the vamp or prostitute redeemed by love, who abandons all her previous aims.
The bad girl tries to satisfy two sets of values, and does not
lose sight of the first for the sake of the second. The inade-
quacy of love without the material comforts that one must
murder to obtain is demonstrated by the bad girl in *The
Postman Always Rings Twice.* She and the hero, having

fallen in love, run away together, leaving behind her aging husband and his promising lunchroom business. As they trudge along the highway where fast cars pass them by, the girl, an ex-waitress, is overwhelmed by the meagerness of their prospects, and insists they turn back. It thus becomes necessary for them to kill her husband in order to take over the business. The financial gain is somewhat more modest than in the case of the previous bad girls, and requires only a single crime, rather than a series of crimes. Having solved her economic problem in this way the girl would have been content to settle down with the man she loved. This is an exceptional case where the hero succumbs to the bad girl's efforts to lead him into crime. In contrast to the man lured by the vamp, who exploited and then abandoned him, this hero, but for an accident, might have lived happily ever after with his partner in crime.

A type related to the bad girl is the home-digger. This is an intensely attractive and emotionally cold girl, suffering from humble circumstances, who is ready to marry any man who will give her the comforts she requires. The beautiful waitress in *The Fallen Angel* encourages the hero, whom she does not love, to join in the competition for her. She differs from the previous girls in that her financial aims are quite modest and do not lead to crime. Instead of taking care of herself, she demands, in the face of a world that seems grudging and untrustworthy, that she be taken care of. While equally free from conscience, she lacks the boldness of the bad girls, and their capacity for love.

American ways of fusing goodness and badness in women start with a good woman and spice her up. The major result of this procedure is the good-bad girl whom we have described, whose goodness is concealed behind a façade of badness. An alternative procedure is to take a girl who appears too good and make her more sexy. In older films like *She Married Her Boss,* the tailored, bespectacled and efficient secretary raged and suffered while her boss carried on with fluffy blondes. Eventually she took off her glasses, put on a décolleté evening gown which made the boss look at her for the first time, got drunk, flirted, and ended up in his arms. Current comedies on this theme tend to avoid having the woman unattractive to begin with. Rather they present a girl who seems very attractive, but who temporarily alienates her man by her sexual unreadiness. She must then demonstrate added charms to win him back.

In *The Sailor Takes a Wife,* the hero falls in love at first meeting with the heroine, a popular hostess in a servicemen's canteen. They are married almost immediately. On the wedding night she appears in "jamies" with her hair in pigtails. When the sailor laughs at her outfit, she indignantly locks the bedroom door. The next night she wears herself out dancing at the canteen, and falls asleep on the couch the moment she comes home. In this more literal presentation of the popular girl, exuberant dancing with dozens of men is an antidote to lovemaking. The third night the hero gets innocently involved with a comic Rumanian vamp who lives in the same house. As he leaves her apartment drunk, she finally succeeds in planting an imprint of lipstick on his cheek. The bride gives a serious interpretation to this, and the couple are about to break up. The following day the vamp comes to their aid. While they are out, she prepares the apartment for a reunion. She provides soft music, perfume-drenched air, and a black lace nightgown which she lays out on the bed. (She is the proprietress of a lingerie shop and the hero had ordered the nightgown from her as a surprise for the heroine.) The heroine assumes that these arrangements are for a rendezvous with the Rumanian. There are further explanations. In the happy ending, the bride appears in the black lace nightgown. In this parody of the once serious issue between a good and a bad woman, the hero is not tempted by the vamp. But he requires that the good girl assume at least superficially some of the vamp's effects.

In *Without Reservations,* the hero is at once attracted to

the heroine. But when he tries to make love to her, he is
warded off by a forbidding talk about spiritual understanding, and he leaves her. The heroine then goes to Hollywood,
where she frequently goes out with film actors, and changes
the plot of her novel (which is to be filmed) so that love replaces politics as the major motivation of her characters. It
is only then that the hero comes back. The sexualization of
the good woman is generally confined to comedy and appears
much less frequently than the good-bad girl. Infusing sex
into the girl who is not sexy enough seems a less stimulating
undertaking than toning down the one who has too much.

French films tend to concentrate on the bad girl. Where a
conflict between a good girl and a bad girl arises, the man
tends to prefer the bad one. However, a variety of devices are
used to etherialize or ennoble her. The prostitute transformed by love still appears. The bad woman is sometimes
presented as a superior being, unaffected by the more sordid
aspects of her life. Her career of seducing men may be invested with a metaphysical significance. The bad woman may
at first appear good, and thus subject the man to deep disappointment. The sequence of the man's impressions of her
is then the reverse of that associated with the good-bad girl.
The French hero idealizes the woman who he later learns
is bad.

In *Macadam,* a prostitute triumphs over a nice girl, but is
then transformed by love. A rather severely good girl has met
a young sailor, and a promising relation develops between
them. The sailor is accidentally implicated in some underworld affair, and, to check up on him, a prostitute is instructed by her pimp to seduce him. The sailor falls in love
with her and immediately loses interest in the good girl,
whom he then treats quite rudely. The prostitute, on her
side, falls in love with the sailor, breaks off with her pimp,
and moves towards respectability.

In *Les Visiteurs du Soir,* the beautiful bad woman is a
supernatural creature sent by the devil to corrupt and de-

stroy. The prostitute and pimp are here invested with a higher significance, and adorned with medieval trappings. In *Les Enfants du Paradis,* the beautiful bad woman moves through her shady life with an air of untouched remoteness. She appears in the sideshow of a fair as a naked Venus, associates with underworld characters, and has evidently lived a promiscuous life. The hero at first sight sees her as an ideal creature. His penetration of her dubious façade is expressed in an episode at their first meeting where he proves that she is not guilty of a theft of which she is suspected. His idealization of her is further expressed in his hesitation to make love to her on short acquaintance, despite her readiness. This has unfortunate consequences, as it results in her becoming the mistress of his friend. However, she loves the hero, and suffers from the series of accidents which keep them apart. She is like the prostitute redeemed by love, except that her love leads to no change in her mode of life. But this love is a sufficient redeeming feature in the image of her life and character. In comparison with this woman, the devoted good girl, whom the hero marries but never loves, is pale.

In *La Passionelle,* the hero worships from a distance a beautiful young girl far above him in station. When one day she invites him to her room, he learns that she has had a lover whom she has murdered. She wants the hero to dispose of the body for her, and offers herself to him in exchange for this service. Unable to forgive her for destroying his dream, he refuses her offer.

American films, in the effort to fuse goodness and badness, take a good girl as the base and try to disguise her as bad, or otherwise to enliven her. French films, concerned with the same problem, proceed in the opposite direction. The point of departure is a bad girl, who may appear to be good, or be redeemed, or carry an aura of idealization. The bad woman may deceive the man as to her character. The woman sent by the devil in *Les Visiteurs du Soir* confides a fictitious story of her unhappy life to engage the sympathy of the man she intends to seduce. However, this wilful deception is not usual. The double aspect of the woman derives more often from the man's tendency to idealize her, his difficulty in seeing her as she is.

British films seem to be less concerned than American and French with goodness and badness in women. Possibly this issue is replaced by that of men's destructive impulses towards women. In *Madonna of the Seven Moons,* a rare film dealing with the mixture of goodness and badness in a woman, the heroine is a dual personality. Most of the time she is a rather prim and stately wife and mother, devoted to her family and to good works. Periodically her other personality takes possession of her. She forgets her usual life, assumes a gypsy-like costume and abandon, and runs away to join her lover, a dark and passionate underworld character. All this is attributed to a girlhood seduction by a dark vagabond. Thus it is the fault of a bad man that the sexy potentialities of a good woman are brought to the surface. There is a much sharper dissociation of the two aspects of this heroine than in the American good-bad girl or in the French mixed types. Her husband knows her only as good, her lover, only in her gypsy role. She herself, when she assumes one character, loses all memory of the other. American and French heroes, though with differing feelings, see the women they love as both good and bad. In the British film, the bad aspect of the woman is evoked by a dark foreigner, the seducer and later the lover, and appears in an alien gypsy guise. Her husband is completely satisfied with her without knowing anything of this other side of her nature. It is only by an unfortunate accident that the good woman develops a sexy character. She is then insane, and eventually destroyed by this abnormal component.

A few observations may be added about the types of men who accompany, or correspond to, various types of women. In early American films, the good girl was attacked by a wicked seducer, and rescued by the hero. As heroines have

become more worldly-wise and able to take care of themselves, there has been a tendency for both the seducer and the
rescuer to degenerate into comic figures. The fatal man, particularly the foreign one, has suffered the same fate as the
vamp. In a transitional stage, *Hold Back the Dawn* exposed
the tricks of the foreign lover. As an emigré, hoping to gain
entrance into the United States, he wants to marry an American schoolteacher. He uses in a calculating way the seductive
tones and looks which in previous films seemed to be inspired by passion. The girl is naïve enough to be taken in.
However, in an eventual reversal of their relationship, the
man falls in love with her. Her patriotic lectures also take
effect; a wish to become a good American is substituted for
his originally cynical motives. In *Lover Come Back*, the foreign charmer is a comic character. He pursues the heroine
with flattering speeches in a heavy accent, with bows, hand-
kissings, and self-congratulations on his irresistible technique.
The heroine has no difficulty in resisting him. A less comic,
but still far from menacing derivative of the seducer, is the
wolf. He is easily converted into a monogamist when he
meets the right girl. In *Those Endearing Young Charms*, the
hero is an Air Force officer who is in the habit of making
easy conquests and not taking them seriously. When the heroine, whom he has taken away from his less exciting buddy,
confides that she has fallen in love with him, he is at first
annoyed that she does not share his frivolous attitude. She
breaks with him, and he is soon hanging around pleading
with her mother to put in a good word for him. In the end,
persuaded of his conversion, the girl throws herself into his
arms.

The rescuer of women is now apt to appear as a case of
arrested development. He is sexually unawakened, a male
sleeping beauty, and overestimates the value of his heroics for
the woman who is usually more competent than he. The hero
in *Ball of Fire* is an unworldly middle-aged scholar. While
compiling a slang dictionary, he interrogates a gangster's

moll. To explain a term, she gives him what is evidently his first kiss. He resolves to free her from her underworld involvements and eventually succeeds, although both the girl and the gangsters take advantage of his naiveté for some time. In the remake of this film (under the title *A Song is Born*) the comic Danny Kaye replaces the romantically serious Gary Cooper in the hero's role. In *Hold That Blonde,* the rescuer is a completely comic figure. The girl whom he is rescuing from involvement with a gang of thieves watches over his blundering efforts and knocks him out when his zeal threatens to get him into real danger. The incompetent hero of *The Paleface* is misled into believing that he has saved the life of the heroine by killing a horde of attacking Indians, while it is really her more accurate shots which achieved this.

Another derivative of the rescuer is what we may call the standing-offer man. He is always devotedly waiting for the heroine, ready to help, and undeterred by her failure to respond. He regularly loses the girl to a more enterprising and demanding suitor. The help which he offers is reduced to routine services which the heroine permits him to render in the interests of her relation with the other man. In *Young Widow,* the heroine's boss is a suitor of long standing. When she repulses his rare efforts at lovemaking, he assures her that he will always be there if she needs him. In the end she takes advantage of this offer by calling him to drive her to the airport so that she can wave goodbye to the man she has fallen in love with. In *The Sailor Takes a Wife,* the heroine uses her long-term suitor to help her move into the apartment where she is going to live with the sailor who has won her in an overnight courtship. Such are the current forms of the devotion of a good man which might once have saved a woman from ruin.

In British films, the standing-offer man has a better chance of being accepted. His restraint does not need to be attributed, as in the American case, to a lack of strong impulses. He is the more acceptable as his opposite, the seducer, re-

mains a danger. In *The Years Between,* the heroine, after the
presumed death of her husband, falls in love with a man who
has loved her for years. Despite his long quiescence, he manifests sufficient intensity when he finally gets his chance. In
This Happy Breed, the girl is glad to return to the devoted
boy from next-door after she has been deserted by the lover
with whom she ran away to Paris. The picture of a good and
a bad man who make conflicting claims on a good woman persists in British films, as we have seen in *Madonna of the
Seven Moons.* The bad man degrades the woman rather than
yielding to her ennobling influence, as he is apt to do in
American films. In *Love on the Dole,* the heroine is continually importuned by a vulgar, affluent gambler, and finally
gives in to him after the death of the good man she loved.
The gambler, untouched by the fact that she comes to him
only because she needs money for her sweetheart's funeral,
proceeds to install her as his mistress just as he had long
intended.

The partner of the good-bad girl in American films is a
good-bad man. However, the double aspect of his character
is connected with violence rather than with sex. As we shall
see later, he is frequently suspected of crimes which he did
not commit. He tends to be absorbed in crime investigation
and in warding off attacks by male assailants. As a result of
this preoccupation, he cannot be as immersed in love as the
earlier great lover or the devoted rescuer. The suspicious
appearance of the girl further tends to evoke a certain wari-
ness. At the same time, the hero's manner with women is sure
and easy, and suggests experience. He talks in a tough ban-
tering style, and without polite preliminaries. The hero of
Nocturne, a detective, first meets the heroine, a murder suspect, as she is climbing out of a swimming pool. His first
words to her are: Why did you kill him? Moderated by this
tough scepticism, the hero's feelings are not likely to become
urgent or overpowering. There is little chance of his being
deceived or swept off his feet like the victim of the vamp.

While assuming a quick though casual tone of intimacy, he makes it quite clear to the woman that he can take her or leave her; and that he will take his time to find out about her. He is carrying on two investigations: one to clear himself, the other to clear the heroine. In the first case he is the suspect, in the second the one whose suspicions are aroused.

§ CAN YOU LOVE TWICE?

THIS problem is perhaps peculiarly American. Many European cultures probably take it for granted that one can love genuinely, later cease to love, and then love somebody else. The intensity of feeling declines, the formerly beloved person becomes boring, and a new person is required to arouse again the whole feeling. In America there is less belief in the inevitable running down of love. The one right person is conceived as a permanent stimulus to the same fully pleasurable feelings. The institution of the second honeymoon indicates the refusal to believe that there is an early high point in a love relation which is not recapturable. If the once beloved person ceases to give pleasure there is apt to be a complaining conviction that this could not have been the right one.

This static character of love is frequently symbolized in films by the recurrent use of a theme song with which the love of a couple is associated, and which continues to evoke the same feelings regardless of the passage of time. The romantically devoted married pair in *Sentimental Journey* take pleasure in the endless repetition of the title song, and there is always an exchange of particularly loving looks when one or the other of them puts it on the phonograph. The undimmed emotional effectiveness of such a theme song may

also indicate the continuity of love despite quarrels and separations. There is nothing irreversible in emotional life.
Whatever happens, it is always possible to get back to normal; that is, to the situation of maximum satisfaction. In
Too Young to Know, the couple are first brought together
by the fact that a certain juke-box tune is their common
favorite. Some time later, after they have married and separated, after he has gone overseas and she has had a baby and
given it away for adoption, they come together again. The
hero half absent-mindedly starts picking out the same tune
on the piano, and the girl admits that it is still her favorite.

The belief in the unchangingness of love is probably related to the tradition of monogamy combined with the demand for continuous pleasure. It is also related to the characteristically American denial of the evanescent aspect of
life. Americans tend not to admit

"... that Spring should vanish with the Rose!
That Youth's sweet-scented Manuscript should close!"

Instead, one plans to move to California, to take a course in
the Charm School. The only kind of change which is readily
admitted is improvement, and this tends to apply to tech-
nology rather than to human relations. There seems to be a
high capacity for retaining early preferences with undiminished intensity. The childhood taste for ice-cream is little
superseded by acquired tastes for more subtle delicacies; and
comic strips continue to be read alongside of Pocket books.
The grown man retains his boyhood enthusiasm for baseball,
and shares with his son the admiration for its heroes.

Over against the image of unalterable romantic love, there
is the picture of the wrangling middle-aged couple frequently
presented in B-pictures (not included in our study) and in
other media such as comic strips. The ideal love of the A-
pictures, and the marital discords of the B's, regularly presented as comic, are disconnected; they are not two stages in

the same series. The discordant married couples probably represent the older generation, with whom we do not identify. They have never been young, while we shall never be old. The American tradition of the younger generation surpassing its parents encourages the refusal to see in them a portent of what we shall become. By contrast, in the French film, *Torrents,* a young couple repeat the tragic fate of their parents. The father of the girl and the mother of the boy had had an enduring unhappy love for each other. The boy and girl love each other, but their marriage plans suffer a similar fatality. In both generations the lovers each marry someone else, and in the end the man is left to mourn the death of the beloved woman whom he could never obtain. In an American film, *Those Endearing Young Charms,* an opposite relation between the generations is shown. The daughter profits by the mother's mistake. The mother's regret for not having married her soldier boy on the eve of his departure for overseas in World War I saves the daughter from repeating this error in World War II. Thus in America the older generation tends to provide a point of departure rather than a precedent. We may observe their frustrations, the petering out of their pleasures, but it has no application to ourselves.

The belief in the one love that will last for life involves the idea of an indefinitely suspended emotional life prior to the appearance of the right person. At the same time the idea of passive waiting is not agreeable. Moreover, it is necessary to demonstrate one's eligibility by never being without a partner. The solution is provided, especially for women, by the image of the girl who is constantly courted but never loves any of her suitors. The capacity for eventually loving greatly appears associated with the capacity for indefinitely suspending any intense feelings.

Besides the idea of the one love, there is the belief that the most desirable man or woman appeals equally to all members of the opposite sex. Instead of the dream of someone who is uniquely suited to oneself, there is the desire for the person who meets certain generally acknowledged specifications, like the measurements of bathing beauties. The tendency to emphasize bosoms more than faces indicates a de-individualization of female love objects. In *Without Reservations,* the heroine, who believes in individual suitability in love, is made to feel ridiculous by the hero who regards love relations as biological. The heroine's novel is about to be filmed, with Lana Turner cast as a woman who is turned down by the central male character because of her wrong political views. The hero scoffs at the plausibility of such behavior on the part of any man. In *Stolen Life,* the hero justifies his preference for the more sexually provocative of two sisters in terms of what would appeal to any man. The good sister is cake, the sexy one is frosting; every man wants the frosting. The hero of *The Blue Dahlia* tells the heroine: every man has seen you before, the trick is to find you.

The American aim to eliminate individual idiosyncrasy, to meet certain widely accepted standards of excellence, makes for the replaceability of the individual. The ideal specifications may in fact be rarely met, but in principle any number of individuals might meet them. The combination of actual rarity with potential mass production introduces a distinctive flavor into the American conception of the ideal. The longing to be an irreplaceable person is thus never quite satisfied. Several others may measure up to the same specifications. Moreover the possession of such excellence is evanescent; the perfect bosom may wax or wane. The lover is aware that his taste is the taste of millions, and his triumph in winning the possessor of rare charms is enhanced by the awareness of how many would desire what he has obtained. The rarity of the ideal is not a matter of a relationship between two individuals peculiarly suited to one another. It is rather the rarity of the man or woman who meets the specifications, the temporary title holder. The affirmation of the irreplaceability of the beloved (corresponding presumably to the wishes of the individual seeking love), and the conception of persisting love for the one right person, have to contend with these factors. The insistence on the one love and the one right person perhaps become intensified in the effort to deny the replaceability of any one person. The basis for choice in love (obscure enough in any case) is rarely rendered convincingly in the movies. The couple seem fated for each other more by virtue of the fact that the actor and actress are coupled as co-stars, than by any development of a relation between them in the plot. The desirability of the hero and heroine for one another is equated with the presumable universal desirability of the stars.

How often have movie heroines had boy friends or movie heroes girl friends before they meet each other? And how often has there been any serious love in these previous relations? Fifty per cent of movie heroines have had some relationship with a man other than the hero, but without ever being in love. Only fifteen per cent of heroines have ever loved before. Thirty per cent have, for all we know, had no admirer before the advent of the hero. The remaining five per cent have had some kind of relationship, but there is insufficient evidence of its loving or unloving character. Of the heroes, twenty-five per cent have been connected with women whom they did not love, while an equal number have been seriously emotionally involved. Forty-five per cent have, as far as we know, always been unattached. The other five per cent have had some kind of relation which may or may not have been a loving one.

Thus if women have had any prior relations with men, the chances are more than three to one that they have stopped short of love in these relations. The emotionally uninvolved popular girl is in the ascendant. In her most dramatic form she is the good-bad girl. In the case of the man, there is a fifty-fifty chance that, if a woman has entered his life previously, he has fallen in love with her. The emotional susceptibility of men is thus considerably higher than that of women. On the other hand, it is more frequently the case with men than with women that there are no indications of any previous involvements in their lives. This is probably in part because it is more taken for granted that a man has had some relations with women, and his eligibility does not depend on his displaying them. It is more essential to the woman's attractiveness that she should be sought after by other men. That she is likely to remain unloving prior to her relation with the hero expresses perhaps a vestige of the demand for female virginity, which now appears displaced from the physical to the sentimental level. A fair number of these cold popular women have entered into loveless marriages before meeting the hero, who, however, has the satisfaction of being assured that they never loved anyone but him. There is some difficulty in showing a man in a situation where a woman loves him while he remains unloving. Such a situation is humiliating to the woman—and women are rarely put in humiliating positions in American films—while pursuing an attractive woman who does not love him is less damaging to the man.

If we examine in detail these loving and unloving histories, we find that the largest number of unloving heroines are girls who have attracted suitors, whom they encourage more or less, without loving them. It is simply the girl's due, and the sign of her eligibility that she should have these men hanging around. In almost as many cases the heroine has contracted a loveless marriage. These women tend to be rather querulantly defensive about their behavior. Life has been hard for them and they had no resource except their attractiveness. The heroine of *The Postman Always Rings Twice* recounts self-pityingly how she had to earn a living as a waitress, and was unremittingly pursued by men until she married her aging and unattractive husband as what seemed to her the only escape from economic and personal sordidness. The unloved husband is not portrayed sympathetically. Another considerable group of unloving women have resorted to relationships with other men in an effort to maintain their self-esteem after having been temporarily rejected by men they love. Another slightly smaller group consists of women who are pursued against their will. The heroine of *Spellbound,* for instance, is subjected to the amorous approaches of a fellow psychiatrist who tries to persuade her that her psychological health cannot be good if there is no man in her life. She discourages him by allowing him to kiss her and manifesting no reaction. Occasionally a woman has become involved with a man she does not love, as a means to an end. This is the case with the heroine in *Because of Him,* who passes herself off as the girl-friend of an aging actor in order to get on the stage.

Where a woman loves twice, she may have been mistaken in her first choice. The heroine of *Love Letters* gave her first husband credit for the lofty sentiments expressed in letters actually composed by his buddy. In *The Well-Groomed Bride,* the girl retains her girlhood adoration for the high-school football hero until she sees him absent himself from their wedding to pose for publicity photos. In another case, the heroine carries on with another man in an unhappy interlude of her marriage, which is later reconsolidated. The second man, a briefly loved playboy, turns out to be less lovable in the long-run than the rather insignificant but loyal husband. (*Mildred Pierce.*)

The real difficulty arises where the first love was well-founded. How then can the woman ever love again? This problem is posed in the case of widows, who undergo an intense struggle about allowing themselves to love a second time. If they find themselves falling in love with a new man, they either tend to get him mixed up with the first, which they find confusing, or they go to great lengths to differentiate the two relations. The title character in *Young Widow* is shown making a difficult transition to a new love, in which the use of the theme song is again symbolic. First she plays what had been her husband's and her own favorite song when she revisits alone the place where they used to live.

Later, in an effort to return to life, she is dancing rather half-heartedly with her new suitor when she hears the song again, feels it is too incongruous with her new partner, and runs away in tears. Later still, when her relation to the new man has progressed, they are shown dancing happily together to the same tune. Thus the woman has not detached herself from the first man to form a new relation with the second. In a sense the new man has become a reincarnation of the husband. This is confirmed when the man kisses her; she finds herself warmly responsive, coming alive again as she puts it, and then confesses in some confusion that she feels as if the man were her husband. While true love cannot die, it can get displaced from one person to another. The second man becomes the heir to the associations the woman had with the first. The story has a war setting; the husband had been killed in the war, and the new suitor is an Air Force officer. For the new man in such a situation there is the guilt of taking the girl of a dead buddy, probably combined with the much less conscious longing to identify with the buddy which takes the dual form: I want to be in his place with his girl, to know the same experiences he has known, because of my feeling of closeness for him; and also I ought to be dead in his place. (In *Dead Reckoning,* the hero makes a conscious effort to see his dead buddy's girl as the buddy had seen her.) The woman may share the feeling: Why should this man be alive and my husband dead? To remove these obstacles to the acceptance of the new man, he is made to die a symbolic death. He and the heroine are in a subway station together when an old woman falls to the track just before the arrival of the train. The hero throws himself on the track and holds her between the rails as the train passes over them without injuring them. It is from this point that the heroine begins to have a strong positive feeling for him. This feeling is intensified when she sees her girl-friend embrace her returned Navy husband who has lost a leg in action. As this occurs just at the moment when the hero is about to depart for renewed overseas duty, the heroine again associates the idea of destruction or mutilation with the hero, and is overwhelmed with tenderness for him. She rushes to the airport to wave goodbye to him, and to call into the air the long withheld "I love you."

In *Till the End of Time,* a young war widow shows a similar tendency to confuse a new man with her husband. In this case it does not apply to the hero, but to a buddy of her husband who tells her about the last weeks of the husband's life. She tenderly kisses him goodnight, and explains afterwards that he almost seemed to be her husband. The hero, a returned veteran, shows a manifest disinclination at first to take the wife of a dead fellow soldier. He even blames her for their initial encounter, having the mistaken belief at first that the husband is still alive, and even later, not realizing how long he has been dead. Here also the new man must undergo almost fatal danger in order finally to be loved. He and some of his ex-buddies get involved in a fight with some semi-Fascist veterans' organizers, and the hero's best friend is almost killed. It is after this fight, and after the all-night vigil in the hospital when the hero waits to see whether an emergency operation will save his friend, and thus demonstrates love and grief for dead and injured buddies generally, that the girl finally comes to him.

A different solution of the widow's problem occurs in *My Reputation.* The detachment of the woman's love from her late husband is facilitated by the fact that he had been incapacitated by illness for several years before his death; already during that time he no longer seemed like himself. In spite of this excuse for changed feelings, the wife continues to love him even after his death just as before. When confronted by her young sons who want to know about her relation to a new man, she admits that she loves him, but insists that at the same time she continues to love their father. No love can ever be like the first, although the later one is also true love. In maintaining the old love side by side with the new, this heroine is a kind of sentimental bigamist. As in the previous films, physical danger to the new man as he is about to be sent overseas helps to release the woman's love for him. The hero, however, is exempted from guilt towards the dead husband, who was not a buddy. Instead he has guilt feelings towards the woman because, in his character as playboy, he feels unsuited to her domestic way of life. Thus in his character, as well as in the feeling he inspires, the second man is here differentiated from the first.

The difficulty of presenting a woman as truly loving two men is expressed in all three films by the fact that we see her only with the second man. We do not see the first man at all, although in *Young Widow* the heroine is haunted by his voice when she first returns to their old home.

Where the preceding heroine was a sentimental bigamist, the heroine of *Tomorrow is Forever* is a real, though unwitting bigamist, for which, however, she compensates by never really loving her second husband. The first husband, badly maimed in World War I, decides to do an Enoch Arden. His grieving wife consents to marry her wealthy boss, while telling him graciously that she can never really love him. After a number of years of this second marriage, which seems to provide a tolerably congenial and luxurious life, the wife again meets her first husband who appears greatly changed but whose disguise she gradually penetrates. Her memories of him as a young husband recur with undiminished vividness, though he tries to persuade her that he is no longer the same man. Immediately following the recognition scene, he solves the wife's dilemma by dying of a heart attack. Since here we have seen the woman with both husbands, since her love for the first was not only reported but shown, it is necessary to deny that she really loved the second.

The legend that true love never dies is supported by these films dealing with the problem of a woman loving twice. One of the loves may turn out to have been a mistake, in which case it was not true love. On the other hand, a beloved

man may die; this is the main situation in which detachment
from a once loved person is seriously considered. True love
never dies a natural death, but the beloved person may die
a violent or premature one. Since the films do not recognize
mourning as a process of emotional detachment, the widow
is left still loving the lost husband. The heroine in *Till the
End of Time* feels she is stuck with her dream. While love
remains attached to the dead man, it is recognized that the
woman also needs a live one. The sympathetic maiden aunt
of the heroine in *Young Widow* sanctions the quest for a new
man, telling her niece that she is the kind of woman who
needs a man in her life, and hinting at the unsatisfactoriness
of her own spinsterhood. The implication throughout is that
a woman once loving never changes her feelings, and that
nothing but the death of the beloved man could ever force
her to become interested in someone else.

A British film, *The Years Between,* dealing with the war
widow theme, acknowledges the possibility of true love dying. The hero, for the purposes of spy work, must change his
identity and be reported dead. His devoted wife, stricken by
this report, is plunged into melancholy and is continually
haunted by scenes of their former happy life. To distract her,
friends persuade her to take her husband's seat in Parlia-
ment, and she gradually becomes absorbed in an active life.
After some time she falls in love again, with a long-term
suitor. She is happy with this second man, whom she neither
confuses with her husband nor struggles to differentiate from
him. Her love for her husband, intense as it had been, has
become resolved in mourning and her subsequent immersion
in work. On the eve of her wedding to the second man, she
learns to her dismay that her husband is alive and about
to return. She is resentful of the deception which has been
practised on her, and finds it all the harder to accept her husband back again since she finds him changed by several years
of imprisonment. As he is ill and appears dependent upon
her, she cannot bring herself at once to tell him of her

changed feelings; but at this point she only loves the other man. Eventually there is a rather contrived reunion between husband and wife, facilitated by the end of the war and a general confusion of feelings. Here, in contrast to the corresponding American films, we see the heroine in genuine love scenes with two men, implying the acknowledgment that love can have an end. The anti-climactic revival of the dead love remains somewhat unconvincing.

Other British films, such as *Brief Encounter,* indicate that after some years of marriage, even though the husband does not die, the wife may fall in love with someone else. Unlike American films, the British sometimes concern themselves with the emotional problems of middle-aged people. In the United States there are no middle-aged people, and, if there were, they would have no emotional lives. There is only young love, and its expectations constitute the only ideology of man and woman relations. Aging actors and actresses continue to portray the susceptibilities of adolescents, eagerly pursuing the one great love, until one day they get cast in father and mother roles, which of course involve no love life.

The fantasy of one love in a life tends on the whole to establish the line of the hero's as well as the heroine's career. The slightly greater allowance of more than one love for the hero may derive from the demand for male gallantry (the hero can't have married a girl without having loved her), and from the greater value attached to the woman's sentimental virginity. Thus men are more easily deceived than women, since the love the hero felt before meeting the heroine was most frequently a mistake. A certain passivity of the hero is implied here: he may fall into the hands of the wrong woman if she gets there first or if, by her quicker approach, she eliminates the right woman (temporarily). In *Leave Her To Heaven,* the hero's relation to the right woman is still in an incipient stage when the impetuous wrong woman throws her arms around him and announces to everyone's surprise (including his) that they are about to be married. As she is beautiful as well as impulsive, he of course falls in love with her. Later, when she has killed his younger brother and demonstrated other unlovable tendencies, he becomes detached from her and resumes the relation with the right girl. In *A Stolen Life,* the hero's relation to the right girl is interrupted by the intrusion of the wrong one who sweeps him off his feet into a marriage which, because of her promiscuity and extravagance, turns out to be unhappy. Thus even for the hero who has loved twice, there is apt to be only one right woman. This one right woman, if she arrives in time, protects the hero from the attack of the wrong woman in somewhat the same way that the love of a good man once protected the frail woman.

§ SENTIMENTAL EDUCATION

WOMEN are frequently superior to men; the reverse is rare. A comparison of the ways in which men and women improve their social position gives an indication of this. (The theme of social ascent seems to have become a minor one; it occurs in about one fourth of our films, and almost never constitutes the main plot line.) When women rise in status, it is mainly due to their abilities. The heroine of *To Each His Own,* rises from being a small town pharmacist's daughter to running an international enterprise; her ascent is achieved through her ingenuity in preparing cosmetics and her business acumen. The heroine of *Mildred Pierce* similarly rises by means of her abilities from being a waitress to owning a nation-wide string of restaurants. Less frequently women rise through marriage.

By contrast, men rise mainly through marriage, sometimes by a fluke (women have no need for such chance aids), and

almost never through merit. The chance rise is usually pictured as comic. In *The Kid from Brooklyn,* the hero, a milk-
wagon driver, accidentally knocks out a champion prizefighter in a street encounter. He is then built up as a fighter,
despite his timidity and ineptitude. After winning a series
of set-up bouts, he defeats the champion by an unexpected
upset (the champion has been accidentally drugged, kicked
by a horse, etc., beforehand). Where the hero gains in social
standing through marriage, it matters little to him in most
cases. In *Stolen Life,* where the hero is a light-house keeper's
assistant and the heroine a rich upper-class girl, they are both
agreed that nothing much matters except sitting by the sea
and thinking about life. In *The Big Sleep,* the hero, who
ends up with the daughter of his wealthy employer, is a
tough private detective who makes his own way very com-
petently. Thus the danger of the hero being put in a passive
position through his dependence on the woman for social
ascent is warded off by his regarding the advantage as unimportant. In *The Guilt of Janet Ames,* a young man is supported by his wife in resisting her rich father's attempt to
take the young man into his business. In the occasional case
where the rise in fortune achieved through marriage is important for the man, it is also apt to be fatal. In *The Strange
Love of Martha Ivers,* a weak man has been pushed into marriage by his conniving father, who has blackmailed a rich
and powerful woman for this purpose. Despised by the woman,
and oppressed by guilt for her crimes which he has helped
to cover up, the man drinks heavily, makes bitter speeches
about his father's ambitions for him, and ends up by committing suicide. In an exceptional case where a man rises largely
through his own efforts, his success (which turns out to be
fatal for him) is attributed less to his·ability than to an unscrupulous drive for power which leads him to treat destructively those who help him as well as those who stand in his
way (*Ruthless*).

Where men rise by a fluke, the unmanliness of being a

passive recipient of fortune is mitigated by comedy treatment. Where men rise by marriage, this danger is warded off by showing the man as indifferent to the advancement. In the less frequent case where he is not indifferent we get a cautionary tale of tragic consequences. Thus, as far as men's social ascent is concerned, the best that can be done is to mitigate the humiliation of passively accepting the gifts of women or of fortune. They mainly lack the recourse which women have of rising on their merits. (We are not speaking here of those successes through achievement which leave the individual in substantially the same social position.) The ability to rise in business seems largely to belong to women. The men who rise by a fluke not only owe their ascent to outside causes, but achieve their rise in some less substantial medium, such as sports or entertainment.

The leading roles for which Academy Awards were given in 1947 and 1948 are perhaps related to these contrasting images of men and women. The men's roles were those of a would-be writer incapacitated for work by drinking (Ray Milland in *The Lost Weekend,* 1947), and an actor who goes mad from the emotional strain of his work (Ronald Colman in *A Double Life,* 1948). The women's roles were those of a wife and mother who goes to work and rapidly rises from waitress to restaurant chain owner (Joan Crawford in *Mildred Pierce,* 1947), and a Swedish maid who becomes a congresswoman (Loretta Young in *The Farmer's Daughter,* 1948).

Given this formidable superiority of women, how is it used in relation to men? According to the film version women use their superiority almost always benevolently, or at least harmlessly. The usual pattern shows the superior woman setting the stage for the man's achievement. She does not put him into a passive receptive position, but arranges things so that he may realize his best potentialities. Thus there is a tendency to deny any danger to the man deriving from the woman's dominant position. This is largely accomplished by locating her superiority in the area of skill, achievement, and success rather than picturing her as dominant in emotional relationships, and by stressing the man's activity. The man feels pleased with his own achievements which the woman's arrangements have made possible. The woman is equally delighted to see what her man can do once he is given a chance. The theme of the woman manipulating the man's career appears most often (though by no means exclusively) in comedies. While the man tends to appear in a more comic light than the woman, the effect of the comic treatment is again to reduce the seriousness of the threat represented by the dominant woman.

In *Stork Club,* the hero wants to become a band-leader, but his attempt to organize a band nearly fails because he cannot afford to keep his musicians together until they find an opening. The heroine, with whom the hero has quarreled temporarily, takes over the whole crew of musicians (she has acquired a large bank account from an anonymous benefactor) and rehearses with them on her pent-house roof. By a ruse she induces the owner of the Stork Club to give them an audition, gets a contract for them, brings the only slightly resisting boy-friend in to direct the successful opening, and more or less steals the show with her singing. The couple are now happily reunited (as the source of her mysterious wealth is virtuously explained). The man feels that the success he has obtained is deserved: he only needed a chance to show what he could do. The girl is proud of him for being a success.

In *Over Twenty-One,* the wife helps her husband to succeed in what he wants to do, and at the same time gives a demonstration of her superior competence. In the beginning she resigns her job as a successful Hollywood script writer to become an army wife, and to help her husband pass his course in an Army Air Force school. The husband has been a successful newspaper columnist, but is out of his element in the army, finding it hard at middle-age to learn so many new things. The wife keeps encouraging him though secretly convinced that he will fail. She feels that to satisfy his conscience it is necessary for him to make the attempt. Meanwhile, to protect him from the urgent demands of his newspaper boss, she starts writing his column and, without his knowing it, turns out the best articles of his career. To her surprise, her husband passes his examinations, and there are even thirty others below him on the list. The wife exclaims admiringly: "My man smarter than thirty other men!" At the graduation ceremonies he is asked to read one of his recent inspiring articles—written by her. While the woman's attitude here seems condescending, she does not reduce her husband's morale by any manifest contempt. She cannot help her superiority, and her whole effort is to use it in such a way as to create the opportunity for her husband to do what he wants.

The heroine in *Uncle Harry* is a successful artist while the hero is a would-be artist inured to designing wall-paper patterns. When he shows her an old landscape of his, she takes up the brushes and transforms his timid work with a few strokes. Her conscious motive is not to demonstrate her superiority but to recall him to the fuller realization of his potentialities. It is the hero's sickly, helpless, and clinging sister who has a paralyzing effect on him while the active heroine revives him.

While women thus promote the careers of their men, they by no means force on them an overwhelming demand for success. On the contrary, they guard their men against excessive absorption in work in the interests of their potentialities for a full life. When the man shows signs of becoming obsessed with his work, often with the consequences of reduced productivity, his wife will recommend that they get away to their house on the island for a few weeks, or that they set off on the long deferred second honeymoon. She may reproach him because she has been seeing so little of him, but her recommendations are also shown to be for his own good. The man's excessive absorption in work is often re-

lated to an involvement with another man, his colleague or
boss, who dominates him. The woman's efforts to rescue her
man from his immersion in work may then take the form of
trying to emancipate him from this other man. Thus the
woman protects the man from the dangers of the man's world,
here represented by too great work absorption, in the melodramas by the threat of violent attacks to which the hero
might succumb if he did not have the woman's support.

In *The Saxon Charm,* the playwright hero has become involved with a domineering and capricious producer who
makes him rewrite his play until he quite loses his sense of
judgment about it. His wife, in an effort to restore his crea-
tive capacities, takes him off to their house on the island, but
the producer follows them and rushes the husband back to
town with him. The two men return to their day-and-night
collaboration and reduce the play to a complete hash. The
wife persuades another producer to read the original version,
the perfection of which she alone recognized: it is accepted
with enthusiasm. The husband finally sees the weaknesses of
the man with whom he has been so unproductively absorbed,
and recognizes his wife as the one reliable authority on his
work.

The same pattern of female management occurs not only
in connection with the man's professional success, but also,
more generally, in connection with his growing up. In *Guest
Wife,* the woman has been mildly irked for years by the fact
that her husband takes a little boyish, hero-worshipping attitude towards his sensationally successful best friend. This
self-effacement in favor of the friend reaches its climax when
the husband agrees to let his wife pose as the friend's wife.
She then arranges the situation in such a way that the husband will finally feel impelled to assert himself as the better
man. Allowing both men to become uncertain as to how
seriously she enters into the pretense, she arouses the husband to feel sufficiently competitive and combative towards
the friend to punch him in the jaw to recapture his wife. She

is confident in advance of this outcome, but nonetheless delighted to see her husband finally assume a long deferred
masculinity.

The pattern of masculine success in a woman-arranged
situation reflects a major aspect of American child training.
As Margaret Mead has pointed out, American mothers are
concerned to a distinctive degree with their children's achievements. The emphasis in their relation to their children is
less on giving to a helpless creature, than on seeing what he
can do. He is supposed to make good in the skills and functions that can be expected of him at each stage, and the
mother rewards him with her love to the extent that he performs well. She arranges situations appropriate to the child's
development at a given stage, which are challenging enough
to make him bring out his abilities but scaled in such a way
that he can experience success. The fact that the situation
has been arranged by the mother is not stressed; the emphasis
is rather placed on the fact that the child has accomplished
something by his own efforts. This emphasis is reflected in
the American belief that one can succeed on one's merits if
only one gets the breaks, coupled with the belief that the
favorable situation will somehow present itself. This child
training pattern is distinguished from those of other cultures
where the child is made to strive for goals beyond his present
ability so that he is exposed to numerous failures, or where
the child is protected from trying out the strength he has.
The benevolent arranging woman is thus modeled on the
type of American mother who plans successful experiences
for her child.

In contrast to the good managing woman there is the bad
woman who tries to control her man's life without regard for
his needs or potentialities. The possessive wife in *Leave Her
to Heaven* distracts her husband from his writing by her constant emotional demands. Her offer to support him (she also
took the initiative in proposing marriage) is debilitating. She
is the kind of active woman who prevents rather than stimu-

lates her man's achievement. Similarly the hero's wife in *One More Tomorrow* impedes his development by her demands that he fit into the scheme of social conservatism which she prefers and which coincides with the aims of his plutocratic father. On the other hand, the hero's girl-friend introduces him into the liberal journalistic venture in which she is involved. She does not make any attempt to force the hero into her pattern, but only exposes him to an opportunity and presents him with the example of her own purposeful activity in contrast to his playboyish aimlessness.

The wrong kind of career-manipulating woman may provoke her husband to murder her. She elevates him socially and financially without allowing him to do anything for himself. Unable to endure this enforced passivity, he is moved to violence. The hero of *Sorry, Wrong Number* has been raised from poverty by an heiress who insists that he assume the perfunctory position of a vice-president in her father's business. If he tries to do anything on his own, she produces a heart attack to force him back into conformity with her wishes. The only way he sees of making money independently is to do it secretly and illicitly. His destructive impulses towards his wife are facilitated by the difficulties he encounters in his illegal enterprise. Blackmailed by a more expert criminal with whom he has become involved, he has his wife murdered to get her insurance money. The hazards for the woman may thus be extreme if she tries to manipulate her man's career in the wrong way. The destructively manipulative woman is apt to lack any skills of her own and to use emotional pressure rather than management as her method of control.

The active woman, especially the woman of independent achievements, generally has a stimulating effect on her man. The successful woman colleague of the hero in *Uncle Harry* awakens him to the possibilities of a fuller life, where his dependent and demanding sister had kept him bound to a restricted routine. In *Lady on a Train*, the hero's fiancée continually quarrels, reproaches, and demands apologies. In this atmosphere the hero remains withdrawn from the world, living in the stories he writes, until the active heroine, intent on solving a mystery in which she is accidentally involved, carries him off with her into dangers in which he is forced to prove himself. The women who appear as foils to the benevolently managing or example-setting woman reflect the negative mother types: the overprotective mother who doesn't want the son to do anything for himself; the mother who wants to force the son into a traditional pattern; the clinging mother who keeps the son close to home and bound by her dependence; the mother who keeps saying, "You've hurt Mother," and exhausts her own and her child's energies in unproductive moral crises.

In an exceptional case, a woman of superior achievements has a paralyzing effect on her man despite her benevolence. The heroine in *Mildred Pierce* is so much more competent than her unemployed husband that he feels humiliated and turns to another woman for comfort. She also puts to shame her second husband, an upper-class playboy whom she supports by successful business enterprise. However, this woman is entirely sympathetic. She does not mean to compete with men, and cannot help the superiority which circumstances force her to demonstrate. In the end she is loved and admired by both her men, her first husband returning to her after the death of the second.

While the woman demonstrates her superiority to the man, and frequently raises his achievement level by arranging opportunities or by the stimulus of her example, the reverse situations rarely occur. Where a skilled professional woman is humbled by a man, it is not by any superior achievement on his part, but by the demonstration that she is still a woman and cannot get along without him (*She Wouldn't Say Yes, Without Reservations*). The woman is associated with higher cultural demands, the man with biological needs. This is the reverse of the picture in the days of the vamp, when women by their sexual allure tended to distract men from considerations of honor, career, and social position. In contemporary films, as we have seen, the man is usually successful in resisting the beautiful woman who tries to drag him into a life of crime (*Dead Reckoning, Framed*). According to the present picture, women influence men in an "upward" direction; men sometimes influence women in a "downward" one. This resembles an older image of woman as morally superior to man and exerting an ennobling influence. However, where the superior woman formerly excelled solely in moral virtue (Marguerite in *Faust* is a stock instance), her superiority in the present version lies rather in professional and other acquired skills. This is probably a reflection of the fact that in American life the main educators of children are women. At home it is frequently the mother who sets up the demands for the child's accomplishments, and appears herself as the model of competence. The father often plays with the children on their own level. It is frequently the mother, for instance, who teaches the children linguistic skills, explains things to them, teaches them to argue, and out-argues them. The father, often feeling outdone by the mother in this higher intercourse, communicates with the children on the level of inarticulate rough-house. In school as at home, women appear as the pedagogues. Not long ago the culturally superior American woman appeared in a negative light, in *Dodsworth* or in *Bringing Up Father*. In these versions the contemptuously superior woman attempted to impose on her more genuine husband the taste for a higher culture which she herself had not assimilated, but which she thought to be stylish. This type, with her bogus aesthetic susceptibilities, seems to be largely replaced, as far as current movies are concerned, by the more positive image of the woman who can do things. Another contrast with earlier related types appears by comparison with *What Every Woman Knows*. Where Barrie's heroine did things for her man and deceived him into believing he was doing it all himself, the managing woman in

American films tends, as we have seen, to arrange for the man to achieve his own success.

The triumphant path of the competent, managing woman reveals along its course, as we have observed, a number of side-tracks marked dangerous, and dead-end. One of the most dangerous of these is the course of the high-brow career woman whose life is not man-oriented. In comedies she is subjected to humiliations and reduced to the position where she is ready to accept on any terms the man whom she has almost alienated and whose paramount importance she has come to recognize almost too late. In a melodrama, she may be subjected to much more severe punishment. The emptiness of her intellectual pretensions is exposed, and she is brought to the point of clinging to the strong man on whom she has learned to depend. In *The Accused,* the heroine is a still young and beautiful but rather stiff and spinsterish professor of psychology. The film proceeds to demonstrate that she has no understanding, for any practical purpose, of her own or other people's emotional lives. Like an inexperienced school girl she goes for a drive in the country with an unbalanced and amorous male student. Intending to seduce her, he listens tongue-in-cheek while she laboriously interprets his case history. When he starts to embrace her she is taken by surprise. He has just time to ask her why she went out with him before she in a panic bashes his head in with a blunt instrument she finds on the car seat. The rest of the film is taken up with her unsuccessful efforts to escape detection. Her careful calculations are of little use. However, in order not to be recognized by the one witness who saw her near the scene of the crime, she alters her schoolmarmish make-up, fluffs up her hair and starts wearing flowered hats. This has a more favorable effect, as the two men investigating the murder both fall in love with her, and one of them successfully defends her at her trial. The woman who thought she was brainy enough to figure out everything for herself ends up as a symbol of prettily suffering womanhood while her man makes the eloquent speeches which will decide her fate. Thus women may be infallible when they devote themselves to managing their men's lives, but they are mistaken if they think they can manage their own.

That the managing woman behaves like a mother to her man is usually not acknowledged in words. In the exceptional case where the man is referred to as a child, there is an alleged extreme emotional dependence on the woman as well as a debt to her in the sphere of achievement. The associations of "mother" and "child" remain those of emotional dependence and do not seem to include the prominent functions of American mothers in promoting their children's achievement. When the wife in *Sentimental Journey* suggests to the husband that they adopt a child, he says: "What's the matter with me? Well, if you want to give me a little brother or sister, I guess it's all right." Later the wife teaches the little girl whom they adopt to take care of the husband as if he were a child. When speaking to the family doctor, the wife remarks that the husband is more of a child than the little girl. Eventually, after the wife's death, the girl assumes the maternal role in the household. When the husband and a friend are absorbed in a discussion late at night, she tells them: "You boys better get to bed." The child-husband is a consistently successful playwright and producer. His dependence on his wife consists in the fact that he only became a success after their marriage, partly because he leaned on her in planning his productions. This leaning, as far as it is shown, consists in keeping her awake at night discussing plans, and making her rehearse rather continuously. It is also agreed by all the friends of the couple that he is entirely dependent on her emotionally. This dependence is demonstrated by his resenting having to share her with a child whom he doesn't find congenial, and by his going into a depression after her death. The wife's assumption of his childlikeness seems to serve the purpose of justifying her arrangement of his life for his own good, even though he does not see the wisdom of her provisions. Knowing that she is dying (a fact which she must, of course, conceal from the husband) she adopts the little girl and trains her to take her own place. That this plan rests on the assumption that he is not to find another woman to replace her remains unacknowledged. Although the infantilism of the husband is throughout more alleged than demonstrated, the wife is shown as entirely unselfish in maintaining this fiction, and the husband as unresisting in accepting it.

The man-as-child is most completely portrayed by Danny Kaye in such films as *The Kid from Brooklyn*. This is a parody on the man's achievement of success in arranged situations. The hero, who hasn't the faintest idea of how to fight, is accidentally launched on a boxing career. As his manager arranges a series of set-up engagements for him and he sees one after another powerful brute hit the canvas as a result of his light blows, he gradually becomes convinced of his invincibility. The man-as-child is here permitted to retain his infantile delusions of omnipotence. He is not required to grow up or to acquire difficult skills, though he does show the cunning of the weak in surprising and comical ways (when he ducks to let two large men knock each other out) and the mixture of skill and lack of skill of the immature (in his songs which are a fluent combination of verbal mastery and gibberish). The fantasy of success descending on the inept man, who is artificially protected from realizing his own ineptitude, is an escape from the burden imposed by Mother's demand for achievement. In this film it is a father-figure, the manager, who enables the hero to succeed without acquiring skill (to win love without having to raise his achievement level), in contrast to the other films which we have discussed, where the woman sees to it that her man really makes good. The comedy expresses the alliance of father- and son-figures in the fulfilment of the wish to evade the woman's relentless demands for achievement.

Occasionally the man is simply the recipient of benefits

deriving from the woman's superior competence. While she turns the tables on him in demonstrating her superiority, her manifest motive is to come to his assistance. In *Spellbound,* the heroine psychoanalyzes the hero, an amnesia victim, in order to recover the memory of his past and absolve him of a murder of which he is suspected. In the course of this relation there is a reversal of position which brings the woman out on top. The hero originally appears as the new director of the psychiatric hospital where the heroine is a staff member. It turns out that he has assumed this false role as a result of his mental confusion. Soon it is discovered that the real director has been murdered, and the hero is suspected of the crime. He flees and, as the heroine comes after him, he is reduced to being her patient, dependent on her help to recover his identity and exonerate himself. The impact of the woman's triumph and of the reduction of the man's position in relation to her is softened by the circumstance that, being in love with him, she is dependent on him for her happiness. Before he is quite restored, he nearly murders the heroine. While this is presented as an expected consequence of psychic disturbance, it conveys a reaction against the hero's passive position. This is more manifest in the similar film, *The High Wall.* After the helpful woman psychiatrist has injected the hero with pentothal, he forces her at the point of a gun to escape with him from the prison hospital and to assist in his capture of the murderer.

In their management of men, women occasionally resort to physical force. A woman may have to knock a man out for his own good. The heroine in *Hold That Blonde* knocks the hero on the head with a rock to keep him from interfering too zealously with the gangsters who would have killed him. In *Stork Club,* the heroine has to knock unconscious the elderly millionaire whom she rescues from drowning. In another instance the knocking out of the man, though equally harmless, lacks the excuse of being for his benefit. In the final scene of *The Kid from Brooklyn,* the hero, who has just won a boxing championship by a series of flukes, is accidentally knocked out by a lively dowager who is demonstrating a punch he taught her.

Men are repeatedly pictured as pawns whom women dispose of between themselves. There are recurrent scenes in which two women discuss an absent man with the assumption that his life will follow the course that they agree on. In *Weekend at the Waldorf,* a young woman on the eve of her marriage pays a visit to the movie star who has been a lifelong friend of the bridegroom. The bride wants to get an assurance that the movie star does not love her man. Being convinced on this point, the bride is confident of marital happiness. She does not have to ask the man whether he loves the actress. As long as the other woman doesn't want him, she feels that he is hers. In *One More Tomorrow,* the hero is entirely subject to feminine manipulation. When the heroine refuses his first proposal and goes off on a jaunt to Mexico, he falls into the hands of a female fortune-hunter who lures him into marriage. Later the heroine returns to confront the wife, to warn her against diverting the hero from the career on which the heroine had launched him. There is an acrimonious argument about which of them knows what is best for him. When the bad woman asserts that after all she is his wife, the heroine answers that this is only because she had previously turned down his proposal. There is here no very high estimation of the man's autonomy. If one woman gets him, it is less the result of his choice than of another woman's permission. Of course, there are also numerous and more frequent films in which the man disposes of himself. However, where a man is shown as being disposed of by women, this is not expected to reflect negatively either on him or on them.

While the dominant position of women is thus usually portrayed as benevolent or harmless, there is an occasional breakthrough of the apprehension that they could damage men. This idea of damage is usually mitigated by a comic presentation. Comic accidents may result in the man's bleeding on the wedding night. In *Easy to Wed,* the wedding night of the hero and heroine, which coincides with the reunion of another couple, is marked by both men's suffering bloodied noses. There is considerable confusion as the hero is supposed to have been married to the other man's girl, but there is no serious hostility between the two men. The hero punches the other man in a friendly spirit, in an effort to help him win back his recalcitrant girl; he expresses the belief that a bloody nose always gets them. The girl then rushes in and punches the hero. Both men show the same somewhat alarmed surprise as they find blood spurting from their noses. While the red stains spread in technicolor on their handkerchiefs, they are consoled by their only slightly distraught women.

In *Janie Gets Married,* the bridegroom's father is painting a gruesome picture of marriage while the young man is shaving just before the wedding. Startled by the father's emphatic statement: There will be times when you'll want to cut her throat, he cuts himself with the razor. Subsequently he appears at the bride's house with a patch of sticking plaster on his cheek. The bride, finding it unsightly, pulls it off, the cut bleeds again, and the bridegroom's mother reproaches the girl for damaging her son.

In other comically damaging marital encounters, the husband may escape with body bruises. The young husband of *The Sailor Takes a Wife* is almost swallowed up by an unmanageable folding bed on his wedding night. A few days later the couple are breaking up housekeeping, although the marriage has not yet been consummated. As both snatch their things out of the dresser drawers with angry haste, his hands, not hers, get repeatedly smashed. In *The Bride Wore Boots,* the hero's divorced wife becomes reconciled to him after seeing his splendid performance in a steeplechase in which he undergoes several painful spills. Swathed in bandages, he is bowled over by her homecoming embrace and lies on the floor groaning about his internal injuries.

Only rarely is the possibility of the man's being damaged by the woman treated seriously, as in *The Macomber Affair*. Mrs. Macomber is the reverse of the helpfully educating woman. She expresses contempt towards her husband when he is weak and inept. When he gains in skill and courage, she so fears losing her dominant position that she kills him. Mrs. Macomber is an exception. She embodies the threat of the emotionally dominant woman, who despises her man, taunts him with his weakness, challenges him to get on top, and releases the full force of her destructiveness if he dares. This woman of bad dreams is continually obscured behind the image of the woman whose dominance is benevolent. It also illustrates a pervasive trend in American films, to deny dangers. As we shall see elsewhere, the danger of suffering through love, the danger of jealousy, the danger of man-man hostilities, the danger of death, all tend to be denied in American films. The conviction that it cannot happen to me guides the fantasy development more often than the imaginary entrance into the danger situation, trying to see what it would be like if it did happen.

In the case of the dominant woman, a potential danger (Mrs. Macomber shows what it is) gets faced in a way. But before it is faced, in the great majority of cases, the teeth are taken out of it. As in the numerous films we have described, the possibility of emotional domination of the woman is excluded. Certain benevolent or harmless forms of domination are selected, by focussing on the area of skill, taking as a model the achievement-encouraging mother, and presenting the outcome of greater activity for the man. Various alternative possibilities, even in the area of skill, are avoided; the possibility, for instance, of the woman humiliating the man by her superior accomplishments or of the man resenting her demonstration of superiority.

§ GOT A MATCH?

WHEN Lauren Bacall appeared in the doorway of a shabby hotel room, gave Humphrey Bogart a long level look and asked in a deliberate throaty voice: Got a match?—when in a later episode she kissed him, and commenting on his impassive reaction, taunted: It's even better when you help —she became a new type of movie heroine (*To Have and Have Not*). She is a woman who approaches men with a man's technique. She presents the man with a provocative, slightly mocking mirror image of himself. Her attraction derives from her combination of masculine and feminine. A man can feel at home with her; she talks his language. In relation to her he experiences none of the discomfort or uncertainty of moving into alien territory, of being required to understand whims, susceptibilities and expectations of a creature different from himself. She does not have the organdy-ruffled femininity of the girl who can be shocked, who must be approached with an artificial delicacy, who holds a man at arm's length while awaiting expressions of fine sentiments. On the other hand, she does not have the equally alien satin couch female quality of the woman who expects elaborate boudoir etiquette and eventual transportation into ecstasy. In contrast to both of these, the masculine-feminine girl has the blunt familiar honesty of the man's world. She provides an answer to the old song, "I'd rather have a buddy than a sweetheart": you can have a sweetheart who's a buddy. Unlike the good girl she admits without euphemisms that she is interested in sex. Unlike the vamp she does not carry an unrelieved aura of it. In her masculine aspect, she is free from the mannishness of women who wanted to be equal to men in a competitive way, felt solidarity with other women, and denied the importance of sex difference. Here a masculine attitude is assumed as an approach to men, and with a constant pleasurable awareness of the difference of sex. This type expresses the stock sentiment of *vive la différence* not by adopting distinctively feminine behavior, but rather by assuming what has been characteristically masculine. It is this combination that we mean to express by calling this type masculine-feminine.

The masculine-feminine girl frequently takes more initiative than the man, both in establishing the initial contact and in sexual approach. This may at first sight look like a reversal of the traditional roles of the sexes. But in effect it rather rectifies the older situation, in which the man was required to assume the initiative, so that an atmosphere of equality results. The girl must prove that she has a masculine attitude; the man is assumed to have it. Another apparent reversal of the usual roles occurs when the girl mockingly reproaches the man for holding out on her (It's even better when you help). Just as a man may, without loss of self-esteem, make repeated overtures to a highly attractive woman though he receives only slight encouragement, this type of heroine continues her approaches to the highly attractive man whom she has chosen even though he maintains for some time an appearance of detachment. While she has announced her readiness, she also maintains a coolly humorous attitude; the man need not feel under pressure from her. She embodies perhaps a man's idealized image of his own courtship behavior.

In *The Strange Love of Martha Ivers,* the heroine assumes the initiative throughout the opening phase of her acquaintance with the hero. She picks him up, using in part stock masculine pick-up lines, in part responses to such lines, without requiring him to give the opening for the response. She is sitting on the steps of her rooming house waiting for a taxi when the hero first appears. She asks him for a match and for the time. Later she offers him a lift in her taxi, and afterwards offers to buy him a drink. She confesses to him that she is lonely, thus giving the reply to the stock male pick-up line (not voiced by the hero): Aren't you lonely? When she learns that the hero is driving to the West Coast, she asks him to take her with him, again giving a positive response to an unexpressed pick-up intention of the man. When the two have installed themselves in adjacent hotel rooms for the night, she comes to his room to trade a Gideon Bible for a cigarette. Her approach represents the characteristic pretense of maintaining contact with the man for the sake of various incidental services to be obtained or offered. This manifest concern with impersonal matters relieves the relationship of the pressure of sexual or sentimental urgency.

In *The Blue Dahlia,* the hero and heroine first meet when she offers him a lift in her car. In *Notorious,* the hero has crashed the gate at a wild party of the heroine's. She, rather drunk, comes up to him, looks him over, and says: I like you. In *Till the End of Time,* the hero and heroine are dancing together at a juke joint where they have just met. She announces: I'm driving you home. When he asks who told her so, she replies: You did, when you sat down beside me. These heroines repeat the most direct masculine line: I like you; and I know you like me—lines whose impact depends on their being used at first meeting, and whose intention is to dispense with preliminaries. A similar taking-things-for-granted line is used at a more advanced stage by the heroine of *The Dark Corner.* In the final scene she announces to various acquaintances that she and the hero have a date at City Hall tomorrow: He hasn't asked me yet, but I always told him I was playing for keeps. This coercion of success, by the brazen assumption that nothing else is possible, is also common to movie heroes.

The masculine-feminine girl is one with whom business and pleasure can be combined without any change of tone. The heroine in *The Dark Corner* is the hero's secretary, and a resourceful ally in his detective work. She is not like the older movie secretary who had to take off her glasses before the boss would notice her. It is clear throughout that she is an attractive girl and she does not conceal the fact that she is making a play for him. Their personal relation is carried on with the same tough, humorous and cagey banter which they use in discussing business. Occasional love-making distracts neither of them from their work. *Tomorrow is Forever* presents a contrasting picture of a boss wooing his secretary in 1918. There is a shift in their relationship when he becomes her suitor, changing from impersonal friendliness to tender protectiveness.

Love is not the whole existence of the masculine-feminine girl. Her approach is casual, deliberate, and knowing. She is not likely to be overwhelmed by unexpected feelings or to have her whole life changed by the coming of a man. All this is a relief to the man, since he does not have to live up to exorbitant expectations, and does not have the guilty feeling that he matters more to the woman than she does to him. The girl conveys this in her attitude that a kiss is just a kiss. Instead of making the man feel that he is taking a fateful step, she assures him that she is mainly interested in appraising the pleasure of the moment. "It's even better when you help" expresses a non-urgent suggestion for having fun, with no strings attached. In *The Big Sleep*, the heroine initiates love-making by asking the hero if he likes her. When he says yes, she taunts him: You haven't done much about it. He kisses her and she responds with: I liked that; I'd like some more. She gets another kiss. Similarly in *Till the End of Time*, the heroine, when the hero first kisses her, remarks appraisingly: I liked that.

In the close-up kisses of the late '20's the screen was filled with two merging profiles. The blanking out of all other sights and sounds expressed the overwhelmingness of the experience. What was probably the most famous kiss of the '46 season, that of Cary Grant and Ingrid Bergman in *Notorious,* showed the couple sauntering through her apartment, interspersing a continuous series of kisses with elated dialogue in such a smooth way that neither seemed to interrupt the other. When he had to talk on the telephone, they still kept on with the intermittent but seemingly continuous kiss. There is less loss of consciousness, less of a break with other activities than in the older style. Talk tends to be increasingly prominent in connection with kissing; the kiss itself, as we have seen, can be discussed. Semi-involuntary movements, such as formerly expressed the melting of the woman, tend to disappear. The heroine being kissed used to begin with her hands braced against the hero's chest, and ended with her arms clasped around his neck. The kiss worked a transformation, revealing to the woman feelings of which she had been unaware. This transforming kiss has now been relegated to comedy. The resistant heroine of *She Wouldn't Say Yes* first begins to love the hero when he kisses her, but her reaction is pictured in a comic light as she looks dazed and staggers slightly. In *The Kid from Brooklyn,* a disgruntled boxer, who wants to pick a fight with the hero, abruptly grabs the hero's sister and kisses her. To everyone's surprise this kiss prolongs itself and produces unanticipated reactions in both partners. It marks the beginning of love, but again the situation is comic.

In the mid-thirties the kiss reaction as an indicator of the rightness of the partner received a romantic comedy treatment in *Tom, Dick, and Harry*. The heroine married the one of her three suitors who made her hear bells ring when he kissed her. The kiss as indicator appears in a more farcical way when the heroine gets hiccoughs (an idiosyncratic reaction to excitement) after the right man kisses her, in *For the Love of Mary*. The indicative function of the kiss remains a recurrent comedy device, though mainly associated with rather immature and simple-minded heroines. For more worldly-wise girls a kiss means less. The heroine of *One More Tomorrow,* for instance, engages in considerable friendly kissing with the hero, but turns down his first proposal of marriage, unaware until much later that she really loves him. The kiss, having become casual for the woman too, brings no revelation and involves no commitment.

The good-bad girl and the girl with the masculine approach, while they are frequently combined in a single prize package, satisfy to some extent different needs. The good-bad girl fulfils the wish of enjoying what is forbidden and at the same time meeting the demands of what we may call (with only apparent redundance) goodness morality. The good-bad girl is what the man thinks he wants when he is told by society and conscience that he must be good. The girl with the masculine approach satisfies a different need. She is related to what we may call (with only apparent contradiction) fun morality. You ought to have fun. If you are not having fun, something is the matter with you. Fun morality, widely current in America today, makes one feel guilty for not having fun. It imposes a new burden, expressed in the stock complaint attributed to the progressive school child: Do we have to do whatever we like again today? The difficulty of meeting the demands of fun morality may be due to the persistent operation of goodness morality on deeper levels. Fun morality threatens to reveal that we have less strength of impulse than we feel we have when confronted with goodness morality on the conscious level. The masculine-feminine girl helps to solve this problem. With an air of authority she indicates how much intensity is required. Casual and deliberate, she teases the man but does not condemn him when he is not carried away by a kiss. If behind the laconic appraisal of pleasant sensations ("I liked that; I'd like some more") there is passion or deep love, it is all to the good; but it is not compulsory. A pretended lack of emotion is a protection against impermanence from outer or inner causes. (This type of girl appears mainly in melodrama where the future of any relationship is made uncertain by a dangerous world.) The masculine-feminine girl not only reduces the demand for overwhelming feeling, but in a humorous, reasonable way permits recesses from sex. She is a pal with whom it is possible to have fun apart from sex, maintaining an awareness that she is a woman, but making few special demands on this score. The vamp, as a woman not only accessible but demanding, is perhaps a danger which has never been successfully faced and overcome. She has been defensively laughed off; but before she became comic, she was frightening because of her insistence on a passion-dominated and woman-centered existence, in which men were helpless before her unpredictable whims. The masculine-feminine girl has the vamp's readiness for love-making without the emotional hazards. Besides reassuring the man about the adequacy of his impulses by not raising too high a demand, she helps him to release feelings which too much femininity tended to inhibit. Her active initiative helps him along, and incidentally relieves him of the apprehension that his advances may be unwelcome.

Since goodness morality and fun morality both operate in contemporary American culture, we frequently find a movie heroine using a masculine approach and appearing as a good-bad girl. The heroine of *The Big Sleep* approaches the hero in the direct manner which we have described, and also appears suspiciously involved with a shady night-club owner. The hero's unhurried reaction to her inducements is rationalized by the necessity of regarding her as a suspect. The heroine of *The Strange Love of Martha Ivers* similarly combines a masculine approach to the hero with an apparent involvement in shady dealings. The good-bad aspect counteracts the tendency for the masculine girl to become too much of a buddy. It demonstrates her attractiveness to other men. At the same time this association with other men satisfies in another way the wish to invest the girl with a masculine aura. In both the good-bad and the masculine aspect it is essential to demonstrate that the girl loves only the hero. We have already seen how this is proof of her goodness. In relation to her masculine approach it is important to establish that this girl who offers herself so freely to the hero has been less free with other men. It is usually conveyed that she has chosen the hero by an act of infallible choice, not impulsively but knowingly, having appraised at a glance his rare qualities. The hero receives the announcement of his election by her easy approach, which is thus not a sign that she is easy to get, but a special compliment to him.

Since this type of heroine assures the man that she accepts him from the start, she relieves him of the necessity of having to prove his worth. He proves it anyhow, but she does not meanwhile suspend judgment. This image of a woman who immediately gives the man assurance that she thinks he is good may compensate for the real-life mother who brought him up on what Margaret Mead has called "conditional love." American children are often weighed and measured, and awarded Mother's love to the extent that they compare favorably with others. The fantasy of the immediate and unconditional award of love by the movie heroine seems related to the suspense and uncertainties of this childhood experience. The occasional taunt of the masculine-feminine girl (It's better when you help. You haven't done much about it.) does not express any doubt about the man's capacities, but rather teases him for not using them.

The masculine-feminine girl may also appear without an admixture of seeming badness. The hero's secretary in *The Dark Corner* is an instance, and even more so the tailored professional woman heroine of *Uncle Harry*. In other cases, for instance in *Gilda,* the good-bad girl may appear without a masculine approach. The heroine lacking the detachment we described is preoccupied with love, demands that the hero love her, and suffers because his suspicions of her postpone their getting together. The hero is saved by these apparently well-founded suspicions from being enveloped by this emotionally demanding woman before the end of the film.

The heroine may, especially in comedies, repeat the mode of amorous approach which the hero has used earlier, either with her or with another girl. Here the girl's taking over the man's technique is spelled out. At the beginning of *Easter Parade*, the hero brings flowers, a bunny, and an Easter bonnet as gifts for the sulky and resistant glamor girl he is courting. In the end, at Easter a year later, the heroine brings flowers, a bunny, and a beribboned top-hat to the hero. The intervening plot details the hero's conversion from the glamor girl to the pal type as represented by the heroine. This is expresed in the style of dance which he performs with each of them. The glamor girl is at first his dancing partner; they perform a ball-room routine in which complementary masculine and feminine roles are expressed. When the glamor girl leaves him, the hero takes the heroine as his partner. After a false start in which she proves clumsy in ball-room dancing, he discovers that she has great talent for tap dancing in which they develop a parallel and interchangeable technique, both performing the same steps. In their most successful number they appear dressed exactly alike as two hoboes. In their off-stage relations, the hero also learns progressively to appreciate the girl who is more like himself.

A type contrasting with the masculine-feminine girl is the bitch, the most dangerous woman to appear since the decline of the vamp. As presented in *Scarlet Street*, she is solely preoccupied with sex. Lounging on an untidy couch, she asks drawlingly, "What else is there?" when her pimp and lover, concerned with business, demands impatiently whether she cannot think of anything else. She is ready to heap contempt on any man who, like the hero, seems inadequate to her demands. Similarly, Mrs. Macomber, in *The Macomber Affair*, takes every opportunity to underscore her husband's weaknesses. A mocking and gleeful witness of his humiliation when he runs away from the lion he has wounded, she ostentatiously bestows her favors on the guide who has been the hero of the hunt. She is a disturbing influence in the man's world, resenting the friendship which later develops between her husband and the guide. When her husband overcomes his fear, she is so piqued at the loss of her dominating and contemptuous position that she shoots him. She is not only intensely demanding, but her demands are impossible to meet. She is the opposite of the masculine-feminine girl who always makes her man feel he is doing all right.

§ ARE YOU COLD?

IN THE early days of courtship in automobiles, a stock line for initiating necking was for the man to ask the girl: "Are you cold?" This device had a number of advantages. It served to get the couple together without their admitting amorous intentions. In this respect it satisfied the demands of goodness morality. To the extent that the couple felt they ought to be having fun but lacked sufficient impetus, the fiction of a non-sexual exigency helped to get them over this hurdle. It was also face-saving for the man in case of a refusal.

Current films make frequent use of related devices. Accidental circumstances throw the couple together, often literally. In *Young Widow,* the hero and heroine, who have just met, are repeatedly thrown into each other's arms by the jolting of the train. An outside agency accomplishes the purpose of incompletely acknowledged impulses. The couple are helped along; they are not left to their impulses which might not give them sufficient impetus, or which might leave them feeling guilty. In an auto accident in *Runaround,* the heroine is knocked unconscious. This gives the hero his first occasion to pick her up in his arms and thus facilitates their first kiss. It is not the impulses of the couple but the automobile which has got out of control.

The hero in *She Wouldn't Say Yes* accidentally knocks the heroine down with a swinging door, and must then pick her up and brush her off. This incident not only facilitates physical contact, but is also a symbol and portent; the woman has previously boasted that she is the reverse of a push-over, but she is destined to fall for this man. The same couple, shortly after this first encounter, are thrown against each other in a train. Later they find, to their surprise, that they have been assigned the same upper berth. Unknown to them the ticket agent who witnessed their first meeting was inspired to play Cupid. As a double expression of the need for outside propelling agencies, the hero in this film is the author of a comic strip in which impish creatures called Nixies aid and abet timid people in doing what they really want to do. The ticket agent, an admirer of the hero's invention, has consciously assumed a Nixie role.

The hero first meets the heroine in *Red River* when he comes to the aid of a wagon train besieged by Indians. The heroine has been shot through the shoulder. He pulls the arrow out, and remarking that it may have been tipped with poison, sucks the wound. The hero in *Somewhere in the Night* is only trying to find a place to hide from pursuing gangsters when he breaks into the heroine's dressing-room. Not only is his intention non-amorous, but his preoccupation with the problem of safety prevents him from wanting to take advantage of the opportunity. In *Easy to Wed,* the hero has been hired to get the heroine into a compromising situation for purposes of blackmail. His efforts to establish an intimate contact are kept going by pressure from his employers.

These indirect devices for achieving contact seem to contrast with the deliberate and conscious approach of the masculine-feminine girl which we have discussed. However, both are related to the difficulty of being impulsive. Neither the couple who have to be thrown together by a jolting train, nor the heroine who slowly and deliberately announces "I like you," or delivers judgment on the quality of a kiss, have much capacity for emotional exuberance. In the case of the heroine with the direct approach, the dictates of fun morality are conscientiously carried out. She helps to make fun achievable and safe, in part, by not requiring overwhelming feeling. Where accidental circumstances take over to bring about the unintended or unacknowledged intimacy, impulsiveness is equally alien to the characters. The unacknowledged impulse becomes embodied in the external agency, the car that gets out of control, the ticket agent who assigns the hero and heroine the same berth. There is a greater atmosphere of goodness morality here than in the case of the masculine-feminine girl; most of these plots are dominated by good girls, and the heroes are compliant to their demands. Thus the major function of the devices described seems to be to allow the hero and heroine to maintain a conscious denial of impulse, while circumstances propel them towards each other. This propulsion may also reenforce or supplement impulse.

Sometimes a representative of authority may step in to demand that the reluctant young people make love. The hero in *What Next Corporal Hargrove?* is ordered by his commanding officer to be nice to the French mayor's daughter who has taken a fancy to him. The officer threatens Hargrove, who is faithful to his girl back home, that he will be put on perpetual garbage patrol if he does not obey. Hargrove, reluctantly escorting the French girl, feels forced to make a show of kissing her when the officer passes by. In *Hold That Blonde,* the hero, who wants to have nothing more to do with women after having been jilted by his fiancée, is ordered by a psychiatrist to get another girl as the only cure for his neurotic symptoms. In *Pillow to Post,* where the hero and heroine have posed as married to solve her housing problem, the hero's commanding officer supervises their reconciliation after an apparent quarrel, demands a more convincing kiss than the hero dared to give. The authority figures here act to decrease guilt and anxiety about the carrying out of impulses. As representatives of goodness morality they give assurance of their approval. Thus they express the fantasy of once forbidding authority figures turned indulgent and approving. They also present a parody of fun morality. They put the weight of authority on the side of impulse, and impose the relentless requirement that people have fun whether they like it or not.

French films tend to present a contrasting picture: where circumstances facilitate intimate contacts, they are apt to be consciously used, or even contrived, for sexual purposes. When the hero in *Panique* discovers that a beautiful woman has moved into the room opposite his window, and that he can easily watch her from this vantage point, he proceeds to station himself at the window every evening. This becomes his main preoccupation; there is no pretense that he gets glimpses of her by chance. The hero in *Les Neufs Célibataires,* having fallen in love at first sight with a beautiful and haughty foreign woman, proceeds to organize circumstances in a way that will bring them together. He institutes an undercover marriage agency to serve foreign women who want to arrange nominal marriages with French men in order to continue residence in France. As he has foreseen, the woman he loves comes to seek his services; after pretending to arrange a marriage of convenience for her, he eventually presents himself as her bridegroom. In *Macadam,* the prostitute who has been ordered by her pimp to seduce the young sailor, takes the room next to his at a low-class hotel. She calls in the hotel keeper, a jolly old woman with an underworld background, and the two of them arrange her bed so that she can make it break down in the middle of the night, call out in alarm, and summon the sailor to her aid. The old woman who helps to arrange things corresponds to the authority figures who bring young people together in American films. The difference is that the young people in the French film are not unwilling.

French films tend to show people as readier to acknowledge, and assume responsibility for, their impulses, and at the same time as more likely to be overwhelmed by unanticipated and disastrous feelings. The hero of *Panique* loves the woman he has seen through the window before he has even spoken to her. This uncalculating emotional commitment eventually leads him to disaster. The American hero who has met a beautiful girl seems rather to have the feeling that he could go for her in a big way—if certain requirements were met. In the case of the good-bad girl as we have seen, his feelings remain tentative while he proceeds to investigate. In less melodramatic cases, his tentative attitude helps him to avoid the humiliation of a refusal. Chance circumstances and people, and non-amorous motives serve to keep the couple together until they can be more sure of each other. The American hero and heroine tend to avoid the dangers in which their French counterparts more frequently become involved. Where French films may demonstrate the disastrous consequences of being carried away by impulse, American films are more likely to show the happy results of impulse kept within bounds. Thus both French and American films seem to express distrust of impulse, but in different ways: the French by facing the danger, the American by denying it.

§ WILL IT EVER TAKE THE PLACE OF BASEBALL?

IN Love Affair, a film of the '30's, a Continental lady-killer is on an ocean liner bound for the United States. A telegram which he has just received from an enamoured lady blows out of his hand. The American heroine picks it up, reads it with an ironical smile, and hands it back to him with the question: "Will it ever take the place of baseball?"

This query (which recalls: Is sex necessary?) suggests a way of achieving detachment. Most of the time, under the pressure of fun morality, we maintain the image of ourselves as being in a state of perpetual readiness to rise to any amorous occasion. But there are moments when, under the guise of comedy or humor, it is a relief to disparage the whole affair. In a similar way, business men may find relief from incessant and strenuous activity by calling it all a racket. For a moment the tension relaxes, and it becomes possible to ask: Is it really worth all the bother? This momentary, joking renunciation of impulse is perhaps the American version of Buddhist retirement from the world. In the movies the comic hero may express this freedom from impulse, or may dare to prefer childlike pleasures to more difficult adult ones. Bob Hope reclines in a harem, surrounded by beautiful girls, and sucks a lollipop (*The Road to Morocco*). At first glance, he appears ludicrous for not taking advantage of his opportunities. But under the comic façade, another pleasure is provided, that of emancipation from the demand for impulse achievement. The comic hero demonstrates a certain wisdom.

American film comedies repeatedly present unused sexual opportunities as occasions for amusement. Their pleasant tone derives partly from a belief that there will be plenty of other chances, partly from the fiction that impulses will always be ready to seize on the next opportunity. But at bottom the missed opportunity seems to be a relief, like being provided with a good excuse for getting out of an examination. Frequently the situation is arranged so that one or both members of the couple have no wish to take advantage of the opportunity, which they have not sought to begin with. In most cases the value of the lost opportunity is diminished by introducing various anaphrodisiac devices: discomforts, distractions, a temporary ludicrousness in the appearance of one or both partners. In *Guest Wife,* the heroine and her husband's best friend are posing as husband and wife. They are not really interested in each other at all. It is just an elaborate hoax that the friend feels forced to play on his boss who believes him to be married. As guests of the boss, the bogus couple are forced to share a bedroom. The wife, to teach the friend a lesson, pretends that she has fallen in love with him. Her advances throw him into a panic. Clad in pajamas which he has clumsily pulled on over his clothes, he takes refuge on a porch where he gets drenched by a shower.

The Sailor Takes a Wife is a comedy about a wedding night that repeatedly fails to materialize. The young couple, who have married after a few hours acquaintance, set up house-keeping in a hastily acquired apartment. The difficulties of initiating marital relations are symbolized by the malfunc-tioning of material appurtenances. The elevator does not work except capriciously and unexpectedly. The windows are stuck shut. The young husband is almost swallowed up by a folding couch which he is struggling to open into a bed. The girl, who had hitherto seemed very attractive, now appears in a pair of heavy, long-sleeved pajamas, and with her hair done up in little-girlish pigtails. When the young man laughs at this costume, she runs to the bedroom and locks the door.

The fairly frequent discrepancy between movie advertise-ments and movie content may have a similar impact to that of the missed opportunity. The advertisements may suggest a greater prominence of love-making than appears in the film. In an extreme case, *The Bells of St. Mary's,* where the two stars played a Catholic priest and a nun, the advertise-ments showed their profiles juxtaposed, with clerical collar and headdress eliminated. Presumably audiences do not manifest too much disappointment when a film reveals less

amorous content than the advertisements would lead them
to expect. They may think of themselves as wanting sex, and
feel relieved to be exempted from it.

Missed opportunities rarely constitute a permanent loss.
There are always plenty of other chances. The couples who
spend the night together without anything happening frequently marry in the end. The classic case was *It Happened
One Night,* the well-known film of the '30's, in which the
hero and heroine reproduced for their wedding night the
circumstances of the earlier night together when they had
divided the room between them. The last scene showed the
falling of the blanket curtain which had served as a barrier.
Similarly in *Lady on a Train* and *Runaround* a harmless
night spent together is a prelude to marriage. In *The Sailor
Takes a Wife,* the three times postponed wedding night is
finally consummated.

In French films, missed opportunities are more apt to be
occasions for endless regret. The lost occasion is not recapturable. There tends to be a fatal discrepancy in the timing
of desire and opportunity. (Failure in various kinds of timing pervades the plots of French films.) When the chance is
provided, the wish to take advantage of it has not yet ma-
tured; when the desire is there, the opportunity is denied.
Fate behaves in a niggardly and mocking way. In the old
René Clair film, *Sous les Toits de Paris,* the hero brings
home to his room a girl of rather easy virtue who has no
place to go for the night. He gives up his bed to her while
he sleeps in a chair. Later he falls in love with her. She is
going to come to live with him, and he happily prepares his
shabby little room, putting flowers on the table, a loaf of
bread and a bottle of wine. An unfortunate chance intervenes and the hero is taken to jail. When he gets out, he
finds his girl already with another man. In his room the mice
are gnawing the bread which was to have been his wedding
cake.

In *Les Enfants du Paradis,* the hero brings to his room the

beautiful woman with whom he has fallen in love. She begins
to undress but he feels there should be more preliminary
soul-searching and mutual avowals, and he leaves her. She
immediately becomes the mistress of his best friend, whose
room is next door. Numerous other difficulties intervene, the
hero and the heroine both marry. It is not till years later
that they return to the same room. They repeat the words
they said on the first occasion and try to deceive themselves
that they can have their chance again. They spend one night
together. Then his wife comes to plead and weep, and the
heroine leaves, presumably never to return. Besides expressing the rarity of opportunities, this film presents a further
contrast to the American pattern. In American films, the
ever-renewed opportunity is always the same; time effects no
changes. The unused chance reappears as bright and shiny
as ever. In *Les Enfants du Paradis,* the attempt of the hero
and heroine to make the later meeting a repetition of the
first points up the hopeless transformation of their circumstances.

The British *Brief Encounter* also presents a lost opportunity as irretrievable. The difficulty here is in raising the
intensity of impulse sufficiently to overcome serious scruples.
The middle-aged man and woman, both married, who have
fallen in love with each other, are ready at one moment to
forget everything but their love. They go to an apartment
which the hero has borrowed for the occasion, but they are
interrupted. The heroine is overwhelmed with shame, all
her reluctance is rearoused; the hero, struggling with his
own bad conscience, lacks sufficient force to persuade her a
second time. Shortly afterwards they separate. Similarly in
Sleeping Car to Trieste, a married man and a young woman
are starting out somewhat apprehensively for an interlude
of illicit love on the Continent. On the train they become
accidentally involved in a criminal investigation and their
intended relation is exposed. When they reach their destina-
tion they part without going through with their plan. Here,

as often happens in British films, accidents have the effect of activating guilt instead of providing exemption. In contrast to *Les Enfants du Paradis,* where the hero and heroine long for a second chance, in these British films internal obstacles prevent them from seeking it. American films usually express the confident expectation that impulses will be sufficiently resolute in the end to bring the couple together, the more so as they are free from guilt; the missed opportunity is a proof of their virtue. American films express an equal confidence in an inexhaustible series of opportunities. This double confidence, combined with a less manifest relief in exemption from love-making, makes the lost opportunity a situation of comedy rather than pathos.

§ LOVE WITHOUT TEARS

IT IS probably a characteristic American conviction that suffering is pointless and unnecessary. In keeping with this, love in American films rarely involves suffering. The numerous possibilities of tragic love, familiar in western literature, find new counterparts here. Lovers do not show the unreasoning obstinate attachment which might involve hopeless longing for someone unattainable, or rage and despair at the loss of the loved one. There is little feeling that it is sweet to be tortured by the loved one; such treatment does not bind the victim to the tormentor, as sometimes happens in British films (*The Seventh Veil, They Were Sisters*). There is a tendency for feelings to become quickly detached from a loved one who has proved disappointing by not loving in return, or by dying, or by turning out to be a criminal. The lover may then decide that this was not love or was not the right person. There is thus little danger of being dragged down by love for an unworthy person; love is awarded to the person who deserves it. Complementing and rewarding this flexibility of feeling is the wealth of opportunity. Replacements, temporary or permanent, are readily available in case of a temporary or permanent defection of the loved one.

This plenitude of possibilities consoles the rejected suitor. In *Two Guys from Milwaukee,* the man who has just been turned down by his girl boards an airplane and is dazzled by the discovery that his favorite movie actress, Lauren Bacall, is sitting beside him. Although Humphrey Bogart comes up a moment later to claim his seat, the impact of the revelation is not lost: there is another dream-girl just around the corner. In *The Well-Groomed Bride,* the heroine, whose bridegroom is diverted at the last moment by an old sweetheart, quickly switches to an even more attractive man who is conveniently at hand. Her disillusionment with the bridegroom and her falling in love with the new man have progressed concurrently, thus eliminating the danger of an even momentary emotional void. In *Wonderman,* when the bride is kept waiting at the church and it seems clear that the bridegroom is not going to show up (he has in fact been murdered, and his place has been taken by his twin brother who is in love with another girl), the bride accepts the offer of the best man to take the bridegroom's place. In *Mildred Pierce,* when the heroine's divorced husband is thrown over by his lady friend, he at once calls up his ex-wife and asks her out to dinner. During the break in her marriage, the heroine has consoled herself with another highly attractive man. However, she now shifts back to her husband. In *The Sailor Takes a Wife,* the rejected suitor of the heroine and the vamp who had made a play for the hero end up by consoling each other. In these rapid changes no one is for long without a partner. The feelings of shame and guilt which Americans seem to associate with being alone are as far as possible avoided.

Emotional entanglements which suggest ironic possibilities are satisfactorily resolved by an appropriate adjustment of feelings. In *The Fallen Angel,* the impecunious hero falls in love with a beautiful mercenary woman. In order to win her he schemes to get the fortune of a small town heiress, a sweet, colorless girl, whom he rushes into a hasty marriage. Immediately afterwards the mercenary one is murdered. Instead of suffering bitter regrets for her loss or for his loveless marriage which has now become pointless, he achieves a quick transformation of feelings which enables him to find satisfaction in the changed circumstances. The day after the murder, he finds that the dead woman has already become unreal for him; at the same time he discovers an unexpected attractiveness in his wife, and is soon genuinely in love with her.

The possibility of lovers suffering prolonged uncertainty about each other is avoided. In *Pride of the Marines,* the young man and the girl have been going together for some time, but when he enters the service, there have been no definite commitments. In saying goodbye, the young man says that they've had a lot of good times together and, considering the uncertainty of things, they had better leave it at that. We then see him pacing the platform of the railroad station alone—he had asked her not to come to see him off—and he looks very lonely. Suddenly the girl appears and throws herself into his arms. It turns out that he has an engagement ring in his pocket, and he has just time to slip it on her finger before the train pulls out.

Lovers who are temporarily deprived of a loved one are apt to be provided with someone to love them in the meantime. They are thus not left in the unpleasant position of being unwanted and lonely. Also, they have a chance to turn the tables by refusing the love of the newcomer. The American remake of the British *Stolen Life* illustrates this. The heroine has just become friends with the hero when her bad twin sister takes him away from her. It is only after a considerable time and several tragic upsets that the heroine, who continues to love the hero throughout, finally gets him. In the British version, she has no consolation in the interim; she mainly goes sailing by herself. The American version supplies her with an attractive suitor whom she in turn repulses. She does not find a new love—after all, she is going to get the hero in the end. But instead of waiting for him in solitude, she is occupied with warding off the not too distasteful advances of another man. *This Love of Ours* has a similar pattern. The heroine has been driven from her home by her husband, who mistakenly suspects her of infidelity. In the long interval before their reunion, she acquires an attractive, understanding, and devoted suitor, whom she in turn rejects.

Where love disappointment is not compensated by the appearance of a temporary or permanent substitute for the lost loved one, other consolations may be provided. The two girl singers in *Night and Day* remain in love with the songwriter hero, who reciprocates only with a comradely affection. One of the singers becomes a top musical comedy star; the other accepts the patronage of a series of millionaires. The ex-marine in *Till the End of Time,* temporarily disappointed by his girl, immediately reverts to the comradeship of his war buddies. They get drunk together and plan to buy a ranch where they will all go off to live.

Where continued attachment to a loved one would involve serious trouble, feelings become detached. This may happen where the hero has fallen in love with a woman who later turns out to be a criminal (*Framed, Dead Reckoning*). This pattern contrasts with one which is frequent in French films. The lover may be thrown into self-destructive despair on learning that the previously idealized loved one is criminal (*La Passionnelle*) or be provoked to murder by her infidelity (*Quai des Orfèvres*). But love once committed to this woman cannot be detached. Women may similarly persist in loving a man who leads them into a life of crime (*Panique*), or who repulses their love (*Falbalas, Torrents*). This feeling of being hopelessly bound is alien to American films. Love tends to be reasonable and righteous. The hero who withdraws his love from the woman who turns out to be bad is exercising the principle of conditional love which he learned from his mother: you have to be good if you want to be loved.

Where a disappointed lover is not provided with a new partner, there is nevertheless little indulgence in grief, rage, or envy, but rather a quick shift to non-painful feelings. In *Adventure,* the heroine's girl friend, who had at first made a big play for the hero, greets the news of their marriage with an effusive, "I love you both!" and immediately assumes the role of friend of the family. The necessity of mourning beyond a minimum for a dead loved one is also denied. A long painful process of detachment of feelings is not recognized. In *My Reputation,* the widowed heroine denies that there is anything painful about the memories evoked by the old house. In *Young Widow,* when the heroine returns to her job after an interlude of being haunted by memories of her dead husband, she expresses regret that she did not go back to work sooner: she has been wasting her time.

The rare characters who submit to suffering from loss of love are apt to appear as comic or weak. The hero of *Hold That Blonde* develops comical symptoms after having been rejected by his fiancée. He becomes a kleptomaniac and his ears wiggle every time he sees a pretty girl. He has to be told by a psychiatrist to get himself another sweetheart. In *The Strange Love of Martha Ivers,* the man who continues to love a woman who despises him is a consistently weak character. He has allowed his father to arrange his marriage, permitted himself to be used to cover up his wife's crimes and to advance her ambitions. All he can do about it is to get drunk. In the end he commits suicide.

With the many expedients for avoiding suffering in love, it is not surprising that few love relations turn out unhappily. If we consider the central love story, and define unhappiness by death or defection, only one sixth of American films have love ending unhappily. French films show love turning out unhappily half of the time. The proportion of unhappy love in British films seems to fall between these two.

The hazards of love are further reduced by the fact that scarcely anyone tries to force anything on a loved one. The lover does not imperiously demand conformity to his wishes, nor does he practise any serious deception to get what he wants. In *My Reputation,* where the domestically inclined heroine falls in love with the playboy, there is little danger that she will be ruined or that he will be trapped. Neither has the inclination to take advantage of the other. The situation is easily resolved by a transformation of his feelings, so that his wishes coincide with hers. In *The Fallen Angel,* the original exploitative intentions of the hero fail to materialize. Almost immediately after he has married the heroine for her money, he confesses this to her, then makes good by falling in love with her. Even the exceptionally demanding and possessive wife in *Leave Her to Heaven* does not feel that she can force on her husband her requirement that they live in complete mutually absorbed isolation. Instead she kills anyone who threatens to invade their solitude. In an exceptional case, *The Killers,* the bad woman uses the hero as a fall guy for her crimes and the enamoured hero allows himself to be used.

Aside from a few exceptions, however, men and women are not made vulnerable by emotional susceptibility. Dangers in American films tend to take the form of external violence, not of inner conflict. The threat of falling hopelessly in love with someone bad or exploitative or unloving, and so having one's life destroyed, seems unreal. The shot in the dark, the beating in the lonely shack in the woods, or the false crime accusation—these are the images of danger. In American films, men and women may, and often do shoot each other. They do not break each other's hearts.

2

PARENTS AND CHILDREN

AMERICAN FILMS tend to picture both hero and heroine unbound by family ties. Homeless, in the main jauntily self-sufficient, they make their way through city streets, night clubs, lunch wagons, and hotel rooms until they find each other, and then pass from our view before they settle down to constitute a new family. More than half of the heroes and half of the heroines have no relations. If they do have any, they are not likely to have more than one.

The most frequent relations of heroes are in-laws and children. This reflects the American emphasis on the family you make, as against the family you come from. The fact that children, when present, almost always make some difference in the plot underscores this point. Following children and in-laws in frequency, and in the following order, come father, mother, brother, and sister. Brothers, though they do not appear frequently, tend to be the only relations of the hero, other than children, who play a decisive role in the story. This is probably related to the American emphasis on rivalry with age-mates, while the older generation is supposed automatically to fall into the background.

Heroines show a stronger tie to the family they come from through their relation to their fathers. Fathers of heroines appear twice as often as fathers of heroes, and also twice as often as mothers of either. In addition, fathers of heroines tend to have some importance for the plot. For the movies, the father-daughter tie is the most significant manifest tie with the older generation. Children are the next most frequent relations of heroines; they, too, tend to be important to the plot. Thus for heroines as for heroes, the family they make is emphasized. Next in frequency, and in the following order, come sisters, mothers, in-laws, and (very rarely) brothers. Of these, sisters alone play a significant role. Thus for both heroes and heroines, only siblings of the same sex are important. In both cases they are rivals.

In contrast to American films, British and French films provide the hero and heroine with family relations more frequently. American and British films resemble each other in the equalization of the sexes in respect to family ties, while the French show the woman as more family-bound than the man. There is some indication that, in French films, the family of origin is more prominent than the procreational family.

* * *

In this chapter we shall consider the image which the films present of various family relationships, the quality of feelings and behavior characteristically shown between parents and children, brothers and sisters. We propose to consider separately the roles of older generation parents and those of the hero and heroine as father and mother; for there is discontinuity between the past and the present generation in American films. The heroine as a mother does not resemble her mother and never will. Attractive and energetic, she will never become the faintly unpleasant, ineffectual older woman that her mother is. Nor will she come to matter so little to her children, to have so little grip and impact on the life around her. Similarly the hero matters tremendously more to his son than his father does to him. This is partly an effect of the spot-light focus on our own generation: in American films the present generation appears rather as outside of the continuous passage of human life. (In a similar way the hero and heroine enjoy prerogatives not shared by those around them. For instance, they are usually the only ones who find love.) Thus we, as represented by the hero and heroine, are exceptional and do not see any precedent or anticipation of our fate in those who went before. American films do not undertake to reconcile us to the transient or otherwise disappointing aspects of life by dramatically evoking them. They fairly consistently deny these deprivational aspects.

A continuity of generations, however, is not entirely lacking. But it takes its starting point in the present and stretches into the future. The hero finds immortality in his son. His father, a mild, colorless, undemanding character, has no immortality, but falls unprotesting into oblivion.

One of the major contrasts between American and French films derives from the difference in role of the older generation father. In French films, this older generation father (typically Raimu) tends to be the central and most interesting character. His grown-up children appear still unformed by comparison with him. His rich emotional life and conflicts about being an aging husband, a father, and a grandfather dominate the scene. His children remain bound to him, and his son learns from him how to behave as a father in his turn. The *Marius-Fanny-César* trilogy takes fatherhood as its central theme, starting from the loving and conflict-ridden relation between the young hero and his warmly devoted, irascible father and ending with the consolidation of a positive relation between the hero and his grown-up son. Throughout, the older generation father is the most active, fully drawn, and decisive personality. (It is characteristic that the last film of the series, in which not only his son but also his grandson assumes major importance, bears his name as title.) He is the fully developed father type in contrast both to his old friend, Panisse, who assumes the paternity of the son's child, and to the son, who until the last film is only a lover and has not learned how to be a father. In American films, which in this respect seem to parallel American life, there is no role of comparable importance for the older generation father either in arranging his children's lives or in acting as a model of character and wisdom. An exceptional American film of the thirties, *Make Way for Tomorrow*, centered around an aging couple, parents of grown-up children. These worthy old people had no place in life; their children found it embarrassing and annoying to have them still around. At the close of the film they were on their way to an old people's home. This prospect was too painful to contemplate and the film was without sequels.

American films tend to present the hero's and heroine's involvement with their parents as finished business. This is often conveyed by showing the older generation parents, when they appear at all, as pale background figures. Where parents or parent substitutes play a more active part, the children tend to effect a quick and complete emotional detachment following a dramatic break. The tragic tradition of Oedipus and Hamlet, where the son's life is overshadowed by his father's death, is not perpetuated. In British films, on the other hand, a son may blame himself for his father's death and devote his life thereafter to self-imposed penance. In American films there seems to be less guilt as well as less positive feeling towards the antecedent generation. A son may do a successful detective job following his father's murder, leave the scene strewn with corpses, but then, unlike Hamlet, go off unscathed and arm-in-arm with his girl. A father may be driven to suicide by his son; disguised parent figures, say the powerful man and woman who rule the hero's home town, may die violent deaths. The sequel is apt to be the same: in the sunny morning following the nightmarish fatalities, the hero and his girl drive off in an open roadster along the beckoning highway. The involvement with parent-figures, even in the case of their violent deaths, is like a dream from which one wakes to the work and promise of one's own life to live.

The escape of the children from protracted involvement with their parents is a point on which several basic trends in American films converge. We have spoken before of the tendency of characters to manifest an easy flexibility in their emotional attachments; wherever there may be disappointment or other danger, love can be withdrawn and redirected to more rewarding objects. The hero is not caught in a hopeless involvement with an unfaithful or otherwise dangerous woman. Behind the woman to whom it is inadvisable to become overattached is the image of the mother, whom one must not love too much. According to the movie fantasy this disengagement is not too difficult. It is facilitated by the wish to turn the tables on the woman, to disappoint her just as the mother has presumably disappointed the little boy. The heroes of film melodramas regularly treat in this way the attractive but possibly dangerous woman who seeks their love. They get satisfaction from her frequent approaches and avowals while they play hard to get. They are thus always in a good position to withdraw whenever that seems advisable. As a reaction against the original involvement with the mother, the film hero seems to be demonstrating the feeling: you need me more than I need you, or, in the words of a popular song, "I get along without you very well."

The image of the mother threatened with rejection also

appears in the relation between the heroine and her son. Usually the child's father is dead or absent. While the boy could thus have the mother to himself, this possibility is little exploited. The emphasis is rather on the mother's suffering deprivation through the son, who means so terribly much to her in these circumstances. The mother is harried by the possibility of losing the son; he is dangerously ill, or someone else adopts him, or, when he gets older, he runs away. The aim of disappointing the mother-figure predominates over that of the son's monopolizing her love. In the melodramas where the hero is usually able to have the beautiful woman who is involved with the older man if he wants her, the most frequent development is that he rejects her either temporarily or finally.

The translation into drama of the emotions engendered in family life usually involves some disguise. In American films, where older generation parents appear as such they are usually negligible figures. We believe that these manifest parent images do not exhaust the feelings and fantasies about mothers and fathers on which film plots draw. The tendency in American life to relegate parents to the background facilitates the displacement to other persons of unresolved feelings towards mother and father. In the films we trace the more intense feelings of sons towards their fathers in the melodramas where the hero is involved in violent conflict with a dangerous older man, often his boss. The mild, ineffectual manifest father of the films represents the father as sons are encouraged to think of him. But this effort to obviate father-son rivalry and conflict does not succeed completely in eliminating the child's image of the father as a big and dangerous man. This image, not manifestly appearing as father, persists in the night-time dream world of the film melodramas where the hero is involved in a conflict of crime and punishment with the older man, his boss, often a lord of the underworld. Like a dream this conflict takes place mostly in the dark, with the illumination perhaps of the neon lights that flash off and on outside the window of the cheap hotel room. The locale is far from home, and the characters are strangers, who, as often in a dream, represent people one has known before. This night-time world in which the hero grapples with a dangerous older man, and wards off entanglement with a desirable and yearning woman, represents the last struggle, as in a dream, with the love and hate he bears towards his parents before he wakes to the morning sunlight of real life in which he will ride off in the shiny roadster with his own girl beside him.

One of the major devices in achieving the hero's triumph over the emotional residues of familial involvement is the projection of these emotions onto others. It is the hero's boss who attacks him and who commits numerous crimes for which he frequently tries to inculpate the hero. The violent impulses of sons towards their fathers, acknowledged in much of western tragedy, find a reverse expression here. The son is in the clear because the older man attacks him first. Everything he does is in self-defense. Any bad actions of which the heroes of other dramas may accuse themselves appear as a frame-up against which the hero must fight. He would be amply justified in killing the unfairly attacking older man, but he is doubly in the clear as this deed is usually accomplished for him by someone else. American film heroes (in contrast to British) do not generally blame themselves for intentions but only for acts. Just as the hero is technically in the clear in connection with violent interchanges with the father-figure, he is free from blame in relation to the mother-figure. It is not he who knowingly or unknowingly seeks to win the other man's woman, but she who persistently and unsought pursues him. The Oedipal formula as transcribed in this film fantasy reads: father attacks me and mother seeks my love. The hero is the innocent object of these bad impulses proceeding from the parent-figures. The assumption in American life that children will surpass their parents may contribute to making the parents eligible to be the bearers in fantasy of the condemned impulses of the children. Perhaps the impact of the immigrant tradition is also relevant here, as it contributed the image of parents as representing an old and bad culture which they tried to leave behind and from which the children succeeded in emancipating themselves.

Our procedure in this chapter has been first to examine the manifest parent images (that is, the parents appearing as such) and subsequently, under the title of the Concealed Triangle, to point out what we take to be the underlying emotional drama of the hero's relations to mother- and father-figures appearing under various disguises. The familial story centering around the daughter seems to provide less dramatic material. The heroine's relation to her manifest father is much more developed than that of the hero with either parent. It thus appears to be less conflict-ridden and leaves less over for disguised expression. Feminine rivalries and hostilities within the family tend to be focused on sister (preferably twin sister) relations more than on those of mother and daughter. Some of the major woman-woman conflicts occur in this relationship. The emphasis on the sister seems less related to a need to mitigate mother-daughter conflicts through displacement than to the idea that, as sex rivals, the two women must be matched in age. This is based on the presumption that a woman old enough to have a grown daughter will have lost her sexual attractiveness. As the relatively recent trend of the glamor mother develops, we may expect more and more to find mothers who look no older than their daughters appearing as sex rivals, as for instance in *Mother is a Freshman.*

Brothers also appear in situations of possible rivalry, but this rivalry tends to be more subdued than that between sisters. Characteristically the motive of rivalry is not ascribed to hero or heroine; the unacknowledged aim of disposing of a brother or sister is achieved for them by accommodating chance. Thus the twin sister who stands in the way of the heroine's happiness is washed out of a boat by a convenient high wave. The hero finds himself thrown by unanticipated circumstances into the position of a richer or more famous twin brother. Here as elsewhere in American films, heroes and heroines are absolved from guilty impulses, while what they might have wished (if they had not been so good) is accomplished for them by other agencies. Where other sorts of dramas have often presented premonitory visions of the dangerousness of fulfilling certain wishes (for instance, those which involve eliminating anyone who stands in our way), American films provide solutions in which such wish-fulfilments can occur without penalties. It is not enough to say that these are wish-fulfilment fantasies. Even in dreams wish-fulfilments often arouse anxiety or turn into nightmares. We shall observe the devices introduced to obviate anxiety in the film wish-fulfilments, as well as the places where, and the ways in which, apprehension of danger breaks through.

Among the most frequent mechanisms used in American films for making wish-fulfilments safe are projection and denial. The impulses in one's own nature which may lead to danger and self-defeating conflict are ascribed to other characters while the hero appears free and innocent of such strivings. Dangers from outside are thus substituted for dangers from within. The hero of the melodramas is surrounded by a world that directs at him forbidden love, violent attacks, and accusations of criminal deeds. Since these counterparts of his own unacknowledged love and hate and self-accusations appear as external he can fight against them. The possible fatality to the hero of external dangers, whether embodied in ensnaring women, the brutal attacks of gangs of men, or the false accusations of obtuse police, are denied. These dangers can be, and usually are, surmounted by the hero if he is sufficiently energetic and shows enough capacity to take it. He will then, despite numerous beatings, emerge eventually unscathed, free, and in the clear. The possibility of dangers residing within ourselves is thus little acknowl-

edged in American films. The conditions of anxiety or happiness tend to be external and subject to control. While the
mechanisms leading to these solutions represent common
human possibilities, they are not always equally decisive in
the formation of dramatic plots.

§ THE OLDER GENERATION

THE hero's father is usually a sympathetic character, and
almost always ineffectual. His relation with the hero is
friendly, but he can give him little more than good will. In
most cases, it would make no difference to the course of
events if the father were eliminated from the story. He is a
non-essential background figure.

In *Till the End of Time* there is a nice solidarity between
father and son in implicit opposition to the uncomprehend-
ing dominant mother. The son has just returned from the
army. The mother embraces him and weeps. The father,
close to tears himself, but with a sensitive feeling for the son's
embarrassment, succeeds in diverting the mother, makes a
gently humorous aside to the son about women's hysterics.
He then offers the son a drink, but the mother protests that
he should only give him very little. She still thinks of the son
as a boy, while the father accepts him as a man. Later, when
the son remains at loose ends and shows no inclination to get
a job, the father comes into his bedroom in the morning, sits
down on the side of his bed and asks him tactfully about his
plans. As the son expresses his need to get reoriented, the
father does not press him further. In contrast to this, the
mother requires full-dress explanations in the living-room.
She forces the father to make a set speech on how disap-

pointed they are in the son, and to demand from him a definite statement of job plans. This, of course, arouses strong resentment in the son, and he rushes out of the house in a rage. Later, father and son share an all-night vigil in a hospital where a buddy of the son's, who has been injured in a fight, hovers between life and death. The father is reminded of how, years before, he waited in the hospital all night when the son was born. The father's memory about the birth of his son is thus associated with man-man solidarity. He feels a closer bond of mutual understanding with his son than with his wife.

A similarly sympathetic father-son relation appears in *Too Young to Know*. The son arrives home from college unexpectedly, with a bride. The situation is awkward, particularly as the mother starts protesting about the son's being so young, and complaining that he did not let them know ahead of time. The father gently smooths things over by reminding her of how young they were when they were married, gradually gets her into a good humor by recalling how pretty she was. Here, again, the mother expresses dissatisfaction with the son and makes the family atmosphere strained, while the father tends to accept whatever the son wants, and tries, in a conciliatory way, to protect the son from the mother's criticisms and to relieve the tension. The father is too weak, however, to play any decisive role in the children's affairs. Later, he is replaced by a more effective extra-familial father-figure, an old judge who takes an interest in the young couple and helps to straighten out their difficulties.

In *Body and Soul*, the hero's father owns a small candy store on New York's lower east side. The hero, impatient to rise from this low status, tells his parents that he has the chance to make a career as a boxer. His mother is moralistically critical about fighting. He brushes aside her objections by asking whether she thinks he wants to grow up to be like Pop. The father, unresentful of this, slips the son money from the cash-register, which he needs to buy boxing equipment. Almost immediately following this the father is accidentally killed by neighborhood gang violence.

Fathers tend to be less competent than their sons. In *Johnny Angel*, the hero's father is killed in a plot which the hero succeeds in exposing. The father is an honest old ship's captain, trusting and simple-minded, who lets himself be used by an unscrupulous employer, and who is murdered so that he will not reveal an act of piracy. The son is an honest young ship's captain who is anything but trusting, knows his way around the underworld, and is proof against the murderous attacks of bad men and the seductions of wicked women. In investigating his father's murder he is exposed to both these dangers, but emerges unscathed. He is not superior to his father morally, and (which is exceptional for the movies) has followed the same profession. His superiority lies in his worldliness, particularly in his distrust of everyone, which insures him against being made a sucker.

In *Lover Come Back*, the hero is a famous newspaper correspondent. His father, a sweet, insignificant little old man, seems to have at least this advantage over his more spectacular son that he has been able to preserve a happy and stable marriage. The son's affairs with women are in confusion and his wife, whom he still loves, is about to divorce him. However, the father is not allowed even this advantage. The son, having followed his wife to Reno in the hope of dissuading her, is amazed to meet his father there, and to learn that his father is planning to divorce his mother on the basis of some ridiculous misunderstanding. The son has to straighten out his father's marital difficulties before settling his own.

In an exceptional case, the father may be unsympathetic. The hero's father in *One More Tomorrow* wants to subordinate the hero's ambitions to his business interests. He tries to persuade the hero to suppress an exposé of the father's dubious business dealings, which is about to appear in a lib-

eral journal the son has been financing. He does not succeed.
Like the sympathetic fathers, he is ineffectual.

* * *

Father-daughter relations are almost without exception
positive. Fathers have a wider range of significance for daughters than for sons, extending from the father who is the main
love object of the daughter's life (*Leave Her to Heaven*) to
the sweet little old man in a far-off city whom the daughter
phones long-distance on Christmas Eve (*Lady on a Train*).
The importance of the father depends on how strongly the
daughter feels about him rather than on any activity of his
or any control which he exercises over her. The daughter
eludes with ease any attempt at protective supervision. When
the daughter in *Lady on a Train* arrives in New York she is
met by her father's business agent who has been assigned to
look after her. The girl immediately escapes him by asking
him to carry a portable radio which turns out to be someone
else's and leaving him to disentangle himself from the irate
owner while she rushes off to investigate a murder she happened to oversee from the train window. Throughout the
film the girl is boldly pursuing her increasingly dangerous
crime investigations, and the ineffectual representative of the
father is vainly trying to catch up with her. In exceptional
instances where the father tries to influence the daughter's
ideas, he is equally unsuccessful. The father in *Notorious* (a
rare bad father) meets with immovable resistance when he
tries to convert his daughter to Nazism.

The father tends to be much concerned with his daughter's
marriage, and is apt to form an alliance with his prospective
son-in-law. While affectionate towards the daughter, he is
not possessive, and may become the ally of her suitor at a
time when she is still resistant towards him (*Easy to Wed,
The Well-Groomed Bride*). Thus, in relation to sons-in-law,
as in relation to sons, the father disarms any possible hostil-

ity. He is ready to exert all the influence he hasn't got for the fulfilment of the son's or son-in-law's wishes. An alliance between father and prospective son-in-law is elaborately developed in *She Wouldn't Say Yes*. The daughter, a handsome and severe career woman, lives alone with her jolly little old father, whose continually expressed wish for a grandchild she dismisses with impatience. The father conceives an immediate warm friendship for her unwanted but persistent suitor. This spontaneous abdication of the father from a position of exclusive possession of a beloved daughter is typical. It expresses, among other things, a mild retaliation against the dominant woman in relation to whom the father and prospective son-in-law become secret allies. The alliance between these two potential rivals parallels the alliance of father and son against the dominant mother. It also expresses the friendly sharing of a woman which is a fairly frequent comedy theme. The use of this sharing as a means of intimacy between the two men is particularly patent here. In a comic reversal of the saying, "It's not your father I'm marrying, it's you," the hero and the father hold hands and exchange vows in a secret marriage rehearsal. In the end, on what was to have been the wedding night, the young man sleeps with the father. His marriage is not yet legal, and the father makes him sleep in the lower berth with him while the daughter occupies the upper. At the same time he mitigates his intimacy with the young man by regarding him as a medium for expressing his love for his daughter. As the young man stands on the lower berth and kisses the daughter who leans out from above, the father delightedly explains to a perplexed conductor: I'm kissing my daughter goodnight. Despite the scheming of this father to ensure his daughter's marriage, his efforts have mainly afforded a comic diversion in an affair which would have developed to the same end without him.

A father may be assisted by other paternal figures, all intensely devoted to the daughter, all concerned with promoting a happy romance for her. The upshot remains the same:

the daughter makes up her own mind and solves her own problems. In *For the Love of Mary,* the heroine, a White House telephone girl who lives alone with her elderly father, is the main concern of four Supreme Court justices and the President. The justices are backing a young lawyer, and become exceedingly distressed whenever the heroine quarrels with him. The President has provided her with a handsome naval aide for escort. In the end she marries a third young man who is unencumbered by paternal sponsorship.

There is a tendency to picture the heroine alone with her father. In the majority of cases where she has a father, the mother is not seen or mentioned. Thus the presumable wish of young girls to get their mothers out of the way and to have their fathers to themselves is gratified in these films. This gratification, however, is without conscious emotional intensity. The father with whom the daughter lives alone is a figure of reduced importance, for whom she feels a moderate affection. In the few cases where the father has a more intense emotional importance for his daughter, he is either dead or absent. Thus, where father and daughter are shown together, their relations are not intense; where their relations are intense, they are not shown together. Though the relation of a daughter to her father is the only child-parent relation which is admitted to retain some importance in adult life, there is a tendency to push this too into the background.

In *Notorious,* the heroine's father exercises a decisive and nearly fatal influence on her life. Shocked and embittered by the discovery that he has been a Nazi spy, the heroine first throws herself into a life of dissipation. However, she is soon offered a more effective way of demonstrating against her father's betrayal. She is recruited by the FBI for intelligence work against the Nazis, with whom, as her father's daughter, she will be able to make favorable contacts. In connection with her work, she is forced to marry an elderly Nazi, a former friend of her father's, who nearly murders her when he finds out that she is a spy. The father never appears except as a voice in a phonograph recording made by the FBI. In *Leave Her to Heaven*, the father, through his excessive indulgence of his daughter, exercises a disastrous influence on her life. The father, who has died before the film begins, had admitted his daughter into his intimate confidence, allowed her to help him with his work and to go with him on holidays in the mountains from which the mother was excluded. The daughter marries a man who resembles her father, and, in an effort to keep him entirely to herself, is led to murder and finally to suicide. The father never appears except as ashes which the daughter, carrying out his wishes, strews from a funerary urn over his favorite mountain-top. The fact that these exceptional important fathers are not shown indicates the difficulty of presenting an older generation father as a decisive character.

The tendency in American films to avoid the presentation of intense father-daughter relations becomes more evident when we compare an American with a French treatment of the same theme. *To Each His Own* and *La Fille du Pusatier* start out from an identical situation: a daughter, living with her widowed father, has an illegitimate baby by an Army flier who disappears into the blue. The French film concentrates on the subsequent conflicts in the father-daughter relation and their eventual resolution. The father is at first indignant, disowns his daughter and sends her away. When he learns that the child his daughter has borne is a boy, and that it will bear his name, he is deeply moved. His dead wife had borne him numerous daughters, but the daughter has succeeded in presenting him with a son. While maintaining a pretense of grudging disapproval he goes to visit the daughter, sees the baby, calls it by his name, weeps, and takes them both home with him. The father is the central figure, and his changing feelings towards the daughter provide the major impact of the film. When the daughter in *To Each His Own* informs her father about her illegitimate baby, he makes a fine speech to the effect that we love each other, we do not

judge each other, and dies in the next reel. There are no conflicts or dramatic upsets in this relationship, which falls into
the background of the main action. The father plays no role
either in complicating or resolving the daughter's difficulties,
which revolve around how she can take possession of her
child and get credit for being his mother after he has been
adopted by another woman. The daughter's frustrations and
triumphs are all concentrated on her own and the next generation. She triumphs over the adoptive mother of her child
because this woman's husband loves the heroine and has
never loved his wife. At the end she triumphs, at least momentarily, over the bride of her grown-up son as the son,
finally made aware of his mother's identity, leaves his bride
on the dance floor and goes over to the heroine to ask: May
I have this dance—Mother?

* * *

Where the mother of the hero appears, she is apt to be a
colorless, background figure. Insofar as she shows any distinguishable characteristics, she is a person you would rather
not have around. While remaining for the most part without
influence, she contributes to tension in the home. Generally
obtuse, she lacks comprehension of her son. She is anxious
about his taking a drink, officious in recommending to him
the bobby-soxer next door (an object for long-term courtship,
when he is urgently concerned with a mature glamor-girl),
shocked by his buddy's profanity, intolerant of the distress
which makes him delay settling down to a job (*Till the End
of Time*). She is ungracious when her son presents his girl to
her, and carpingly critical of her daughter-in-law (*Janie Gets
Married, Too Young to Know*). Less frequently she may appear as a technicolored Christmas card figure, the gentle,
white-haired lady who presides over the stately country house
to which the hero returns for rare family reunions (*Night
and Day*).

In *Body and Soul,* the hero's mother plays a more serious role, but she is still unsympathetic and ineffectual. She opposes with moralistic contempt the hero's ambition to become a boxer, and would rather have them live on a social service allowance after the father's death. The hero angrily throws the visiting social worker out of the house and proceeds, despite his mother's criticism, to work his way up in the world as a fighter. This mother's anti-fighting ethic is just as unassimilable for her son as the less serious anti-profanity and anti-drinking morality of the mother in *Till the End of Time.* When, in the end, the hero retires from the ring, it is because he has learned for himself about the corruption of the fight racket and not because he has accepted his mother's ideals. (The relative prominence of the hero's parents in *Body and Soul* seems related to the fact that the family is presented as Jewish.)

The exceptional *Swell Guy* presents a mother who does exert some influence on her son. This influence is entirely negative, as the son reacts intensely against her severe morality and is at the same time demoralized by her disapproval. The father, who is dead, had been an easy-going character, neither very honest nor very successful, with whom the son felt closely allied. When the son returns home after a long absence, his mother makes it clear that she has not relaxed the contempt she had always maintained for both him and his father. When he makes a successful speech at a picnic, she walks out when the crowd applauds. When he is in trouble, and begs her for a last chance, she tells him he is just no good. He replies bitterly: You had me tagged from the start. This woman is Mrs. Macomber in a manifest mother role. Nothing her son does can alter her disparaging attitude towards him. As we have seen, such destructive potentialities of women are rarely acknowledged in American films. However, a hint of them comes through in the persistent unpleasantness of the usually insignificant older generation mother.

Thus the image of the hero's mother is in contrast to the

more positive image of the father. It would seem that negative feelings towards the father and positive feelings towards
the mother cannot be expressed on this manifest level. Since
it is unlikely that such feelings should be absent, we shall try
to see later whether they do not find expression in disguised
form elsewhere. Where the heroine's relation to her father
becomes intense, they are, as we have seen, not shown together. For the mother-son relation more elaborate distortions
seem required. The wish-fulfilment situation of the daughter
living alone with her father, which we found to be frequent,
rarely finds a parallel in the grown-up son's relation to his
mother. The hero of *Nocturne,* a detective who is hardly
ever at home, lives alone with his mother who stays out all
night playing bingo. The eccentric character of the mother
prevents her from being an object of intense feeling. The
insignificance of mothers for the most part, and the attenu-
ated feelings they evoke, suggest that the more serious feelings of sons for their mothers are expressed under disguises.

* * *

Heroines have mothers less frequently than they have
fathers, and their relations with their mothers tend to be less
important and less agreeable. For both heroes and heroines
the father is thus the more pleasant parent. While for the
hero the mother tends to evoke vague uneasiness, the heroine's conflict with her mother may focus on more definite
issues. In *My Reputation,* the heroine quarrels with her
mother over the issue of conventional forms versus genuine
feeling. As against the mother's perpetual mourning for her
long-dead husband, the heroine refuses to wear black after
her husband's death. She shocks her mother by allowing her
young sons to go to the ball-game shortly after their father's
funeral. It is what their father would have wanted, it is what
they want, and she doesn't care how it looks. Later the heroine defies maternal disapproval in pursuing a relationship

with a new man (a relationship which is harmless but arouses gossip). Underlying the mother's submission to convention and her attempt to impose it on her daughter is the circumstance that the daughter continues to be sexually eligible while the mother has ceased to be so. The emotional impact of this issue is reduced by making the mother a stereotyped, stiff, white-haired dowager, whose own frustrations and claims to sympathy are not elaborated. The unsatisfied longings of aging women seem to be too unpleasant to contemplate, with the result that such women appear as willfully obstructive to the happiness of their young and beautiful daughters.

In *Leave Her to Heaven,* the malign daughter taunts her long-suffering mother with the claim that she (the daughter) achieved more intimate communion with the father than the mother ever did. However, the mother is not her main opponent; it is rather her young step-sister, who wins the disputed young man in the end. The center of contention is, as usual, shifted from the older generation to that of one's age-mates. The mother, a wise, good, and uninteresting woman, has no essential role in the action. On occasion she is the confidante of her step-daughter or of the young man.

While mothers tend to be rather foolish in relation to sons, they may show some wisdom or shrewdness in relation to daughters. The heroine's mother in *The Bride Wore Boots* understands that the heroine still loves her divorced husband, and engineers a reunion between them. She gives a dinner for her two grandchildren, encourages them to overeat, and when they are put to bed with severe indigestion, brings the parents together at the children's bedside. While the son-in-law is taken in by this ruse, the daughter, characteristically, sees through it and resists its effects. A final reunion remains to be effected by the young couple themselves. The efforts of this shrewd mother, as those of older generation parents generally, remain ineffectual.

In the rare case where a mother plays an active and decisive role in a heroine's life, it may be an adoptive mother.

In *Love Letters,* the devoted adoptive mother of the heroine breaks a poker over the head of the brutal husband who is making the heroine unhappy. The shock of this causes the adoptive mother to have a brain hemorrhage and she remains for a considerable time unable to speak. The heroine reacts by amnesia. Since neither woman is able to tell what happened, the heroine is found guilty of murder and serves a prison term. It is only at the end that the adoptive mother recovers and tells her story. Up to this point we have seen her only as a paralyzed old woman in a nursing home. When in the last few moments of the film her decisive importance in the heroine's life is revealed, one sees that her role has a dual aspect. She tells of her love for the heroine, whom she adopted in childhood, and whose every wish she strove to gratify. She also tells of the crime which she committed impulsively on the heroine's behalf, and which nearly wrecked the heroine's life. This mother is a fairy-godmother and witch rolled into one. Again, where a parent assumes a decisive role, where some of the strong and mixed feelings associated with the parent begin to come out, some disguise is necessary. In this case an adoptive mother is substituted for a real one.

In *The Locket,* too, the mother-figure who exercises a decisive, and even more destructive, role in the heroine's life is not her real mother. She appears first as the rich lady in whose house the heroine is a servant's child, later as the heroine's prospective mother-in-law. In the childhood episode which ruins the heroine's whole life, the rich lady falsely accuses her of stealing. The rich lady's daughter, a devoted playmate of the heroine, has been given a valuable locket for a birthday present, and passes it on to the heroine to compensate her for not being permitted to come to the party. The rich lady impatiently takes the locket back and when it is later lost, accuses the heroine of stealing it. This scene terrifies the child and its effect remains undiminished when her own mother exonerates her by finding the lost locket at-

tached to the rich girl's dress in the laundry. The real mother
is anxious lest her child's behavior reflect on her; she is on
the girl's side but ineffectual in comparison with the other
powerful and hostile mother-figure. In adult life the heroine
has an irresistible impulse to steal jewels, and may kill anyone who stands in her way. She drives her fiancé to suicide,
later has her psychiatrist husband committed to an insane
asylum when they begin to suspect her activities. Still later,
she meets the rich lady's son, who had always been away at
school when she lived in the house. He falls in love with her
and they are about to be married. The rich lady no longer
recognizes the heroine and accepts her as her prospective
daughter-in-law. Just before the wedding she presents her
with the fatal locket (it is a family heirloom, she explains,
which passes from mother to daughter, and she gives it to the
heroine because her own daughter has died.) The room in
which the heroine is given the locket is the same in which, as
a child, she was falsely accused of stealing it. Disoriented by
this evocation of the past, the heroine suffers a psychotic
breakdown and is led away to an asylum. Her ex-husband
(the psychiatrist who has by now ceased to be a patient) explains the case to her prospective bridegroom. In this plot
the kindly, ineffectual real mother disappears with the heroine's childhood. The powerful accusing mother-figure remains, but now assumes some of the gentler qualities of the
real mother. She is now ready to give the grown-up girl what
she withheld from her when she was a child; but this does
not make up for the earlier withholding.

*   *   *

Where heroes or heroines suffer from psychic disturbances,
these are most frequently traced to overindulgence by the
father or deprivation by the mother. For the normal hero or
heroine, as we have seen, the nice father and the unpleasant
mother tend to be equally without impact. In the abnormal

case, they produce neuroses, psychoses, and a variety of criminal behaviors. It is not clear whether in abnormal cases the affection of the father and the nastiness of the mother are accentuated, or whether the child overreacts to a common family experience.

The indulgent father usually appears opposite the overly attached daughter. It seems difficult to give full emotional significance to a corresponding father-son relation. Intense tender feelings of a son for a father are apt to give rise to the transformed image of the father as the dangerous attacker, which we find under the disguise of the melodramas dissociated from its familial origin. An approximation to an indulgent father of a son appears in the weak, good-natured father of the hero in *Ruthless*. He would be friendly and helpful to the son but the severe mother has thrown him out of the house, and the father's disagreeable mistress (serving a similar function to that of the depriving mother) prevents him from giving the boy money. The boy grows up to have an insane greediness for money and power, discovers in an elderly financier the strong and dangerous father he never had, and concentrates his schemes on outdoing and ruining him.

Tender relations with fathers can be more fully elaborated in the case of daughters, although here too, as we have remarked, the tendency to devalue older generation parents may lead to the relationship being more told about than shown. The disagreeable mother may interfere in the relation between the little girl and the indulgent father. She prevails on the father to reenforce her discipline in depriving the child of a toy or sending her to her room. This has the disturbing effect of making the little girl feel hostile towards the beloved father, and subsequently guilty for this hostility as the father dies shortly afterwards. She grows up to be psychotic (*The Snakepit*). The impact of the depriving mother on the son, like that of the indulgent father, is more apt to find expression in disguised forms, as we shall see particularly in the fantasy of the mother being deprived in turn: the heroine as mother being threatened with the loss of the son, or the mother-figure of the melodramas vainly pleading for the hero's love.

§ THE HERO AS FATHER

IT IS, as Margaret Mead has pointed out, characteristic of American family life that parents tend to bring up their children differently from the way in which they themselves were brought up. This has been partly related to immigrant backgrounds, partly to the more general expectation that children should surpass their parents. Correspondingly, movie heroes and heroines tend to have relations with their children which are different from those their parents have with them. The hero's father, we have seen, is usually well-disposed and inconsequential. The hero as father tends to exercise more influence on his son's life. Where the hero's relation to his father has been prosaic, the hero's relation to his son tends to be dramatic, a matter of life-and-death. In *Adventure,* the hero, who has been away at sea for months, returns home to find to his surprise that his wife (who had been estranged from him when he went away) has just given birth to a son. The child, however, seems to be stillborn; the doctor is working over it without noticeable results. The hero, elated at the appearance of the son, confident that the son will live, takes the baby from the doctor's hands and breathes life into him. In *Too Young to Know,* the hero returns from the war to find that his estranged wife has borne a son and given him away for adoption. The hero is anxious to get his son back and succeeds in retrieving him. In *Tomorrow is Forever* the hero's wife bears him a son after he has been presumed to be lost in the First World War. The hero, who has been badly maimed and has allowed himself to be considered dead, turns up in disguise many years later as a visitor in the house of his wife, who has since married again. He is elated when he discovers he has a son and assumes an influential role in relation to a major decision in the son's life. It is early in the Second World War, before America's entry, and the boy is eager to enlist in the RCAF. The hero recognizes in his son the same idealistic motives which had led him to volunteer in the First World War, and strengthens his resolve. The mother, fearful for her son's safety, resents the influence of this stranger, as she takes him to be, and nearly throws him out of the house. In the end, the hero succeeds in communicating to the mother his enthusiasm for the son's enterprise, and the son goes off with the mother's blessing.

The hero's son is his immortality. This is explicitly stated by the child's mother where the hero is, or is presumed to be dead (*To Each His Own, Tomorrow is Forever*). It is not easy to picture the hero as being in the same way a perpetuation of his insignificant father; in any case, this idea is never expressed. The continuity of generations extends forward, not back.

The hero tends to receive more love from his daughter than the older generation father. As we have seen, the daughter frequently has the older generation father to herself but does not derive intense gratification from this monopoly. In contrast to this, the younger generation father inspires intense love in his daughter, who strives unsuccessfully to get exclusive possession of him. In *This Love of Ours,* the hero for a time lives alone with his daughter. When the girl was very young, he had taken her away from her mother, whom he suspected of infidelity. He has told her that her mother is dead, and she maintains a shrine to her mother's memory in the garden. This situation, agreeable to the daughter, is disrupted by the reappearance of the mother. The father has known for a long time that his suspicions of her were ungrounded. He finally succeeds in finding her, and persuades her to come home for the daughter's sake. The daughter, who is told that this is her father's new wife, bitterly resents her intrusion. She prefers the old dead mother with the shrine in the garden to the new live one who usurps her place in the house. She tells her father that things were nicer when there were just the two of them, and tries to turn him against the mother by communicating her discovery that the mother had been a night-club entertainer. She almost succeeds in driving the mother away. But after getting hints from an old friend of the family, she recognizes her as her real mother and stops her just as she is going out the front door, suitcase in hand.

A step-father may allow a fuller expression of the daughter's longings. In *The Secret Heart,* a daughter's devotion to her father reappears as love for her step-mother's suitor. In the beginning the girl's father appears as a querulant drunkard who devotes himself mainly to playing soulful music on the piano. The daughter idealizes him, feels she is the only one who understands him, and intensely resents her step-mother, who sometimes manifests impatience with the father. In an alcoholic depression the father walks off a moonlit cliff. The daughter becomes moody, withdrawn, hypochondriacal, and spends her time playing her father's favorite pieces. She revives when an attractive, long-term suitor of her step-mother reappears. The girl misinterprets his friendly interest in her, believes that he reciprocates her love, and gets a shock when she overhears an affectionate passage between him and the step-mother. She rushes out into the night and contemplates stepping off the same fatal cliff, but is stopped in time. Eventually she is led to see that her father was not as wonderful, nor her step-mother as bad as she had thought; that her prospective step-father is not for her; and that the nice boy of her own age who has been hanging around is acceptable.

In *Mildred Pierce,* the daughter of the heroine despises

her mother and loves first her father, then her step-father.
She has an affair with the step-father and kills him when he
tells her that she is silly and her mother admirable. In *Sentimental Journey,* a less mature adopted daughter is left alone
with the father after the mother's death. The girl tries to
carry out the wish of the mother, whom she had loved devotedly, to take the mother's place and take care of the father.
The father resists this substitution. After protractedly rejecting the little girl, however, he becomes reconciled to her out
of obedience to his dead wife's wishes.

These younger generation fathers of daughters tend to be
colorless and intensely loved figures, whose fate is incidental
to a central mother-daughter drama. Their stiff emptiness is
perhaps related to the fact that they always make the con-
ventionally correct choice, preferring the older to the younger
of the two women, regardless of whether the younger one is
a possible love object. This tendency to avoid any disturb-
ingly intense love of the hero for his daughter or step-
daughter recalls the tendency to make his mother emotionally unimportant for him. Thus there is, on the manifest
level, a tendency for familial women to evoke no serious
feelings.

An exception occurs in *The Red House,* in which an adoptive father intensely loves his adopted daughter. In contrast
to the previously mentioned fathers who are bland, handsome, youngish and docile, this father is aging, ugly, crippled,
dominant, terrible in his rage, dangerous, and, as it eventually appears, mad and a murderer. He lives alone with his
old sister and a beautiful young adopted daughter, on a
lonely farm next to an allegedly haunted wood. The wood is
in fact guarded by a brutal young man hired by him. The
secret of the wood, unveiled in the end, is that the father had
years before murdered the mother of the adopted daughter,
whom he loved, together with her husband, and buried their
bodies in a house in the wood. The adoptive daughter, towards whom he is possessive, falls in love with a young man.

They explore the forbidden wood, pursued by sudden blows on the head and rounds of shotgun fire. The father becomes patently mad, confuses the adoptive daughter with her mother and almost reenacts the earlier murder with the girl as victim. Her young man comes to the rescue at the last moment and the old man commits suicide.

In French and British films a father or father-surrogate may intensely love a daughter without assuming the stigmata of the father-figure in *The Red House.* In French films, the father-figure is apt to be the hero who suffers out of love for a familial woman, typically a daughter-figure instead of a mother-figure. This love of an aging man for a daughter-figure is likely to be a second edition of a love for a forbidden woman, which reaches from one generation to another but now with the age relations reversed. The father-figure is portrayed sympathetically, as a man overcome by inappropriate feelings which cause suffering to himself as much as to others. He is not violent. In the end he may prevent others from getting what they want, but without fulfilling his own wishes. In *Symphonie Pastorale,* a pastor falls in love with his adopted daughter, a beautiful blind girl whom he has rescued and educated. An intense rivalry develops between him and his son for the girl's affections. After an operation which restores her sight, she falls in love with the younger man. But the possessive father drives him away, and in the end the girl drowns herself. In *Le Silence est d'Or,* a comic variant of the same theme, the father-figure, who loves the girl and could prevent the happiness of the young couple, becomes resigned and brings them together.

In British films, a father-figure may have an intense possessive love for a daughter or daughter-surrogate in a way which differs from both the American and French versions. While remaining partially sympathetic, this English father-figure tends to be somber and cruel, and at the same time fascinating, binding the daughter to him in spite of her mixed feelings. In *The Seventh Veil,* the heroine's guardian

maintains an aloof and domineering attitude towards her.
When he discovers her musical talent, he becomes a severe
task master, keeping her at her work and promoting her successful career. When she falls in love, he enforces his authority as her guardian, reminds her that she may not even leave
the house without his permission, and takes her away on a
concert tour where he and she are constantly together.
Eventually, in spite of his watchfulness, she falls in love
again, and, being of age now, threatens to leave him. He falls
into a rage demanding that she stay with him, and when she
refuses, beats her with his cane. She runs away with her new
young man, is hurt in an auto accident, becomes disoriented,
attempts suicide, and is treated by a psychiatrist. Finally,
presented with the two still devoted suitors and her guardian
to choose from, she goes to her guardian. This English
father-figure is domineering but weak; he rages out of fear
of being deserted. Before his ward comes to live with him, he
lives alone in an austere mansion where the portrait of his
haughty and beautiful mother (who had run off with a foreign musician when her son was a child) occupies a prominent place. His moroseness and cruelty, and especially his
rage at the threat of being deserted, are related to his past
disappointment and loneliness.

This terrifying but weak English father-figure may easily
pass over the boundary between sympathetic and unsympathetic. The father in *They Were Sisters* brutally exploits the
mother and selfishly monopolizes the daughter. The mother
devotes herself with timid servility to his needs and is re-
warded by contempt and mockery. She is so afraid of him
that she hardly dares to stay away for a day on a holiday with
her sisters. On rare occasions she feels that she cannot bear
any more of his oppression and resolves to leave him. He
then produces a simulated heart-attack, becomes helplessly
dependent, and implies that he would die without her. This
father (in contrast to the typical father-figures in American
films discussed above) prefers his daughter to his wife. The

daughter, whom he presses into service as a secretary, is his indispensable companion and confidante, and he treats her with respect. He is possessive towards her and detroys without a qualm the letters addressed to her by a young man in whom she has become interested. The wife, after a particularly devastating quarrel, runs out of the house and, blinded by tears, collides with an on-coming automobile and is killed. In the subsequent legal investigation of the accident, a question is raised about the state of mind of the dead woman immediately preceding the fatal event. The husband, preoccupied with his good repute, tells about the serene happiness of their family life. The sister of the dead wife denies this with asperity. It becomes an urgent issue for him whether his daughter will support him or not. At this point the daughter again meets the young man she loves, learns that he has been writing to her and infers that her father has suppressed the letters. In a final encounter between father and daughter, he appeals for her support and she refuses it. We see him last in the hall of the law courts, alone.

§ THE HEROINE AS MOTHER

AMERICAN movie heroines tend to find motherhood full of anxieties and frustrations. Where the heroine has a son, the child's father is usually dead or absent (*Adventure, My Reputation, Tomorrow is Forever, Too Young to Know, To Each His Own*). In the heroine's relation to her son, quarrels, separations, fears of separation, and disappointment about his insufficient love are prominent.

In *Too Young to Know*, the heroine gives birth to a son after her husband has quarreled with her and left her. She allows her child to be adopted by a childless couple. In *To Each His Own*, the heroine gives birth to a son after her lover, a World War I ace, has been killed. It is when the father of the child is already dead, that a heroine is apt to show an intense wish to have the child. One rarely finds a heroine manifesting comparable eagerness to bear a child to a man who is still alive. The heroine in *To Each His Own* risks her life to give birth to her son after her doctor has advised an abortion for medical reasons. She then devises a scheme to make the baby appear to be a foundling so that she can adopt him without arousing suspicion. The scheme miscarries, and the child is adopted by another woman. A series of humiliations and disappointments develops as the heroine tries to get her son back and win his love. She applies for the job of nursemaid in the house of the adoptive mother, but is refused. Later, she virtually blackmails the adoptive mother into giving the boy back to her. But he suffers from loneliness for the adoptive mother and the heroine sends him back. Many years later she meets the son, now a Second World War aviator, introduces herself as an old friend of the family, and offers to put him up at her apartment while he is on leave. He goes to stay with her, but again she suffers rebuffs and disappointments. The son wants to spend all his time with his fiancée, and rudely brushes aside this spinsterish, inexplicably sentimental old friend of the family. It is only at the last moment that he learns her identity and calls her Mother.

In *Tomorrow is Forever,* the heroine gives birth to a son after her husband is supposed to have been killed. Later, when the son is grown-up, the mother suffers from the typical anxiety about losing him. While she is untroubled at the prospect of his loving someone else, and behaves graciously towards his fiancée, she is panicky about his wish to enlist in the RCAF. Her opposition to her son's plans, rationalized by her political isolationism, precipitates family quarrels. The reappearance of her first husband helps to resolve the conflict; the heroine's anxiety about her son becomes less acute, and she is able to let him go.

In *Claudia and David,* a more temporary absence of the
father creates the typical situation in which the mother is
left alone with the son and suffers anxiety about losing him.
The young couple go off to a party leaving their little son at
home. The husband becomes absorbed in a business deal and
cannot be disturbed. The wife is overwhelmed by an apprehension that the child has become ill during their absence,
and asks another man at the party to drive her home. They
find the little boy having convulsions, and he is barely saved
by the combined efforts of the party guest and the old house-
keeper. When the husband returns, the wife is furious with
him for having been absent in this emergency. Here the presumable rage of the heroines of the other films against the
absent fathers of their children, rendered inexpressible because of the real or supposed death of these fathers, finds its
outlet. Later in this film, the other component of the con-
stellation, the death or near-death of the father, occurs: the
husband is almost killed in an automobile accident.

In *My Reputation,* the heroine, whose husband has just
died, is left with two pre-adolescent sons. They are about to
leave for boarding school, and the mother plans a picnic
celebration on the eve of their departure. Just as they get
into the station wagon, a bunch of the boys' friends drive up
and invite them to a party. The mother urges them to accept;
they leave her with alacrity, and she is left holding the picnic
bag. Some time later the mother, after an interlude of intense loneliness, falls in love with a new man. This relationship arouses gossip and the boys, when they return for the
Christmas holidays, are snubbed by their friends because of
it. They become enraged with their mother and run away to
their grandmother's house. The mother comes after them,
and with tearful explanations succeeds in reconciling them.
The major role of the sons in the life of this heroine is
deprivational.

Johnny Belinda presents perhaps most fully the legend of
the heroine and her son. The father is not only absent, but

the heroine does not even remember her single sexual contact with him. She is a deaf-mute whose native cleverness and prettiness have been brought out by the kindly interest of a young doctor. A neighborhood rowdy, impressed by her transformation, rapes her. (This is a backwoods variant on the theme of the plain girl getting prettied up and getting her man. Evoking lingering puritanical misgivings about sexual attractiveness, this story relates: a plain girl gets prettied up, gets raped.) The heroine, rescued from life-long loneliness by the appearance of her son, adores him. However, like other young mothers in films, she is in danger of losing him. The father of the child, who alone knows of his relationship, turns up and is moved by paternal feelings for the handsome infant. He tries to take the baby away and the mother shoots him. Here the death of the father recurs, and the hostility of the mother towards him, suggested by other films, is manifest. The heroine, on trial for murder, is separated from her son, suffers intensely from his absence, but finally has him restored to her.

A recurrent theme in these films of the heroine and her son is the absence of the father, who may descend from heaven in an airplane to beget the child and then fly off never to be seen again (*To Each His Own*). We may recognize in this the American film version of the widely recurring myth of the birth of the hero. In its rudiments the myth (told of Buddha, Jesus, Romulus and Remus, etc.) reduces the relation of the mother and father to a transient contact; the father, a supernatural being descends briefly to beget the son and then disappears, so that the mother remains virtually a virgin with the son as the only man in her life. This fantasy, as analyzed by Otto Rank, gratifies the son's longing to exclude the father and have the mother to himself. If we try to see what is distinctive in the American treatment of this myth, it seems to be partly the emphasis on the independence and competence of the mother left to herself (notably the brilliant career woman of *To Each His Own*), partly the stress on her hostility to the father (which is clearest where she kills him in *Johnny Belinda*). The emphasis in the American treatment falls even more on the threat to the mother that she will lose the son, that she will be disappointed in her love for him. This theme is underscored in the melodramas which we shall analyze presently where the hero is frequently bent on disappointing the disguised mother-figure who seeks his love, who seems to have been involved with another man but really loves only the hero. This disappointment of the mother by the son is a major trend in the movie plots reflecting mother-son relations, and suggests as a possible source a specially intense love disappointment of the son in relation to the mother, a disappointment for which compensation is sought in these fantasied reversals of the situation.

The myth of the birth of the hero also recalls *The Miracle of Morgan's Creek*. There the heroine has become pregnant from an overnight marriage with a soldier who has disappeared and whom she has forgotten completely due to a blow on the head which she suffered on the same night. Her position is that of an unwed mother-to-be. She is shown at Christmas time with her old father who is trying to cheer her up. The father, alluding to her imminent maternity, reminds her of the birth of Christ, who was also born in humble circumstances, and, as he might have added, of a virgin mother. The allusion may have seemed out of key in the comic context, but is justified as comparative mythology. The heroine's father in the film goes on to prophesy that her child may become president of the United States. The heroine does in fact achieve great fame from her maternity as she gives birth to sextuplets. Needless to say, they are all boys. The relation of these films to the myth of the hero's birth is confirmed by the circumstance that it is a son (or sons) not a daughter who is born to the mother alone. Another recurrent feature of these films is that the heroine finds an obliging, unaggressive, devoted man who unprotestingly assumes the paternity of her fatherless son or sons. In *The Miracle of Morgan's Creek,* he is a particularly pronounced sucker type, who, incapable of having got a girl in trouble, gets himself into all kinds of scrapes in his efforts to protect her. In the end he is dazzled and disoriented by being given credit for the sextuplets.

The heroine's relation to her son contrasts with her relation towards her father. As we have seen, the relation with the father is undisturbed by the intense and painful feelings which appear in relation to the son. The heroine suffers disappointment for unrequited love, fears of separation, separation, and fears of death in connection with her son. None of these feelings is apt to appear in connection with her father. This again illustrates the tendency of American films to direct intense familial feelings towards the present and future, and away from the past generation.

The heroine is frequently apt to assume a maternal role towards her father or a father-substitute. In this relation she is likely to be more sure and better appreciated than in her relation to her son. Her maternal relation to an old man may be symbolized by her pulling him out of the water, saving his life. Thereafter she feels responsible for taking care of him, nicknames him Pop and takes him to live with her (*Stork Club*). She may support her old father, and when he misbehaves, threaten to withdraw his allowance (*She Wouldn't Say Yes*). The exchange of the father-figure who remains so devoted and easy to mother for the son who is so hard to hold on to occurs in *Apartment for Peggy*. The heroine twice saves the life of the old professor with whom she lives (who reminds her of her grandfather and whom she calls Pop). She loses her son, who dies at birth. (This episode is associated, as usual, with the absence of the child's father.) The old professor, consoling the heroine for the loss of the child, tells her that she has restored him to life.

The frustrations of the heroine in relation to her son contrast with the picture of the hero in relation to his daughter.

As we have seen, the hero as father is greatly loved by his daughter who is usually disappointed in not being able to win sufficient love from him in return. In the total balance sheet of love and disappointment, the hero tends to be more loved than loving in relation to mother, daughter, or mother-substitute. The most stressed theme is the disappointment of the familial woman.

The heroine also tends to be unhappy in relation to her daughter, whom she loves intensely and who does not love her in return. As with the son there is suffering through separation, but there is not the same anxiety about the possible death of the daughter. Instead there is the threat of the daughter's hostility. The mother-daughter conflict, which is expressed only weakly and incidentally in the older generation, is here fully developed. In *Mildred Pierce* the heroine loves her daughter more than anything else. The girl remains hostile and competitive towards the mother throughout. The heroine is extremely ambitious for her daughter, and impatient with her rather ineffectual husband who fails to provide the family with the means for a life of sufficiently high status. The husband finds a less exacting woman to comfort him for his unhappiness at home, and the heroine goes to work, at first as a waitress. When the daughter discovers this, despite her mother's efforts at concealment, she taunts her mother with being a low class woman and says it is not surprising that the wellbred father should have left her. The daughter maintains this attitude even when the competent mother has easily and rapidly risen to being the owner of a large chain of restaurants. The girl takes advantage of the wealth now at her disposal to lead a fast life, mainly running around with an upper class playboy who has previously had an affair with her mother. When the mother reproaches her, she replies that the mother naturally cannot understand or share their mode of life. The mother slaps her face, and the girl runs away from home to become a singer in a low-grade night-club. The heroine, after an interlude of distress, decides to marry the playboy, who is impecunious and attracted equally by her charms and her business. She wants to offer the playboy's family mansion as a home of such high status that the daughter will come back. The ruse succeeds and there is a brief happy reunion of mother and daughter. However, the daughter pursues her affair with her new step-father. After a short time he becomes bored with her; she reproaches him for his withdrawal and he retorts by telling her how much less interesting she is than her mother. Piqued by this, she kills him. The mother, discovering his body, infers what has happened. First she tries to make another suitor of hers the fall-guy for the crime. When this fails, she confesses to it herself. The daughter, brought face to face with the mother in the police station, attacks the mother for having, as she supposes, betrayed her, and thus gives herself away. The movie ends with the daughter being led away to jail, while the mother leaves the court-house at dawn, accompanied by her first husband—he has come back to stand by her, and they become reunited.

The daughter tends to express mixed feelings about the mother's ambitions for her. As we have seen in *Mildred Pierce,* she uses the fulfilment of her mother's ambitions as a weapon against the mother: having acquired, in response to the mother's demands, standards appropriate to a higher status, she turns them against the mother, and despises her as less wellbred than herself. Alternatively she spites the mother by threatening to move downward in the status scale, when she becomes a singer in a low class cafe.

In *Desert Fury,* the mother, a bootlegger's widow, runs a successful gambling house in a small western town, where she is snubbed by the women of good society. Ambitious for her daughter, she keeps sending her away to upper class boarding schools. But the girl always tells her schoolmates about her mother's business, precipitates snubs from them, and then leaves school in a rage, driving home in her flashing station-wagon-style roadster. She insists to her mother that she wants to come to work in the gambling place. There is a long drawn-out conflict between mother and daughter over the mother's demand that the girl rise higher and the girl's wish to imitate her mother. This conflict becomes acute when the girl falls in love with a gambler-gangster with whom the mother had been connected in the past, and whom the mother knows to be a thoroughly bad lot. Against her mother's strenuous opposition, the girl runs off with this man, becomes disillusioned with him just in time to escape being murdered by him. The mother is so relieved to see the girl safely returned that she is ready to yield on the point of the girl's working in the gambling place. However, by now the girl has sufficiently satisfied her rebellious low-life strivings, and is ready to settle down with a nice young man. His accepted place in the community will make it possible for her to become dissociated from her origins.

This Love of Ours is another film whose central theme is a mother's great love for her daughter, her suffering about being separated from the daughter, and the daughter's hostility and contempt towards her. It is frequent in Western culture for the daughter to feel more or less consciously that the mother (who has sexual relations with the father) is a low woman, while she (whose communion with the father is spiritual) can satisfy the higher side of the father's nature which the mother fails to understand. The American pattern of family life, in which each generation is supposed to surpass the preceding, and where the mother particularly is the bearer of this ambition for the children, gives a special emphasis to this common theme. The daughter's sour-grapes attitude towards the mother as a love rival may easily assume the form of social snobbery.

The characteristic demand for achievement which American mothers make on their children presumably works considerable emotional hardship on them: they feel they must fulfil the mother's ambitions in order to be loved. By their provocative behavior the daughters in *Mildred Pierce* and

Desert Fury rebel against the mother's achievement demands. The daughter turns the fulfilment of the mother's demands into a weapon against the mother. She retaliates for her mother's making love conditional by refusing to love the mother. Alternatively, she tries to test whether the mother will love her anyhow, flouting the mother's achievement demands by plunging into low life or obstinately adhering to the level of her origin. Presumably this expresses a longing for the mother's unconditional love, and a wish to be like her instead of having to become alienated from her by superior achievement.

Sentimental Journey is a wish-fulfilment fantasy which provides for the joint gratification of the mother's wish to elevate the daughter and the daughter's wish to identify with the mother. It is a "family romance" in which a fine lady adopts a poor orphan girl. The child is spiritually the true daughter of the mother, enjoying a delicate fantasy life similar to that which the mother recalls from her childhood. Thus the external elevation of the daughter simply makes it possible for her to express her soul, and brings her into communion with the mother instead of forcing her away. The mother, knowing she is soon to die, has adopted the girl to take her place with her supposedly childlike husband. The girl is inducted into such routines as bringing her adoptive father breakfast in bed, and instructed in the practices of over-protection. When the mother dies, this is the last thing the girl would wish, since the mother is the one person she loves, and she has not yet achieved a good relation with the father. Following the mother's instructions, frequently reenforced by spirit communications, the girl tries to take the mother's place with the father. However, he has never liked the girl, resenting the close tie between her and the mother which seemed to exclude him. It was, in fact, as the result of a quarrel, in which the father demanded that the girl be sent away, that the mother suffered a fatal heart attack. The girl was thus unwittingly guilty of setting the dilemma: either

Mother goes or I go. After the mother's death, the father hesitates to go through with his plan to send the child away. However, the girl is eventually so impressed with his distaste for her that she runs away to the seashore where she first met the mother. The father is prompted by the voice of the mother, in the form of a phonograph recording (the more ethereal child receives posthumous messages from the mother without material mediation), to realize how much it means to the dead wife that he should love the child in her place. He rushes out to the nocturnal shore in time to snatch the distracted child from the waves.

In this film the daughter concentrates all her love on the mother. It is probably significant for the American situation that this variant occurs where the conflict between mother and daughter over the mother's ambitions for the daughter is obviated.

§ BROTHERS AND SISTERS

IN THE most significant brother theme, twin brothers are placed very differently in the scale of success and fortune; circumstances throw the more lowly placed brother into the position of his twin, for whom he is naturally mistaken; and he does much better than his brother. The treatment of this theme in current films differs from that of related older films such as *The Prisoner of Zenda* and *The Masquerader*. In earlier films, the lower status hero fell in love with the wife or fiancée of his more favorably placed and less worthy double. He felt guilty wishes to replace this double permanently. Current treatments (*Wonderman, Pardon My Past*) are comic. The hero does not want his twin's wife or fiancée, and suffers chiefly from the embarrassments incurred through mistaken identity. As in other American film comedies, there is much renunciation of forbidden wishes in these movies. This has not always been a difference between comic and serious drama. On the contrary, tragedy has usually demonstrated the fatality of striving to fulfil forbidden wishes, while comedy has frequently given these wishes free play. American movie melodrama, however, usually provides for the fulfilment of forbidden wishes in an atmosphere of danger; American film comedies frequently present heroes ostensibly free from urgent impulses that might get them into trouble.

The story of a hero who slips into the position of a more highly placed or successful person has some specifically American nuances. Behind it is the still plausible belief in upward social mobility. But there is now uncertainty about whether this upward movement can be achieved by ability and hard work or whether it depends on capricious circumstances beyond the individual's control. The plot which arranges by a series of accidents to precipitate the hero into a higher position (in which he is not distinguishable from the original incumbent) expresses the idea that this is all a matter of chance. The query about the highly placed person: "What's he got that I haven't got?" is answered in terms of "breaks." However, the hero does not feel any wish to retain the position which he gets in this way. He feels uncomfortable in a place which he has merely fallen into, and in the end he is glad to escape from it and to set out on his own independent career.

The hero of *Pardon My Past*, a veteran who plans to start a mink farm together with an old buddy of his, gets entangled in the affairs of his millionaire twin (they were orphans and had been adopted in childhood by different families). The hero settles the affairs of his weaker twin, exposing a malign uncle and arranging a reconciliation between the twin and his estranged wife. In the course of this he meets a beautiful young girl whom he mistakenly supposes to be his brother's wife, but who turns out to be a relative of the adoptive family. In the end he goes off with the girl, his buddy, and the first pair of minks with which they are going to start their farm. In this comedy any frustration arising from the increasing real-life difficulty of social movement upwards is denied. That differences in position are a matter of chance is accepted ostensibly without rancor—partly perhaps out of the feeling that chance may at any moment rearrange things. In the end the confidence of the individual to go ahead on his own initiative is reaffirmed. Any love conflict is avoided by providing another beautiful girl for the hero so that he has no need to covet his brother's wife. The solidarity of the men who might be rivals (the hero does his brother a series of good turns) is achieved by eliminating any cause for rivalry. Male solidarity becomes possible through the denial, rather than through the reconciliation of competing strivings. By contrast, in the melodramas, where serious impulses of love and hate are expressed, the hero tends to stand alone. Serious man-man relations tend to take the form of violent hostilities. The limited impact of many film comedies may, in part, result from the effort to achieve all-around good feeling among the characters by denying any intense impulses.

The highly and lowly placed characters (who might be, but are not, rivals) are twins. This probably reflects the American tendency, which Margaret Mead has pointed out, to measure achievements from childhood on by strict comparison with one's age-mates. The aim in growing up is not so much to be able to fill the position of one's forebears as to measure up to and surpass one's contemporaries. Contemporary is often defined quite narrowly since, for example, norms for child-training and child-development may be modified every few years. The definition of contemporary thus approaches twin as a limit.

In *Wonderman* the more obscure brother is less confident and adept when thrown into his double's position. While he achieves success, and in effect surpasses his brother (since he brings to justice the gangsters who killed the brother), he is

mainly in a harried, jittery, uncontrolled state. In desperation he invents an unusual solution to his problems, largely
dictated by uncontrollable circumstances. He rushes onto an
operatic stage to sing his exposé of the gangsters to the police
commissioner in a stage box. (This is the typical Danny Kaye
success story, in which the infantile, hyperactive, inept, adept,
boastful and diffident hero triumphs in the end. A series of
incongruous circumstances confirms his fantasies of omnipotence.)

A younger brother of the hero is apt to be killed. In *Spellbound,* when the psychoanalyst heroine restores the amnesiac
hero's memory, he recalls a childhood episode in which he
accidentally killed his younger brother. This event is supposed to account for his readiness to suspect himself of other
crimes, which he did not commit. In *Leave Her to Heaven,*
the hero's beloved younger brother, partly crippled by infantile paralysis, is drowned by the hero's possessive wife,
who dislikes having to share him with anyone. She did not
see eye to eye with the hero about the pleasures of taking
the invalid boy along with them on their honeymoon. The
hero, in this case, is guiltless of his brother's death, but he
serves a jail sentence as an accessory after the fact: when his
wife confessed the crime to him, he did not immediately
reveal it.

Thus, both the hero's rivalry (towards the twin) and
hostility (towards the younger brother) are expressed indirectly. The hero has no wish to take his brother's place or
to kill him, but other agencies accomplish both aims. In the
second case, the hero tends to be implicated, by his conscience or by the law. In *Wonderman,* where the hero reluctantly takes the place of his murdered brother (at the
insistence of the brother's ghost who charges him with catch-
ing the killers) he is in constant danger of being murdered
by them.

The hero's relation with his brother is thus on the surface
good, like his relation with his father. However, more rivalry

and destructiveness appear, indirectly, in relation to brothers. Brothers are more likely to get killed than fathers. The hero does not assume the father's position, which is usually unenviable. The substitution of the brother for the father as the object of hostility and rivalry is a common device for mitigating father-son conflicts, but it is especially suitable to American life, where the father is protected from attack by being automatically demoted.

The greater conflict of rivalry and guilt in relation to a brother-figure as compared with a father is illustrated in *Body and Soul*. There the hero's devoted father, whose low status in life appears unenviable to the son, dies a violent death and is immediately forgotten. The son's life, however, becomes involved with that of a rival prizefighter, a champion whom he defeats and irreparably injures in so doing. This rival fighter may be regarded as a brother-figure (they are both members of disadvantaged minorities, the hero a Jew and the other a Negro). The hero was led to injure his rival unwittingly as his crooked manager omitted to tell him that the champion was suffering from a previous injury. After the fight in which the hero becomes champion, he adopts his now incapacitated rival, and they become and remain closely bound to each other until the death of the Negro. The hero, despite his attempts at restitution, has the other fighter very much on his conscience, and after his death renounces the fighting game. The role of a brother-figure as the focus of rivalry (in contrast to the father who is automatically left behind), and the association of this rivalry with destructiveness and guilt, is fully expressed here in relation to a disguised brother-figure; with a manifest brother these tendencies are more apt to be muted or denied.

In the case of a rarely occurring older brother we may get a combination of father and brother connotations. The older brother, like the father, is surpassed by the hero. Unlike the father he is a reproach to the hero; the hero's career unintendedly causes the brother's death. The hero's older brother in *Force of Evil,* who has made sacrifices to send him to college, condemns the hero for using his professional skill as a lawyer for a racketeer. The moralizing of the older brother rests on a dubious basis as he himself operates a small branch of the same racket. The hero, trying to help his brother financially, succeeds instead in getting him killed by the racketeer's gang. He blames himself for the brother's death, and (like the hero in *Body and Soul*) is impelled to renounce his crooked career. The destructive connotations of surpassing the father, and associated guilt feelings, which are rarely expressed towards the manifest father, come out in this rare instance in relation to the older brother. We shall see that similar feelings find frequent expression in the melodramas in relation to a latent father figure.

*   *   *

Sister relations are apt to be more overtly hostile than brother relations. Sisters tend to be love rivals, and the defeated one may have little scruple about killing the other. When a twin is thrown by chance into her sister's place, she is not apt to feel, like a brother, that this is an embarrassing situation from which she would be happy to escape. She is likely to have desired this position for a long time.

Of the twin sisters in *The Dark Mirror,* one is good and one bad. (Twin brother plots, as we have seen, are not apt to show this opposition.) The bad sister, equally attractive at first glance, is incapable of inspiring love. Her suitors fall in love with her twin when they learn to differentiate them. Piqued, the bad sister kills a rejecting boy friend. The crime is traced to one of the twins. As the police are unable to distinguish between them, and the girls do not help, no arrest can be made. A young psychiatrist offers to study the two girls to determine which one would have been capable of murder. We see him plying them with the Rorschach, and responding like all the other men in their lives, seeing the coldness of the one and falling in love with the other. The bad one, recognizing the pattern, tries to kill her sister, pretending to the police that the good one is the murderess. The hero, who knows the Rorschach score, intervenes in the nick of time, and the bad sister is taken off to jail. The good sister, only slightly jarred, embraces the psychiatrist.

In *Stolen Life,* the bad twin is a successful flirt who diverts all the men from her nobler, less showy sister. When the good one has fallen in love with a dreamy young man, whose taste for solitary islands and lighthouse tops she shares, the bad one impersonates her sister at a rendezvous, captivates the young man and soon afterwards marries him. She forces him into money-making and fast company, and the good sister gathers they are not happy. Sometime later, the sisters go for a sail together and, at the insistence of the bad one, risk getting caught in a storm. The boat is almost capsized, the bad one is thrown overboard and, despite her sister's desperate efforts to save her, is drowned. The good sister is rescued in an unconscious state. When she comes to, she discovers that everyone mistakes her for her sister; she was found clutching her sister's wedding ring which she had accidentally snatched from her hand in the unsuccessful attempt to pull her out of the water. The girl allows the mistake to go unchecked, believing that only by impersonating her sister can she have the man she loves. This scheme boomerangs as she discovers that the sister and her husband were more estranged than she had suspected, were indeed on the verge of divorce. She finds herself entangled in the residues of her sister's life, importuned by a lover and despised by the husband. Eventually she establishes her identity, and resumes her relation with the hero where they left off when the sister intruded.

In these films the wickedly hostile, unfairly competing sister is disposed of by external agencies. The good sister can get the disputed man with a clear conscience. This fulfilment of wishes by external agencies occurs, as we have seen, throughout American films. A boy and girl may be thrown into each other's arms by the swaying of a railway carriage as an unwanted sister may be disposed of by the tipping of a boat. This automatic wish-fulfilment seems to express well preserved infantile fantasies of omnipotence, and has a doubly happy effect; one gets what one wants without effort and without guilt.

In *L'Amour Autour de la Maison* an older sister, bitter, passionate, and perpetually frustrated in love, is intensely jealous of her gentle, pretty younger sister. As her sister's guardian she mediates between the sister and her suitors, and manages to break off every incipient relationship, sometimes telling the suitor that her sister is incurably ill, sometimes telling the sister that the suitor is only interested in her money. The younger sister is intensely bound to the older one, believing in her protectiveness and becoming panicky when they are apart, even briefly. When she discovers her sister's deception, and realizes that the sister sent away the man she loves, she kills the sister. After this, she goes mad, and wanders around the house in a blank and dreamy state, affirming that her sister is asleep, waiting for her to awaken. This French film seems to say that you cannot get rid of an obstructive person without some penalty; a conflict involves both participants, and a fatality to one cannot leave the other untouched. Both affectionate and hostile feelings towards the same familial person are acknowledged. In American films, the good sister is apt to have nothing but friendly feelings towards the bad one; she neither attacks nor mourns her. The good sister in this French film is more deeply bound to the sister whom she kills; the remainder of her life is overshadowed by the sister's death. American films tend to express the feeling that one easily puts the encumbrances of family attachments behind one, and becomes absorbed in extra-familial love. In the French films, the family ties are more sinister and more tenacious.

coincide with what we are told. In *The Fallen Angel* the heroine's older sister tries to prevent her from marrying the hero, a dubious character. While her intentions are of the best, what we see is a sour-faced aging spinster who interferes with the promising love life of a more attractive younger sister. Thus sister jealousy and rivalry seem to be expressed even where the relation is positive on the surface.

§ THE CONCEALED TRIANGLE

THE emotional significance of manifest familial figures tends, as we have seen, to be minimal in American films, particularly for the hero. We have connected this with the American real-life pattern of concentrating interest on the family one makes rather than on the family one comes from, and of expecting that the son will surpass his father rather than look to his father as a model of achievement or as a patriarch whose position he [the son] will one day inherit. American movies thus reflect the tendency to put the older generation parents into the background, to register one's emotional involvement with them as finished business. This is not apt to be the whole story. A child's relations with his parents are likely to leave lasting, though partly unconscious, impressions. Where adult life minimizes the importance of such residues, their expression will be the more disguised. The harmless, good-natured, ineffectual father and the colorless, slightly unpleasant, emotionally impactless mother, who stand as shadowy figures in the background of the movie hero, probably do not exhaust the emotional significance of father- and mother-figures. We shall therefore look for the expression of this significance in relationships which are not manifestly familial.

In movie melodramas the hero frequently becomes involved with a strange man and woman. The man is usually older and in some position of power. He and the hero are opposed to each other in violent hostilities. Both men are involved with the woman. We shall seek in these triangular melodramas for some of the latent feelings of familial love and hate, with the strange man as a father-figure and the strange woman as a mother-figure in relation to the hero.

The father figure in the melodrama is bad and dangerous. He is sometimes the hero's boss, frequently powerful as a gang leader, a nightclub owner, or a public official or policeman concealing his crimes behind a façade of respectability, or in a position of wealth and high standing, but secretly using underworld characters to carry out criminal designs. This man attacks the hero directly or indirectly, and without provocation. The manifest image of the American father as harmless, well-disposed and ineffectual does not, we may presume, eliminate the fantasy of the father as powerful and dangerous. However, the real-life tendency to divest the father of moral authority is paralleled by the lack of moral significance of the fantasied father. His attack upon the son is not a just punishment. The extended meaning of the term "punishment" in American usage is perhaps relevant here. The term has come to apply not only to morally rationalized deprivations but to any instance of beating. It is punishment in the non-moral sense that the hero undergoes at the hands of the bad father-figure of the melodramas.

In *The Blue Dahlia,* the hero returns from the war to find that his wife has taken as a lover a middle-aged night-club owner and gang-leader. Shortly after his return, the wife is found murdered and the hero is suspected of the crime. Hoping to get evidence to exonerate himself, the hero pursues the gang-leader, who has his henchmen carry the hero off to a shack in the woods where they beat him up. The gang-leader enters. While the hero and one of the henchmen are struggling for the possession of a gun, the gang-leader is accidentally shot and killed. Eventually an elderly caretaker known as "Pop" confesses to the murder of the wife. In the course of his investigations the hero has met a beautiful young woman who turns out to be the estranged wife of the gang-leader; they fall in love and are happily united in the end. The father-figure here is split. There is "Pop," of whose crime the hero is falsely suspected, and there is the gang-leader who attacks the hero, has stolen the hero's wife, and whose wife the hero wins in the end. Similarly, there are two disputed women. When the hero falls in love with the gang-leader's wife (not knowing who she is), this is all the more justified because the gang-leader has already stolen the hero's wife.

In *Gilda,* the hero appears at the beginning as a small-time gambler in a low waterfront locale. He is befriended by the middle-aged owner of a gambling house who later turns out also to be an international schemer and crook. He makes the hero his right-hand man and gradually reveals to him the extent of his enterprises. Returning from a trip, the boss brings back with him a newly acquired beautiful young wife who turns out to have been the hero's mistress (they had broken up because of his jealousy). After some time the boss murders one of his colleagues for business reasons and flees. To avert pursuit, he fakes an airplane crash and is supposed to have perished. Just before his flight he has had a glimpse of his wife embracing the hero whom she still loves. Supposing her husband dead, the heroine persuades the hero to marry her. Still unforgiving towards her and loyal to the boss, he shuts her up in an apartment dominated by the boss's portrait. Keeping away from her, he devotes himself to the large enterprises which have now fallen under his control. Eventually the boss returns and, mistakenly believing that the hero and heroine have betrayed him, is about to kill them. He is stabbed in the back by one of his own henchmen, and the hero and heroine, with their misunderstandings finally straightened out, are happily united.

In *Cornered*, the hero sets out to find the escaped Nazi leader who was responsible for his wife's execution. He traces the Nazi through the latter's wife. She eventually turns out not to be the Nazi's wife, but only posing in this role for some involved reason and the hero falls in love with her. In his pursuit of the Nazi, the hero is approached by sinister agents who try to divert him, and is almost killed by anti-Nazis who do not know his identity. He finally comes face-to-face with the enemy, who has him tied up and beaten, gives a speech about the eventual comeback of Nazism and shoots a disloyal henchman in the face. Somehow the hero gets loose and has an all-out fight with the Nazi. In the course of it he is hit on the head and, as a result of an old head wound, loses awareness of what he is doing while he continues to batter the Nazi. When he comes to, he is surprised to find that he has killed his enemy, whom he had meant to turn over to the anti-Nazis. The killing of the hero's opponent, which is usually performed by someone else, is here done by the hero, but with the mitigation of his being unconscious.

In these melodramas, it is always the bad and dangerous father-figure who attacks the hero. Thus the fantasy of the son attacking the father is reversed. The son's impulse to attack the father is denied on the son's side, and attributed to the father. The crimes of murder (of the father) and stealing (of the father's wife) are consistently dealt with in this way, as the father-figure appears as a murderer and thief. Money theft is frequently substituted for love theft. But quite often the villain has stolen the hero's wife or sweetheart (as in *The Blue Dahlia*, and *Gilda*), or deprived the hero of his wife or sweetheart by killing her (*Cornered, The Fallen Angel*). The villain often attacks the hero because he fears that the hero will uncover his crimes. Also, recurrently, the hero is wrongly suspected of the villain's crimes, while in some cases the villain frames the hero. In view of all this, the hero feels relieved but never guilty when the villain is killed. If he had killed the villain, it would have been self-defense. But usually someone else does the killing.

Since the American father is not built up as a moral authority, his strength as imagined and felt by the child may seem only dangerous and not righteous. When, in fantasy, the father is powerful, he is apt to be a lord of the underworld. The real-life father frequently functions as a secular arm of the mother. She may pronounce judgment on the child's behavior and only delegate to the father the task of physical punishment. The cabin in the woods to which the movie hero is frequently carried off for a beating may be a melodramatic counterpart of the traditional woodshed. That the hero is often beaten by the villain's gang rather than by the villain may reflect the real-life father's effort to dissociate himself from the punishment he is charged with administering ("I hate to do this, son,"—a disclaimer which the son may accept on the surface as genuine while feeling at bottom that it is hypocritical). The absence of strong moral authority in the father, together with the fact that the son is encouraged to think of the father as someone to whom he is potentially superior, makes the father eligible to become the bearer of the son's bad impulses. The father is burdened with the impulses from which the son strives to dissociate himself as, on the more manifest level, he may occupy a social position which the son leaves behind. With very few exceptions, the son-figure triumphs in the end. While this corresponds to the real-life expectation that the son should surpass the father, these films suggest that this expected surpassing is not free from fantasied fears of reprisal and other dangers. Surpassing the father may also leave the son with guilt feelings. The fantasy of the father as bad may have the further function of warding them off. If the father is bad, he deserves what he gets and the son is exempted from self-reproach for having outdone him.

While the hero's struggle with a powerful and dangerous older man usually appears detached from any manifest family setting, occasionally a family background is shown. The hero in *Ruthless* is a self-made financier. The major encounter of his career is his triumph over a powerful and unscrupulous older rival, whose young wife he steals, and whom he ruins financially. The hero's life history leading up to this triangular involvement is traced from childhood. It is complete with a family in humble circumstances, a moralistic and scolding mother, a good-natured ne'er-do-well father, adoption into a better family, and a series of upward progressions in each of which he leaves behind those to whom he has been attached. The real father of the hero is friendly, ineffectual and not very admirable. He has separated from the mother (who considers that she married beneath her), lives by gambling, and has a flashy, blonde, ill-natured mistress. The harmlessness of this real father is complemented by the image of a wished-for and feared strong father, the old financier who is later the main opponent of the hero. Lack of moral authority is common to both. Since this film shows not only the bad dangerous father whom the hero is justified in outdoing, but also the friendly harmless father whom he leaves behind in childhood (a figure that appears a second time in the kindly adoptive father whom the hero treats ungratefully), the hero is less in the clear than in the usual melodrama. The film reproaches him for his "ruthless" leaving behind of those with whom he has been associated at each stage of his upward climb. In the end he is overtaken by the ruined older financier (whose former wife he has in the meantime cast aside); the two men engage in a struggle on a yachting pier, fall into the water and, still struggling, sink and drown together. The love-death of the hero with his male attacker is an outcome which is usually avoided, but the possibility of which is occasionally suggested in other melodramas as we shall see.

Love rivalry is rarely a central motive in the hostilities between the hero and the father-figure. The struggle between them is usually initiated for other reasons. In addition, various devices are used to dissociate the fighting between the two men from love rivalry. The involvement of one of the men with the woman may be tenuous. The father-figure may turn out to be only apparently related to her, as in *Cornered* where the heroine is only nominally the wife of the Nazi. The hero may repudiate the woman, despite her pursuit of him, as in numerous cases which we will discuss presently. Another character, associated with the hero, may be interposed to carry on the relation with the woman, as in *The Dark Corner*. The relation of the father-figure to the woman may be a fatally violent one. The hero strongly repudiates any wish to take his place—that of a murderer rather than a lover. Another aspect of the fantasied brutal father appears here. (*The Blue Dahlia, The Fallen Angel, Cornered, The High Wall.*)

In the fight between the two men, winning means mainly escaping from false accusations and physical attacks—the sudden gunshot in the night, the brutal beating—by permanently eliminating the source of these dangers. These films are usually dramas of danger, not of guilt. The hero does not often feel moral indignation against his adversary, but fights in self-defense against the imminent threat of annihilation. He is justified in fighting because he has been attacked, but he rarely endows his struggle with sentiments of righteousness. Where the hero is a professional detective, he may not always be forced to fight by being attacked or falsely suspected. But here, too, he refrains from giving any moral rationalization for his activities. When asked why he is risking his life, he is apt to answer that it's a job, or that he likes to eat. In the melodrama world making a living and fighting for one's life come close to coinciding. Where the hero is falsely suspected, he usually had good reason to commit the crime, but he is untroubled by Hamlet-like self-accusations for acts committed only in intent. The only issue is with external actions. Similarly, at the end, when his adversary is killed, the hero is usually in the clear because someone else does it. Self-accusation for a murder one would have wished to do is attributed to the outside world. In the form of false suspicions directed against the hero by others, it becomes a danger of unwarranted punishment to be warded off by energetic struggle.

In the exceptional case, *All My Sons,* the father-son conflict is stated in moral terms. The struggle between father and son, usually expressed under the melodramatic disguises which we have described, appears here in a manifest family setting. In contrast to most older generation fathers, the father is not weak and easily surpassable. He is a factory owner who has risen by his own efforts, and is benevolently domineering towards his son whom he has taken into the business. His older son was reported missing in the war, and the mother still refuses to admit that he is dead. A conflict arises because the remaining son wants to marry his brother's fiancée. It is in connection with the girl that the son is led to uncover his father's past crimes. The girl is the daughter of the father's former partner, who is now serving a prison sentence for having issued defective airplane parts, which caused the death of dozens of fliers. As it eventually appears, the hero's father has framed his partner for this crime of which he was guilty himself, having preferred issuing the defective parts to financial ruin. When the hero confronts him with his discovery of this, the father first denies, then admits it, and tries to justify himself in terms of the struggles he underwent to rise in the world and how difficult it would have been to renounce all he had worked for. The hero almost chokes him, later tells the girl it was only chance he did not kill him. He wants to make his father aware of his moral degradation, to make him judge himself. The girl gives him the means by turning over his brother's last letter, which she has hitherto suppressed. It tells how, when he heard of his father's involvement in the airplane affair (the father had been tried but exonerated), he had decided to go out on a suicide mission. The hero shows the letter to his parents. The father, assuming the blame for his son's death, now also assumes the blame for the death of the other fliers ("They were all my sons") and goes upstairs and shoots himself. The hero rides away with his brother's fiancée to start a new life.

While this film substitutes a moral triumph of the son for the more usual triumph over physical dangers, it resembles other melodramas in several respects. The father is criminal, frames an innocent man for his crimes and indirectly attacks his son(s). The son is justified in his counter-attack, but he does not kill the father. The father kills himself. This connects with a trend of the melodramas in which the father-figure is sometimes killed by his own henchmen (*The Big Sleep, Notorious*), by his own weapon (*Gilda*) or in his own car speeding riskily at his command (*The Chase*). In *The Strange Love of Martha Ivers,* the father-figure also killed himself. Thus the father is to blame for everything, even his own murder. The hero in *All My Sons* also wins the disputed woman, the dead brother's girl, without guilt. The father, not he, is responsible for the brother's death.

The non-authoritarian father, presumably frequent in real life, who is a pal to his son and an ally against the mother of whom they are both a little afraid, may have a further latent emotional significance which links in with that of the dangerous attacker. The boy may feel tempted to take this father, from whom he gets more gratifications and fewer demands than from the mother, as an object of intense love. He must then struggle against assuming a passive role to which frightening, as well as gratifying, fantasies are attached. In the film melodramas, the hero is repeatedly tempted to yield to the attacker, to let him have his way. In *The Dark Corner,* the hero at one point cannot see a single clue to follow to exonerate himself of the murder for which he has been framed. He tells his secretary that it's no use, and self-pityingly conjures up a picture of himself being led to the electric chair. The secretary, a resourceful girl who loves him, prevents him from giving in to this despair and rouses him again to activity. In *The Killers,* the hero, lacking such womanly support, lies in his room, awaiting the fatal attack which he knows is coming. *The Chase* pictures two alternative outcomes to the hero's conflict with his criminal boss, one (a dream) in which the hero succumbs, another, in which he triumphs. The hero, an unemployed veteran, is taken on as a chauffeur by a coarse, brutal man of great apparent wealth, who turns out to be involved in various shady affairs, and who lets recalcitrant business colleagues be torn to bits by hungry hounds. The boss's beautiful wife, whom he keeps virtually a captive, appeals to the hero to help her escape. On the eve of their flight, the hero has a dream. He sees himself and the woman in a crowded night-club in the city to which they have fled. She is suddenly stabbed. The hero is accused of murdering her. He breaks away from the police and tries to collect evidence to exonerate himself. But he finds that every witness has been bribed, each piece of evidence falsified. He is finally cornered and about to be shot by the boss's henchman when he wakes up. He and the woman then make good their escape, while the boss and his henchman, pursuing them, are killed in a collision. The dream embodies the more deeply repressed fantasy of passivity. Deprived of the woman, the hero becomes defenceless before the irresistible attack of his male opponent. However, this is only a dream. In the "real" ending, the father-figure is killed and the hero escapes.

The temptation of the hero to yield to the father-figure's attack suggests a connection between the manifest and latent father-images. Where films show the father of the hero, he tends, as we have seen, to be a likeable character with a warm understanding for his son, in opposition to the unpleasant, disapproving mother. However, this father is pictured as insignificant; the intense feelings which he may inspire in the son remain unacknowledged. The son's love for such a father, and tendency to prefer him to the mother, may oc-

casion passive longings to be loved by the father. Such longings in turn give rise to the fantasy of the father as a dangerous attacker who must be fought off—the image of the father
which appears under the disguise of the melodramas.

Sometimes the insight that the father-figure is dangerous
only in fantasy finds expression in the manifest content of
the film. In *The Woman on the Beach,* the hero meets a
beautiful young woman who lives in a lonely beach cottage,
taking care of her aging blind husband (once a successful
painter). The husband is friendly towards the hero, but the
hero is suspicious. He does not believe that the husband is
blind, imagines that he is watching the hero and the wife.
He tells the wife that he thinks the husband only feigns
blindness to keep her bound to him. The woman says she herself blinded her husband in a drunken quarrel. The hero,
however, cannot be dissuaded from his conviction. To make
a test, he leads the husband to the edge of a cliff and leaves
him there. The husband falls over the cliff. He is not killed,
however, and in the end the hero accepts his proffered
friendship and renounces his aim of breaking up the couple.
In *The Web,* the hero is hired as a body-guard by a rich and
powerful man. The boss wants to liquidate two of his partners in grand larceny and plans to make the hero appear
responsible for the murders. First he persuades the hero that
an elderly former partner has threatened to kill him. He
arranges a situation in which the elderly man appears to have
broken into the house, then summons the hero who shoots
the intruder. Later the hero learns that the old man was
harmless. He is reproached by the old man's daughter who
tells him what a gentle man her father was, how he used to
put out crumbs in the snow for the little birds. *The Web* is
less decisive than *The Woman on the Beach,* however. While
one father-figure who was thought to be dangerous is proved
harmless, another embodies the usual threats: the hero's boss
almost succeeds in saddling the hero with his crimes.

In French films dealing with familial themes (which are

usually less disguised than in American films), the central conflict tends to be a love rivalry between an older and a younger man. The two men are usually on friendly terms; there are rarely any violent hostilities between them. One or both of them suffer a severe love disappointment. A major plot type shows the older man falling in love with a young woman who might more appropriately pair off with the younger man. This love of the older man is a misfortune for all three, but he is hardly to blame. He usually has entered into a protective relation with the young woman, and is then overcome by unanticipated feelings. While he may be unable to get the young woman for himself, he can prevent the young man from getting her. It is the father-figure who determines the outcome. Where the American latent father-image is made up largely of violence, the corresponding French image is apt to be the bearer of mistakenly directed love. The father-figure in the French films may thus become the suffering hero of the familial love drama—with a daughter-figure substituted for a mother-figure as the object of rivalry. American films are preoccupied with who is to blame for a crime of violence. French films tend to express the feeling that no one is to blame for the conflicts that arise from misplaced love.

In *Symphonie Pastorale,* a Protestant pastor of a little mountain village is happily married and has two children. He rescues an orphaned blind girl who is running wild in the mountains. Feeling entrusted by God to raise and educate her, he takes her into his house and she soon becomes his favorite child. As she grows up into a beautiful young woman, he falls in love with her without realizing it. His son, who has been away at school, returns home and also falls in love with her. The father opposes the son's wish to marry her on the ground of her blindness. The son suggests that she have an operation that might make her see. The operation is successful. When the girl first sees the son after her sight is restored, she mistakes him for the father and throws herself into his arms. (He is introduced into her hospital room by his last name.) Later, when she sees the father, she is disappointed; he is an old man. The father now impresses the son with how dependent the girl has been on him (the father), how no one could ever be to her what he has been; even if the son married her, the image of the father would always be between them. He succeeds in driving the son away. His demands on the girl become more overt; he tells her that he cannot live without her. After a night in which he sleeps in a chair in her room while she sits beside him, she runs out and drowns herself. The final scene shows the pastor carrying home her lifeless body.

In *Le Silence est d'Or,* a comedy variation on the same theme, an aging movie producer of the early 1900's assumes a fatherly role towards a young man in his employ. He consoles the young man for an unhappy love affairs and gives him instructions on how to pick up a girl. While the young man is out of town, a young girl seeks the boss's protection. She is the daughter of an old love of his who long ago rejected him for another man. The boss takes the girl to live in his house and gives her parts in his films. Anxious about the threats to her innocence in the big city, he severely chides his employees for so much as looking at her (they assume that she is his mistress), and accompanies her everywhere. Sitting in a cafe with her, listening to sentimental music, he discovers that he has fallen in love with her. The young man returns to the city and meets the girl by chance on one of her rare excursions alone. He uses the techniques which the boss had previously demonstrated to him to strike up an acquaintance with the girl, and they quickly fall in love. When the young man discovers that she is involved with the boss, he refuses to pursue the affair. The boss is angry with her for not loving him, and the girl is about to return to her home in the provinces. She and the young man play a final scene in the film in which the boss is directing them. The studio is being honored on this occasion by a visit from an oriental potentate and his entourage who watch the scene being filmed. In the scene the girl is a harem beauty and the young man her lover. The prince to whom she belongs enters and finds the young couple in each other's arms. Enraged, he has the young man carried off by harem guards, and the girl, in despair, throws herself from the window. The visiting potentate does not like this ending to the film; he protests that the girl is too beautiful to die. The producer is persuaded to contrive a happier ending. He will have the prince be magnanimous and renounce the girl. The actor playing the prince, however, resents this revision, which he says will make him look ridiculous. The producer persuades him that he will on the contrary appear all the more noble if he admits his age and withdraws in order to let the young couple be happy. In this speech he expresses his own renunciation of the "real" girl. In the film within the film, the young couple are happily united. The power of the father to separate or to unite is represented in comic fashion by the two oriental potentates, the one in the film and the one in the audience. The father is strongly inclined to prevent the young man from having the young woman, even though he (the father) cannot have her either. But he is subject to benevolent whims, and may unexpectedly set everything right. The final scene shows the producer in a movie theater watching the happy ending of the harem film; he has his arm around another young girl.

The love disappointment which the father may inflict on the son in French films is apt to be outweighed by the disappointment which he suffers. The son's difficulty in acknowledging his father in the role of a lover is countered by the father's difficulty in recognizing that he is getting too old for this role. Resentment against the father tends to be resolved in sympathy and pity. The father image which French films strive to achieve is one in which the discrepant functions of lover and father are fused. In *César,* a young man learns after the death of his presumptive father that his mother had a lover and that he is really the son of this stranger. He is thus confronted with two fathers, one the familiar, loved paternal figure, the other a dubious outsider. The young man goes in search of this second father; as a result the lover finally assumes his paternal role, and the son is able to see the two aspects of the father combined.

The effort of French films to reconcile discrepant aspects of the father seems to express a preoccupation with the father image which extends into the mature life of the son. The real-life father presumably remains a person of importance for his grown-up son. As the relation continues to be a present emotional reality, the son tends to bring to his understanding of his father his own later experience in becoming a lover and a father and in facing the prospect of growing old. Accordingly childhood impressions of the father become transformed; the father image continues to develop and formerly irreconcilable elements tend to merge. American films suggest an opposite picture. It seems likely that the real-life father (like the manifest father in films) recedes to a position of relatively slight importance for his grown-up son. As a result, later experiences are not related to the father; childhood fantasies about him remain isolated and unmodified. The image of the fantasied dangerous father persists side by side with that of the manifest innocuous father.

In contrast to both the American (latent) image of the father as violent, and the French image of the father as amorous, British films on occasion present an ideal father-figure, free of sex and of aggression. The son is not as good a man as his father, and while he may be blameless towards him on the surface, tends to suffer from a bad conscience and to punish himself. The son in *Notorious Gentleman* is an attractive ne'er-do-well, whose sympathetic widower father helps him out of numerous scrapes and protects him from the wrath of his formidable aunt. Eventually the son exhausts the father's patience. They quarrel over the son's making love to the father's secretary. In French films the father interferes with the son's relations to a young woman because he (the father) has designs on her. Here the father is disinterested. His protest is based on the suffering which the son's philandering causes the son's wife. The son takes the father's rebuke with a bad grace, gets drunk, drives recklessly while returning from the country with his father and the two girls, and has a smash-up in which the father is fatally injured. The son, with his arm bandaged, comes to the hospital to see the father who says with grave concern, "You've hurt yourself," and dies. This scene haunts the son and he enters on a course of virtual self-destruction, taking a series of degrading jobs. The father's secretary discovers him as a taxi-dancer and tries to rescue him. She declares her love for him (the wife has meanwhile obtained a divorce), and they have a brief happy interlude in a cottage in the country. However, he apparently cannot accept this happiness and goes away. Eventually he dies gallantly in the war.

The American son is on all counts the winner over the father; manifestly he relegates him to a background position, on a deeper level he triumphs over him in a life-and-death struggle. The French son's happiness depends on the father's permission. And the English son, Hamlet-like, may deny himself happiness as an act of posthumous obedience to a noble and beloved father. The most ideal father-image as well as the most intense sense of guilt towards the father thus appears in English films.

While father figures are not always perfect in British films, there tends throughout to be the presumption that they ought to be. A bitter reproach is apt to be leveled against the father who has not subjected his own impulses to complete control and who thus fails to provide a model of such control for his son. The loss of control imputed to the father, or realized in the son, is apt to relate to the impulse most strongly guarded against, that of destructiveness towards women. *Wanted for Murder* expresses the protest of a son against a father whom he regards as an imperfect model. He feels that the father, behind a respectable façade, was destructive, and argues that his own destructive career, though it lacks the social acceptability of his father's, makes him no worse than his father. The father, now dead, was a public executioner with great relish for his work. It is hinted that his wife suffered greatly through exposure to his unseemly pleasure in his career. The son, a handsome and moody man, lives alone with his aging, solicitous mother and devotes himself to wooing young women and later murdering them. After one of his crimes, he visits the wax-works chamber of horrors, where his father is represented, and in a rage knocks off the father's head with his cane; he blames the father for making him the way he is. In the end, pursued by police and swimming away in a lake, he cries they will never hang him, that he only did what his father did; he submerges himself and drowns. One may see here, among other motives, a temptation of the son, against which he defends himself, to get into the position of the father's victims. This differs from the temptation of the American hero to yield to the father's attack in that the English father appears not merely as dangerous, but as an official punisher; he is invested with moral authority. Instead of fighting off an external attack by the father, the English hero struggles against his own unconscious imitation of and submission to the father's destructive aspects.

* * *

In American melodramas the woman in the triangle, whose relations to the older and younger man make her position correspond to the mother's, is invariably young and beautiful. Americans find it difficult to associate sexual desire with a mature maternal figure. When Eugene O'Neill's *Mourning Becomes Electra* drew a mature mother figure with an active sexual life, who became the object of tragic love rivalry, the role on the stage was assigned to Alla

Nazimova, on the screen to Katina Paxinou, thus expressing the feeling of the alienness of this character, its incongruity with American womanhood. When a British company brought *Oedipus Rex* to Broadway (in 1946), some New York critics remarked on the implausibility of the Greek legend, which asked one to believe that the hero could fall in love with a woman old enough to be his mother. The older generation American mother seems to have established herself as anti-sexual, not indulging herself, and tending to withhold and forbid indulgence to her child. The breasts of the young movie star express their appeal to a generation of bottle-fed babies. The current trend to glamorize mothers does not attempt to infuse sexual warmth into aging women, but rather to maintain an illusion of perpetual youth.

Most frequently the woman in the triangle loves only the hero, while he rejects her temporarily or permanently. In *Johnny Angel,* the hero is pursued by his boss's beautiful young wife who, despite an apparently active sexual life, has never loved any man except the hero. She wants to kill her enamoured, repulsive husband, whom she has bullied into committing grand larceny, and to share the proceeds with the hero. The hero is unmoved by her charms and her passion for him. He meets her only to see if he can get information about his father's murder, which he is investigating. His apathy towards her is further guaranteed by his falling in love with a good girl whom he meets in the course of his investigations.

In other melodramas, the hero's rejection of the disputed woman is a passing phase, a temporary punishment or probation to which he subjects her before conceding his love. This holding back on the hero's part is most often motivated by doubts about the woman's goodness. She seems involved with the other man (or with other men), and he is sceptical of her professed love for him. In *Gilda,* the heroine continually pursues the hero and assures him of her love, but he, doubting her, maintains for a long time a resistant and punitive policy. In *The Blue Dahlia,* the hero learns that the beautiful woman who has picked him up on the road at night is the wife of his gangster enemy. He wants nothing more to do with her, but she pursues him with offers of help, and with assurances of her estrangement from her husband. In the end the hero accepts her. In *The Big Sleep,* the detective hero correctly suspects that the heroine's flirtatious approaches are efforts to distract him from his investigations of the activities of a night-club owner with whom she is mysteriously involved. He coolly evades her advances until her character is cleared. The heroine of *Notorious* had for a short time been leading a fast life, which ceases when she meets the hero and falls deeply in love with him. He recruits her for spy duty and receives the task of assigning her to marry an elderly, powerful Nazi. After the marriage, the hero is overcome by his previously suppressed doubts about the heroine and torments her with gibes about her easy virtue. She repeatedly and tearfully pleads with him to believe in her regeneration. At the very end he relents, after she has nearly been killed by her husband.

In other films the hero eventually rejects the woman after an interlude in which he has accepted her. In *The Strange Love of Martha Ivers,* the hero returns by chance to his home town, which he finds under the rule of a powerful rich woman, his childhood sweetheart, and her weak, alcoholic husband whom she has promoted to be district attorney. The couple are bound together by secret crimes. The woman has murdered her rich aunt, whose large estate she has inherited, and the husband has helped her to cover up the murder, getting a tramp convicted for it. The husband is alarmed at the hero's reappearance in the town, believing that he knows about their crimes. He has the hero severely beaten to dissuade him from staying. The woman experiences a revival of her love for the hero, whose manliness contrasts with the weakness of her husband. She makes advances to the hero, tells him how she wishes she could share her domain with him rather than with her husband. The hero at first repulses her. Then, in the course of a violent physical struggle—she tells him about her crimes, discovers he did not already know about them, and attacks him in a fury—he finds himself passionately embracing her and becomes temporarily enthralled. Shortly afterwards she repels him by urging him to kill her husband whom they find dead drunk. He leaves the couple, assuring them that he pities them. The husband, revived, shoots the wife and himself. The hero witnesses this through the lighted window. He has, in the meantime acquired a girl of his own, with whom he blithely leaves town the following morning.

Just as the manifest image of the harmless father fails to eliminate the latent fantasy of the father as dangerous, so the manifest anti-sexual mother image does not obliterate the fantasy of the sexually seductive mother. What is striking in the hidden fantasy images of both parents is the attribution of the child's forbidden strivings to them. It is, as we have seen, not the son who attacks the father-figure, but the reverse. Similarly, it is the mother-figure who makes advances to the hero, not he to her. This is in keeping with the pervasive trend in American movies to deny dangerous impulses on the part of the hero and attribute them to the world around him. He is thus freed from responsibility and, carried along by outside forces, may achieve the fulfilment of his wishes without guilt. In the usual course of the melodramas the father-figure is killed and the hero can have the mother-figure if he wants her. However, these ends cannot be achieved without danger. The hero of the melodramas is surrounded by an almost completely dangerous world—danger replacing the guilt or divine vengeance which have oppressed and pursued other dramatic heroes. The melodrama hero is threatened by the attack of the father-figure (his own projected hostility), the seductions of the mother-figure (his own projected forbidden sexual wishes), and the false suspicions of the police (his own projected self-accusations).

Since outer danger replaces internal conflict, the hero can fight, and in the end he is usually able to overcome the threats against him. The fulfilment of forbidden wishes is thus only dangerous, not fatal.

In the most recurrent pattern of the hero's relation to the disputed woman, he gets full assurance that she loves only him, while he enjoys the position of deciding whether to take her or leave her. This appears to be, in part, a fantasy of turning the tables on the real-life mother for her adherence to the principle of conditional love. The woman loves the hero unconditionally (there is no one with whom he has to compete), while he withholds his love, waiting to see whether she is good before he bestows it, or withdraws it altogether. This reversal is particularly manifest in *Notorious,* where the heroine repeatedly implores the hero to affirm by his renewed love his belief in her goodness.

The hero's detached attitude towards the woman, his tendency to reject her at least temporarily, has a variety of meanings. The involvement of the woman with the father-figure must be denied, but the difficulty of making good this denial is expressed in the hero's doubts. He refuses to believe what he would like to believe, and awaits external proof. Meanwhile, the hostilities between the hero and the father-figure are kept clear of any admixture of sexual rivalry. The hero fights because he was attacked and not because he wants to take anything away from the other man. The hero must also be kept clear of too direct inculpation in the death of the father-figure, in which a too ready attachment to the woman might involve him. In *The Strange Love of Martha Ivers,* the hero is able to refuse her demand that he murder her husband, because he is not unduly bound to her. In *Johnny Angel,* the hero remains detached from the beautiful woman who pursues him, and who not only wants to murder her husband for his sake, but turns out to have been responsible for the murder of his father.

The lesser importance of the woman for the hero is also

an obvious corollary of the preoccupation with relations between men. As we have indicated, the hero's absorbing involvement with the attacking man probably conceals an intense attachment. Where the dangerous man has murdered the woman in the triangle, the hero takes her place as the target for the dreaded and wished-for attack. The desirability of concentrating on the masculine relationship is reenforced by the confidence that the hero can nearly always win in this situation. Presented with the challenge of the other man's attack, he knows how to be both tough and shrewd enough to ward it off. On the other hand, attachment to the woman makes him exceedingly vulnerable in case she and the opposing man should unite against him. Where this happens, the hero is apt to succumb (*The Killers, The Gangster*).

The hero often pursues the relation with the woman for non-amorous reasons. In *Cornered,* he invades the apartment of the woman whom he believes to be his enemy's wife to find out his enemy's whereabouts. In *Dead Reckoning,* he pursues the beautiful young woman whom his buddy loved, in connection with his investigation of the buddy's mysterious death. He feels it is essential to understand what the buddy saw in her; for this purpose he becomes absorbed in listening to her night-club singing. Other exonerating factors are frequently introduced in the hero's relationship with the woman. He may come to know her before he learns that she is the other man's wife, and may withdraw as soon as he discovers this, as in *The Blue Dahlia.* In *The Postman Always Rings Twice,* he has just accepted a job at a roadside lunch-counter when he sees for the first time the beautiful young wife of the boss. At first he does not know who she is. When he finds out, his first impulse is to leave; but he sees the boss already burning the "Man Wanted" sign. This provides a further exoneration: it is the fault of the father-figure that the hero is forced to stay in contact with the disputed woman. The boss repeatedly throws his wife and the young man together, suggesting that they dance while he plays the guitar, or that they go for evening swims alone together. Another device which may clear the hero of the motive of sexual rivalry is to have him know the disputed woman first, as in *Gilda.* The father-figure then becomes the interloper.

With all the reservations which hedge the relation bétween the hero and the disputed woman, they often end up happily together. Where she turns out to be a bad woman, or where she is murdered, the hero is usually supplied with another girl, who reduces his temptation and eliminates disappointment. The relation to the mother-figure is more conflict-ridden than that to the father-figure. Where the hostilities between the two men tend to follow a uniform course, the relation of the hero to the mother-figure is subject to a number of variations. It is not only less clear-cut, but it also tends to be pushed into the background, allowing the more straightforward hostilities between the men to occupy the center of the stage.

The mother-figure sometimes reflects the presumable expectations of real-life mothers that their sons will help them to fulfil ambitions which their husbands have left unsatisfied. In *The Strange Love of Martha Ivers,* the ambitious powerful woman dreams of eliminating her weak husband (whose political career she strives to advance by making speeches for him while he stays at home drunk) and sharing her domain with the competent hero (a boy from the wrong side of the tracks who has boldly made his own way). Similarly in *The Postman Always Rings Twice,* the beautiful young wife is contemptuously dissatisfied with her middle-aged husband's lack of ambition. One of the first things that bring her and the young hero together is their agreement on how to improve the husband's roadside lunchroom. After their murder of the husband, the wife achieves her dream of fixing the place up as a stylish garden restaurant, and for a time she and the hero share this flourishing enterprise.

In a few exceptional films a doubt appears as to whether the son can surpass the father. Where daughters, as we have seen, show an energetic rebellion against their mothers' ambitions (*Mildred Pierce, Desert Fury*), an irresistible fate may assign the son-figure to the same position as the despised father-figure. In *Nightmare Alley,* the hero is a young ambitious carnival employee who becomes involved with a couple of middle-aged performers. The wife is still carrying on an active career though recalling days of greater success when she and her husband had a famous mind-reading act. The husband has now become an incompetent drunkard whom she supports saving him from what would otherwise be his fate, the lowest job in the carnival: that of a "geek," who is given a quart of whiskey a day to pose as half-man half-beast and bite off the heads of live chickens. The hero is intent to learn the secrets of the couple's former act. He makes love to the wife and plies the husband with the liquor which his wife tries to keep from him. By accident he gives the husband a bottle of poisonous cleaning fluid, of which he dies. Subsequently, the hero and the wife become partners in the mind-reading act of which she now reveals the secrets. The hero becomes involved with a pretty young girl whom he is forced to marry, leaves the carnival and his aging mistress behind, and with his wife as partner, starts a new act with which he has great success in more luxurious settings. As he becomes increasingly daring, he assumes spiritualistic pretensions, over-reaches himself and suffers a dramatic fiasco. Further persecuted by a woman psychologist to whom, in a state of anxiety, he had confessed the accidental killing of the carnival drunkard, and abandoned by his wife, he quickly sinks. We see him in a group of tramps, impressing them with a verbatim repetition of the lines which he had learned from the deceased drunk. He also becomes a drunkard, eventually rejoins the carnival—to become what he has always most dreaded to be, a "geek." After one day of this he is rescued by his still devoted wife, who has also returned to the carnival. Presumably he will assume the role of his predecessor and be helplessly dependent on a wife who protects him from the depths of ignominy. Elsewhere, and much more typically, we have seen the son's triumph threatened, though not prevented, by a dangerous father-figure. Here the son is punished for his easy superseding of a weak father-figure. Despite the eventual consignment of the son to the previous position of the father, the largest part of the film describes the hero's rise, and only a brief final sequence his fall.

The usual treatment of any major theme in American films is a wish-fulfilment in which dangers and fatalities are circumvented and denied. By contrast, a minority of films on the same theme are cautionary tales, in which forbidden impulses are recognized as such and their fulfilment penalized. *Nightmare Alley* is an example. In a few other instances, the usual immunities of the hero collapse. This is apt to occur where he is not sufficiently detached towards the disputed woman, and may thus get involved in murder for her sake or be killed himself. In *The Postman Always Rings Twice,* the hero is prevailed upon by the woman to collaborate in the murder of her husband. They succeed in making this crime appear to be an accident. In the end, however, the hero accidentally kills the woman in an auto crash, and this accident is mistaken for a crime, for which he is sentenced to death. Thus even where the hero is guilty, he suffers from false accusations. In the last scene he is trying to prove to a priest who visits him in the death cell that it was the husband he killed and not the wife (although he knows this will not affect his sentence). The final problem remains not one of guilt, but of getting the record straight before a falsely accusing outer world. In *Suspense,* the hero is from the first intensely attracted to his boss's wife; he does not show the usual detachment of the melodrama heroes. Eventually he murders her husband (who had previously tried to murder him), and is himself killed by a disappointed girl-friend. In *The Killers,* the hero falls hopelessly in love with a beautiful underworld woman, the wife of a gangleader. She uses him for her advantage, and tricks him into bearing the blame for a grand larceny from which she and her husband alone benefit (they make the other members of the gang believe that the hero has cheated them all). In the end, the gang leader sends hired killers to murder the hero.

In French films there is usually a greater emotional involvement of both the older and the younger man with the disputed woman. This contrasts with the American tendency to deny or avoid involvement on one side or the other. Thus, in French films one of the two men is bound to be disappointed; sometimes both of them are. The older man frequently has superior claims to the disputed woman for services he has rendered, which balance the greater attractiveness of the younger man. In *Fanny,* the older man has married the abandoned sweetheart of the younger man and provided a home and a name for her child. When the younger man returns to profess his love for her, his father, closely aligned with the elderly husband, demonstrates to the son the insufficiency of his claim. The young woman, though she still loves her former lover, agrees with the father's judgment. In French films the conflict of the older and younger man tends to be directly about the woman, but is rarely violent. In American melodramas, as we have seen, this conflict is violent, but not about the woman. As against both of these, British films tend to avoid contact between the two men involved with the same woman. In *Brief Encounter,* the heroine's husband and would-be lover never meet, and the husband does not know of the other man's existence. In *Madonna of the Seven Moons,* as a result of the heroine's split personality, her husband and lover do not know of each other's existence. In *I Know Where I'm Going,* in which a young man wins the heroine away from her wealthy old fiancé, the older man never appears except as a voice over the long-distance telephone. By this separation the ideal father image, so important in British films, can be kept clear of sexual and destructive associations which would attach to him if he appeared as an active love rival.

3

KILLERS AND VICTIMS

THE DESTRUCTIVE potentialities present in every human being, though in markedly different degrees, find only very partial overt expression. Even the murderer acts out only a fraction of his destructiveness, while many of us hesitate over hostile words and restrain an angry look. What destructiveness means to us, the unexpressed impulses in ourselves and others, the feared and wished-for things which these impulses might accomplish, is more fully realized in fantasy than in action. It is a perennial function of drama and literature to present images of what violent impulses, usually restrained in life, might look like if more fully expressed. The typical fantasies of violence which find such dramatic expression vary according to time and place. Who the killer is and who the victim, what the relation between them has been, whether they are strangers or former lovers or rivals or seeming strangers who without knowing it are intimately related; what exigencies in human relations provoke fatal violence; the degree of mystery surrounding a murder, whether the drama lets us see the deed or conceals it, whether we watch the pursuers close in on a murderer whose identity we know or whether an unknown murderer must be identified among many suspects; who carries out the investigation; what the penalties are for crime, whether the criminal is pursued by the Furies or conscience or the ghost of his victim or the police; whether the killer is sympathetic; whether the victim is regrettable—the choice among such alternatives provides for a wide range of possible plots.

Dramas of violence in the three groups of films we are considering follow distinctive and contrasting lines. In American films, violence is seen not as a threat of one's own possibly uncontrollable impulses, but as a danger from outside. Accordingly, the hero is rarely the murderer. The murderer is apt to be an alien and unknown person, the suspicion for whose crimes falls unjustly on the hero. The internal struggle to clear oneself of self-accusations is dramatized in terms of the hero as the falsely accused, the police as the representatives of an overly suspicious conscience, and the real murderer to whom the deed is eventually traced. There is no attempt to get free of guilt for bad wishes; only actions count. The hero usually has a motive for the crime of which he is falsely accused, but someone else performed the act. The investigation focuses, characteristically, on material clues rather than motives. The split between the hero and the murderer is that between mere wishes and action. Human beings have a tenacious susceptibility to feel guilt for mere wishes. The American film melodrama expresses the effort to eliminate such guilt. The hero who has the motive but did not commit the act succeeds in clearing himself of the false accusations of the police, who represent by projection his own conscience. The struggle to fight clear of undeserved blame is a difficult one. The belief that only actions count is incompletely established and contends with the deep belief in the dangerousness and blameworthiness of bad wishes. For this reason the hero's motive for the crime he does not commit is not stressed. There is a tendency to concentrate dangerous impulses no less than actions in the real murderer.

The hero is always in danger; he is threatened not only by false accusations but also by his projected destructive impulses embodied in external agencies ever ready to attack him. He may be ambushed in a dark alley, pushed into a waiting car and carried off to a lonely shack where he is bound and beaten. As he walks down a street at night a ten-ton truck may suddenly lunge over the curb to strike him down. Equally, at any time falsely incriminating circumstances may envelop him. When he comes home to his shabby hotel room, he may find a corpse on the floor and thus be precipitated into a desperate struggle against a false murder charge. Behind the façade of the suspicious and attacking world there is usually one man, the real criminal, of whose crimes the hero is falsely suspected, who may have framed the hero, and who attacks him to discourage investigation. Thus the hero's moral struggle is overdetermined by a persecutory fantasy in relation to his male opponent. We would guess that in the underlying fantasy this dangerous attacker is loved. Since such a sentiment is inadmissible, the hero's opponent is usually presented as an object of negative feelings only, although in a few cases a positive relation between the two men is suggested. A devoted woman is the hero's best safeguard against the threats of engulfment in the man's world. In rare cases where she is absent, he may succumb to the attack of his opponent.

The constituted authorities, as we have already suggested, are usually incompetent in American films. The hero must carry on the necessary investigations himself. This is a doubly dangerous job since the criminal tries to deter him by violent attacks, and he must manage to keep out of the way of the police who, so far from being a source of protection, falsely suspect him. However, just as the attacker can be overcome, the police can be convinced once the hero has collected the appropriate evidence. As so often in American films, proving a point constitutes a central issue. The hero, like the good-bad girl, has not done anything; what is accomplished in the course of the plot is to replace a deceptive appearance by an exonerating reality.

Violence in American films may be fast moving and noisy or technically intricate; it is less apt to be emotionally involved. The pair who are joined in fatal violence are not likely to have had a previously complicated or intimate relationship. The predominant motive for murder is to get somebody out of the way who has become an obstacle in the pursuit of certain interests. The murder victim thus tends to be reduced to a thing, a block in the path, rather than an object of intense feelings and possible regret. Death is not very real in American films. There is little lingering attachment to the one who gets killed: he was in the way or he deserved what he got. A murder is the starting point of furious activities (setting off the process of investigation), or marks the end of such activities (when the murderer is eliminated), thus leaving the hero free to take a holiday. Murderers are not haunted by their dead, but only by the crime investigator. Ghosts (appearing mainly in comedy) are likely to be gay enlivening creatures who impel their survivors to enjoy life rather than to mourn. Thus the dead tend either to be forgotten or not to seem very dead. For the most part death remains inapplicable to the hero.

British films are more concerned with the threat of destructive impulses from within which may get out of control, and especially with the possibility of attacking the weak. They are more apt to make the murderer known to us and to present him as at least partially sympathetic. He is the hero who is overwhelmed and destroyed by his own violent impulses. His relation to his victim may have been intimate, and his motive one of vindictive rage for a love disappointment. The murderer has sometimes committed several murders, and may announce to the police or to his victim his intention of committing the next one. We become anxiously involved with the murderer as he moves toward this crime and also with the intended victim. Drawn into a double identification, we do not know whether we want the murderer to succeed or not. For his sake we half wish to see his plan go through without a hitch, half wish he will be stopped in time; on behalf of the victim we wish he may escape, and also (probably less consciously) wish to see him undergo the fatal stroke.

Where American film melodramas are based on a persecutory fantasy, British films of violence center on the act of destroying and being destroyed. While in American films the aim of the fantasy is to avoid involvement in this act, British films induce our imaginative participation in it. Accordingly there is less possibility of avoiding feelings of guilt. Even characters who are indirectly connected with fatal violence, though technically in the clear, are likely to suffer from self-accusations. The constituted authorities are usually wise and just. The soft-spoken, courteous, understanding Scotland Yard man, who is nevertheless relentless in his pursuit of truth, speaks like a father to the hero, the victim of his own wayward impulses; the hero tries to appear nonchalant, but has the sickening suspicion that the other sees through him. Justice is sure in British as in American films, but is usually accomplished by the regular authorities rather than in spite of them.

French films are less concerned with the internal or external dangers of violent impulses. Where crimes of violence occur, the central theme is more apt to be that of the irony of human justice. There is none of the confidence that we

find in both American and British films that everything will
be cleared up and everyone get his just deserts in the end.
As is frequently the case in French films, the story is a rebuke to naive human wishes, an attempt to inure the spectator to the disappointments which are inevitable in this
life. The world does not coincide with any imaginary or ideal
moral order. The impersonal crowd is prejudiced and the
authorities usually wrong. They do not bother to understand
the human heart but are guided by superficial and stereotyped ideas. The eccentric recluse whom no one understands may despite his nobility be falsely suspected of crimes.
But also the real criminal, who appears superficially to have
a character incompatible with crime, may clamor in vain to
have his deeds acknowledged. Where the truth is discovered
it is by an accident, and it is equally a matter of chance
whether the discovery is made a moment before or a moment after the death of the falsely accused.

French films see murderer and victim, the falsely accused
and the police, each as mixtures of good and bad impulses.
Nor is there anyone of complete and reliable competence.
Thus neither the ideal Scotland Yard man nor the American
private investigator who will surely bring everything to light
and set the record straight, finds any regular counterpart in
French films. The falsely accused lacks the drive of convinced innocence; he is more apt to commit suicide than to
put up an energetic struggle to clear himself. He seems to
feel that at bottom no one is really innocent, that his false
inculpation is only one part of a generally discouraging life
situation and that there is probably no one who will bother
to understand him. In keeping with the acknowledgment of
disappointments, French films present death as very real. A
funeral may be a central event in a film, or may move incidentally through the background of even a comedy. The
impossibility of being morally in the clear appears related to
the admission of the hero's mortality, just as the opposite
positions are related in American films.

§ FALSELY ACCUSED

TO ELABORATE on the crime pattern of American films, the hero is likely to be a stranger in town, or just returned from a journey, when a murder is committed in which the circumstantial evidence points to him and he finds an alien world closing in on him with fixed suspicion. He is forced to flee and hide while he carries on the urgent investigations to find the real killer in order to exonerate himself. In *The Blue Dahlia* the hero has just returned from overseas. At his first meeting with his wife he learns that she has been unfaithful, quarrels with her and leaves. Shortly afterwards she is found murdered and he is suspected. In *The High Wall*, too, the hero returns from overseas to find that his wife has been unfaithful. They quarrel; shortly afterwards she is found murdered and he is suspected. In this case the hero half suspects himself; at the height of the quarrel he had fainted (after-effect of an old head wound) and later suffered from amnesia about the incident. In *The Dark Corner*, the hero, after having been cheated by his partner, moves to another city to make a new start. He soon finds that he is being tailed, catches his pursuer, beats him up, and forces him to confess that the partner has hired him. This is a ruse to involve the hero in a frame-up. Shortly afterwards the hero meets the partner again, quarrels with him and knocks him down. Next day he finds the partner's body in his apartment. In *Dark Passage*, the hero escapes from prison to which he has been sentenced for life on a false conviction for his wife's murder, and returns to the town where he once lived, to see if he can pick up the trail of the murderer.

These heroes and many others like them feel like strangers in a world that is alien, hostile, accusing. They have always suffered, they have never had a break. To top it all they are framed and the whole world begins pursuing them for something they didn't do. They tend to be laconic, unsmiling, weary (Humphrey Bogart). They occasionally pity themselves in moments of confidence to a sympathetic woman: I never had a chance in life (the hero of *The Fallen Angel*), I'll end up in the chair (the hero of *The Dark Corner*). But more often they ward off self-pity and depression with a somber humor. The hero of *The Big Sleep* remarks to one of a seemingly endless series of assailants: Everyone seems to be pointing guns at me. They are not indignant; they only want to be let alone. Their suspicions of everyone they meet are justified by the circumstances. They are hunted men, moving among strangers. How do they know who will turn them over to the police? How do they know who is the murderer? Events frequently indicate how difficult it is to be suspicious enough. The hero of *The Blue Dahlia* has been tempted to trust a beautiful woman who he later learns is the wife of his gangster enemy. In *Somewhere in the Night* the hero accepts the proffered help of an influential nightclub owner who later turns out to have committed the grand larceny and murder of which the hero is suspected.

A rare counterpoint to these fantasies in which the hero is really persecuted by the world and where his suspicions are more than justified occurs in *The Treasure of Sierra Madre*. There the hero is shown developing paranoid delusions in relation to men who have no intention of exploiting him. He becomes convinced that his partners in a gold-mining venture mean to rob him. He shoots one of them, believing like the heroes of the previously described melodramas that he attacks in self-defense; only, in this exceptional case, the external danger is imaginary. (Humphrey Bogart, who has so often played the hero who successfully wards off real persecutions, appears here as the man who succumbs to imaginary ones.)

The hero, who is suspected though innocent, suffers as if

he were guilty. He is outcast and alone, hunted and in constant danger, and rarely escapes fairly severe physical damage. Usually he is beaten up by his opponents who want to render him temporarily unconscious or to warn him against further investigations. The henchmen of his main adversary may carry him off to a lonely shack in the country where in a brutal fight of many against one he only escapes as if by a miracle. While beatings are common, the hero is rarely shot or stabbed or subjected to any other form of damage that involves penetration of the body. There are exceptions, however. In *Ride the Pink Horse,* the hero, who is carrying on unwanted investigations, is lured into a dark alley and stabbed, though not fatally. The hero of *Dark Passage,* escaped from the penitentiary, has a plastic surgery job done to his face so that it will be impossible to recognize him. In the dawn after the operation, with his face swathed in bandages which reveal only a suffering mouth and eyes, half-fainting, he makes his way across the city. As he trusts no one, he must go on foot, struggling up steep hills, until he comes to the one place where he can briefly hide. Some workmen whom he passes on the way think he is returning from a drunken brawl and call after him mockingly.

In the course of the hero's investigations, under the constant danger of being overtaken by the police, two sorts of events frequently add to the atmosphere of anxiety and guilt: other crimes are committed by the criminal, whom the hero unwittingly provokes; and the hero himself commits (usually minor) violations of the law. The hero's opponent is apt to murder witnesses whom the hero is about to interview. Arrived at the rendezvous where he is to meet a crucial informant or a rare friend, the hero finds a corpse. In connection with the original murder the hero usually had a strong motive; in the case of the secondary crime he had every reason to want to keep the person alive. However, he is frequently suspected of this crime, too. In addition, his flight tends to involve him in various violations of the law. The flight itself is an evasion of the police who, as he knows, demand his surrender. Illegal devices may be necessary to get evidence or to elude further incrimination. In *The Dark Corner,* the hero, pursuing a crucial witness, catches up with him just after he has been pushed out of a high window. The victim's suitcases, which may contain a clue, are in a momentarily deserted taxi. The hero jumps into the taxi and drives away—police sirens are heard in pursuit. The hero of *Out of the Past,* finding himself framed in a murder case, conceals the corpse to gain time and to surprise his opponents into making a false move. Such falsification of evidence (moving bodies, removing finger-prints, etc.) is frequent on the part of innocently incriminated heroes. They seem to feel that anything will be more readily believed than the truth. Our uneasiness about the falsely suspected hero is strengthened by the fact that he really does something wrong. In the frequent chase sequences, external pursuers take over the role of the hero's guilty conscience. This is in keeping with the pervasive tendency to substitute outer for inner sources of anxiety. Fast cars and police sirens are the Eumenides of American films.

Perhaps the thing from which the hero suffers most, and which contributes most to the semblance of his guilt, is that he is alone. As Margaret Mead and Geoffrey Gorer have pointed out, Americans tend to feel uneasy alone; they feel they are unloved and therefore unworthy of love—there must be something wrong with them. They need the constant reassurance of the positive response of others to feel that they are lovable, hence good. The image of the outcast, misunderstood dreamer or genius is uncongenial. Thus if the hero is alone, even though we know that the suspicions against him are unfounded, he tends to retain an aura of guilt. It is as essential for the hero to escape from his isolation as it is for him to free himself from false accusations, and the two escapes frequently coincide. The girl whom the hero almost always finds in the course of his investigations serves a significant function in loving him, even though he often has so little time for her and can spare her only a hasty and almost absent-minded kiss. In *Somewhere in the Night,* the hero, a returned veteran who suffers from amnesia and thus literally knows no one, meets by chance a beautiful singer. Later, after having been beaten up by unknown assailants, he comes staggering to her doorstep. Out of pity she makes up a bed for him on her living-room couch. Thereafter she helps him in his efforts to clarify his mysterious crime-involved past. He still has to go on many lonely errands, and meets unfriendly, vicious, and dangerous men and women; and for some time he himself does not know whether in his forgotten past he committed a murder. But none of it is as bad as it would be if he did not have the girl to come back to. In *The Fallen Angel,* the hero, a footloose ne'er-do-well and a stranger in town, is suspected of the murder of a beautiful waitress whom he had been courting. He takes flight, but the trusting girl whom he has hastily married for her money (with which he hoped to win the mercenary waitress) goes with him. In a shabby hotel room, she persuades him that she loves him even after he has confessed how bad he has been. Suddenly she becomes important to him and the other woman unimportant. Moved by her poetic (For love alone can make the fallen angel rise) and practical (Don't run away, go back) inspiration, he returns to the place of the crime and discovers the real murderer.

The feeling of how dangerous it is to be alone is evoked in *Sorry, Wrong Number.* The heroine's initial uneasiness and annoyance at finding herself alone in the house at night develops gradually into panic fear which is justified by circumstances. The lonely woman's reminiscences and attempts to communicate with absent people by telephone all confirm her feeling of being unloved. Her father, whom she calls long distance, is in the midst of a gay party; the old schoolmate who was more popular than she is happily married and busy with her family; her doctor is out dancing and tells her brusquely that he cannot be bothered, there is really nothing

the matter with her. Keeping pace with this increasing awareness of emotional isolation, there is an accumulation of factual clues which indicate that she is the intended victim of a
murder plot. Her husband, whose absence has left her alone
and provoked the feeling of being unloved, has hired a murderer to kill her for her insurance money. The catastrophic
feeling associated with being alone is shown to be justified. A
person in this position is helpless to ward off the murderous
attack which is always imminent in the melodrama world.

The falsely accused rarely clears himself entirely by his
own efforts. In a number of cases, the hero, while resourceful and active, with a strong punch and great powers of recuperation, still needs the emotional and practical support of
a loving woman at a crucial moment. In other cases, at the
opposite end of the scale, the falsely accused is powerless to
do anything on his own behalf. The hero may then be the
inquisitive reporter or the scrupulous prosecuting attorney
who becomes convinced of the innocence of the accused and
undertakes to win his acquittal (*Call Northside 777, Boomerang*). Where the falsely suspected is dependent to a high
degree on someone else's efforts to clear him, this other person is more likely to be a man than a woman. Where it is a
woman, her indispensability derives from a professional skill.
The man's dependence on the woman is mitigated by con-
necting her capacity to help with acquired equipment. In
Spellbound, the falsely suspected amnesiac hero depends on
the efforts of his psychoanalyst sweetheart to extract clues
from his dreams. In *The High Wall,* another amnesiac hero,
imprisoned on a false charge, has his memory revived by a
sympathetic woman psychiatrist who injects him with penta-
thol.

The suspicious circumstances surrounding the hero and
his incriminating acts have made us feel anxious since we are
at a loss to see how they can be satisfactorily explained. But
they do not have to be explained at all because, in the end,
the real murderer is found. The haunting burden of false

suspicion is suddenly lifted by the revelation of the real murderer. The effect is not dissimilar to that of a less frequently used device where the hero, apparently hopelessly incriminated, suddenly wakes up and finds it all a dream (*The Chase*). The murderer usually gives himself away, either verbally, when confronted, admitting or even boasting of his crimes, or by renewed attacks on persons who he fears may discover his secret. In *The Blue Dahlia,* the old peeping-Tom caretaker, briefly holding his pursuers off at the point of a gun, tells how the contempt and stinginess of the beautiful woman he was blackmailing goaded him into murdering her. In *The Dark Corner*, the murderer, about to shoot the hero who has tracked him down, pauses to boast of his criminal ingenuity. In *The High Wall,* the murderer confesses, under the influence of a truth serum. The murderer in *Spellbound,* thinking he will kill the heroine immediately afterwards, confides to her the motive and method of his crime. (This fatal last-minute prolixity of the murderer, which precedes or induces his death or capture, reverses the convention of classical tragedy where the fatally wounded hero postponed his demise to deliver a speech.)

The presentation of the murderer seems to be essential to clearing the falsely suspected. Apart from satisfying the curiosity of the audience, this seems to be necessary to relieve the falsely suspected of self-accusations. In an exceptional film, *They Won't Believe Me,* the hero appears guilty of the murder of his sweetheart. He is not, but neither is anyone else. There had been a series of accidents and coincidences. On the witness stand, the hero tells this highly improbable true story which reveals him as a not very admirable character but innocent of murder. He is believed by the jury, but unrelieved of self-accusations—he says he listened to his own story and judged himself. Presumably still doubting that he will be believed, he jumps out of the court-room window just before the verdict of not guilty is to be read. In *Boomerang,* based on a real-life story of an unsolved crime, an honest district attorney fights successfully for the exoneration of an innocent man. The movie supplies a fictitious character, who, we are given to understand, is the murderer and who is killed in an auto accident in the end. The defense of the falsely suspected is conducted not by stressing his true story, but by an attack on the construction which incriminates him. The attack is concentrated on a detail involving the height of the suspect and the angle at which the shot was fired. The district attorney proves his point by allowing the suspect to fire at his head and thus to demonstrate that the gun fails to fire at the angle at which the suspect would have had to hold it. In subjecting himself to this ordeal the defender of the falsely accused undergoes some of the suffering usually inflicted on the falsely suspect himself. He is also subjected to social ostracism (the murder victim is a beloved clergyman, everyone believes that the suspected stranger is guilty, and the party in power is eager to get a conviction). The element of trial by ordeal in the clearing of the falsely suspect, which comes out most clearly here, is also present in the films where the hero must survive many dangers and beatings to prove his innocence.

In some rare cases the falsely accused hero is not cleared. He may unwittingly precipitate too many murders: he is then forestalled by the killing off of all witnesses. In *Dark Passage* persons approached by the hero immediately die without his touching them. The hero, escaped from prison, visits his only friend, who is going to provide evidence to clear him. Immediately afterwards the friend is murdered. Eventually the hero confronts the woman who has committed the murders of which he is suspected, and whose confession alone can clear him. Terrified when he identifies himself (she did not recognize him as his face had been transformed by plastic surgery), she backs away from him and falls out of a high window. The hero, however, has apparently suffered enough for the crimes he did not do. The last scene, like the awakening from (or beginning of) a dream, shows him on a

moonlit balcony above palm trees and with him the beautiful girl who loves him, the one person who believes in his
innocence.

The theme of looking guilty but being innocent, recurs
persistently in various forms throughout American films. The
good-bad girl, as we have seen, creates an impression of wickedness which in the end turns out to be a false appearance.
A young couple may spend a night innocently alone together
or pose as husband and wife, but only to get a tourist cabin
or serve some equally non-sexual exigency. A man may be
seen entering the bedroom of his wife who is at the time, for
harmless reasons, masquerading as someone else's wife. In
such scenes the audience knows that the couple are innocent,
but onlookers in the film regard them as guilty. The appearances tell a falsely accusing story. There is much less than
meets the eye; and it is not always easy to prove it.

This recurrent pattern in which the main characters know
they are innocent (except where they have amnesia), but are
accused by a leering or ostracizing or punishing world with
which they struggle to clear themselves, may be related to
various factors in American life. The older drama of conscience, where the conflict was internal and the individual
suffered from feelings of guilt, has been transformed into a
conflict between the individual and the world around him.
Self-accusations have become accusations of others, directed
against the self from outside. In the upbringing of Americans
today there is a particularly mixed ethic. A great many standards have to do with how things are going to look to the
neighbors, with what will impress other people. These standards are probably the more explicit. Along with this external
ethic, there continues an often less articulate code incorporat-
ing convictions that certain things are right and others wrong.
This inner ethic occasions self-accusations which tend to be
perceived as accusations coming from outside.

The movie hero, warding off false accusations, suffers almost as much as if he were guilty; his feeling of relief in the

end, and the freedom he wins, are in part paid for by this
suffering. Sometimes, as we have seen, he even mistakenly
suspects himself. He is not simply the victim of a miscarriage
of justice; he is framed, the world is conspiring against him.
(By contrast, the films based on real-life stories put the falsely
accused into the background and do not build this persecutory structure around him.) This nightmarish picture seems
related more to intense self-accusations than to the real external dangers of crime and legal ineptitude. The end of the
film demonstrates the advantage of this handling of self-
accusations. If the accusations come from outside, then the
case is closed once they are disproved. "You can't be tried
twice for the same crime" is a rule of legal justice, though
not always of conscience which may pursue and punish end-
lessly for a crime that was never committed except in intent.
The feeling that the end is unconvincing (though a welcome
relief) may derive in part from the indestructibility of the
underlying self-accusations. While real-life stories (like
Boomerang and *Call Northside 777*) deal with a single crime,
the fictional melodramas present a proliferation, in which one
crime leads to another; where when one danger is warded
off another appears; in the attempt to answer one false accusation the hero finds himself faced with another. There is
a sense of relief in the hero's last-minute demonstration: it
wasn't so, it was the other fellow. But, as he emerges from
the night-time world of persecution, and we see him speeding off down a sunny highway with his girl beside him, we
may have the feeling that this relief can only be temporary.
Just as, at the beginning of the film, the hero came to a new
town to make a fresh start, but found himself still followed
by the old ill-fortune, so at the end, his moment of respite
lacks finality. We will see the same hero again in another
film, and another and another, warding off false accusations,
surrounded by the same mistrustful and attacking world.
The repetitiveness of these plots is related not only to certain
surface production factors but also to their psychological

basis, which involves an endless repetition, and admits of no development or stable resolution.

There are a number of variations on the crime plot just outlined in which the murderer is unknown and the hero suspected. In some cases, while the murderer remains unknown, the hero is not inculpated in the crime which he is investigating. Nevertheless, parts of the persecutory pattern usually appear. The hero is suspected of something else, or exposes himself to attack by some forbidden act, or is beaten and shot at because he is carrying on unwelcome investigations. In *Lady on a Train* (a comedy mystery), the hero, a mystery story writer who is investigating a murder, is falsely suspected by his fiancée of having an affair with the heroine. In *The Unsuspected,* the hero, who appears under false pretenses for purposes of investigation, is mistakenly believed to be a fortune-hunter. In *The Red House,* the hero is exposed to sudden violent attacks because he has entered a dark wood that he was warned not to cross and whose mystery he resolves to penetrate. Elsewhere (*The Big Sleep, Dead Reckoning, Lady in the Lake*) the hero, a private detective, is subjected to routine beatings and assaults with deadly weapons.

In some of the false-suspect plots, the murderer may be known to the audience, though unknown to the characters in the film. In another variant, *The Big Clock,* the identity of the false suspect is unknown to everyone except the suspect himself. The audience and some of the characters know that the hero's powerful boss has committed the murder. The hero is forced by the boss to locate and frame an unknown man who had been seen with the victim just before the murder and whom the hero knows to be himself. He must keep up a pretense of pursuing the investigation while doing his best to sabotage it, elude witnesses, and collect evidence against the boss. Elsewhere, the false accusation theme is absent; the central problem is that of eliminating the danger that emanates from a murderer known to the audience: How will they discover him? How will they catch him? Will they

Movies: A Psychological Study

stop him before he kills again? This known murderer differs from the known murderer in British films, whom we see, almost in spite of himself, fulfilling a self-imposed plan to kill, and with whom we may feel a painful sympathy. In the British *The Upturned Glass,* the hero, lecturing on criminal psychology, tells his class the story of a perfect crime. We then learn that he has described the plan of a murder he is about to commit, the murder of a heartless woman who has driven his sweetheart to suicide. We see him with his intended victim, and we follow the announced plan step by step. Will it go through all right? Won't he turn back? No, he has to do it. The murder is an intimate act. The hero has been carrying on a flirtation with his victim, and he kisses her as he draws her to the window from which he throws her out. We watch the hero of *Wanted for Murder,* who suffers from a compulsion to kill, attempt unsuccessfully the murder of the girl he loves and who rejects him. We are drawn into identification with the murderers in these British films, who are driven towards their victims by intense feelings which are rendered sympathetic in a way. In contrast, the known murderer in American films is usually presented as unsympathetic, alienated from us, an inhuman, destructive force. His relation to his victims is undiscriminating. He simply kills anyone who gets in his way. Someone who may have been related to him becomes merely something to be eliminated once he (or she) becomes a threat to safety. Thus the disguised Nazi in *The Stranger* is ready to kill his wife as soon as she begins to suspect his crimes. The Nazi in *Notorious* undertakes to poison his wife when he learns she is a spy. The murderer in *Crossfire* kills his friend who, he fears, might give him away.

Occasionally the killer may be known both to the audience and to other characters in the film; the problem then is not to discover but to trap him. In *The Street with No Name,* an FBI agent poses as a member of the killer's gang. Suspense revolves around whether he will be able to expose the killer before the killer finds out about him. The strongly guarded-against tendency to fuse tenderness with violence comes through in the brief camaraderie between the hero and the gang-leader, who are bound to end up in a fatal struggle. The gang-leader, having chosen the hero for his gang, draws him aside to congratulate him on his (faked) criminal record, and to express the feeling that they are worthy of each other. This intimacy preceding fatal violence is devalued by the fact that the hero is only play-acting and by the incapacity for real attachment on the part of the gang-leader, a pathological killer, who takes pride in his clever arrangements for the hero's murder as soon as he discovers who he is. In addition to his unsympathetic character, the known murderer is usually alienated from us by other features—by being a professional criminal, a Nazi, a crude exponent of religious prejudice (like the anti-Semitic killer in *Crossfire*). Incidents may also be introduced which render him specially unattractive. The killer in *Kiss of Death* throws a crippled old woman downstairs. The killer in *The Street with No Name* is brutal to his pretty blonde wife. French and British movies on the other hand may introduce incidents which make a murderer especially sympathetic. In *The Upturned Glass*, the murderer, who is a physician, saves the life of a little girl. *Non Coupable* has an identical episode.

The American movie killer seems to be an embodiment of our destructive impulses, put at a distance from us, just as false accusations coming from outside may stand for self-accusations. American films find it difficult to present sympathetic characters overwhelmed by bad impulses, sexual or destructive. Destructive impulses tend to be felt not as internal, but as an external threat, and to get embodied in unsympathetic and eventually safely defeated characters. The concentration of badness in one thoroughly bad character, and the image of this character as a threat to everyone around him, is summed up at the end of *Key Largo*. A good old man is reproaching himself for having been an unwitting agent in two murders engineered by the gangster. The gangster's ex-moll answers: You weren't to blame, no one was to blame for anything except Johnny Rocco; and nobody's safe as long as he's alive. Here, as usual, the concentrated embodiment of badness is destroyed, leaving the world, for the moment, free for good people.

Only occasionally are there films in which the struggle of the good and bad is fatal to both. In *Brute Force,* the convicts (essentially fine fellows) die in an attempt to break out of a prison ruled by a sadistic warden. The hero, fatally wounded, climbs the tower where the warden stands, grapples with him and throws him over the parapet; the prisoners in the yard below close in over the body. This joint death of the good and bad recalls the end of Dr. Jekyll and Mr. Hyde. In *Out of the Past,* the hero is unable to escape from the bad woman who has killed the last witness who could clear him. He tips off the state troopers. As the woman tries to drive away with him, they are ambushed and killed. The rarity of a character who combines good and bad within himself is indicated in the exceptional film, *Swell Guy,* which presents such a character as its hero. The film is prefaced by a statement explaining that such characters exist.

Occasionally the hero commits the murder of which he is more often falsely accused. Even here the complaint persists: You got me wrong; I didn't get my due. In *The Postman Always Rings Twice,* the hero and heroine have murdered her husband, and it seems as though they will get away with it. However, this situation of being guilty and looking innocent shifts into the reverse. The woman is killed in an auto accident, and the hero is falsely convicted of having murdered her. In the last scene, in the death cell, the hero, in conversation with a priest, is struggling to get the record straight. In *Nightmare Alley,* the hero accidentally kills a man by giving him a bottle of cleaning fluid instead of gin. The memory of this incident occasionally troubles him and he confesses it to a lady psychologist. The two of them become collaborators in a shady and lucrative business. In the end, she robs him, holding over him the blackmailing threat that she has recorded his confession on a phonograph record —and who will believe it was only an accident? Thus the hero, technically blameless, is burdened with false blame. In *Scarlet Street,* the hero murders a deceiving woman who has exploited him and allows her falsely suspected boy-friend to go to the chair for it. The hero had been a painter of unrecognized genius, whose works had been promoted by the boy-friend as the productions of the girl. The paintings, which he can never claim, achieve great success. In the last shot, the hero, an outcast derelict, passes a swank gallery through the door of which his masterpiece is being carried while well-dressed bystanders admire it. The impression of the hero's crime and guilt becomes oddly distorted with the complaint that he did not get his due rewards.

A woman is rarely the center of a persecutory plot. Women may be suspected of murders they did not commit, but the development and emotional tone is different than in the case of men. The woman is usually subject to suspicion for a shorter time than the man; the oppressive pall of accusation does not pervade the film. Nor is there a proliferation of the original crime of which the heroine is suspected into additional crimes charged to her, or incidental misdemeanors which she commits. The heroine may suffer little anxiety about the suspicions against her; she may not even be aware of them until they are dispelled. She is apt to undergo little deprivation. In contrast to the desperately struggling hero, she is apt to move serenely through the episode. There are few occasions when American film heroines show less fight and more passivity than when they are subject to false charges of murder. In *The Dark Mirror,* the heroine has a twin sister who resembles her completely except that she has a vicious character. A murder is traced to one of the twins, and a psychologist is called in to determine which one was capable of murder. The vicious twin, not realizing that she has given herself away, tries to frame her sister. She almost succeeds. The good twin does not realize her danger until it is past, and remains unperturbed throughout. In *Love Letters,* the heroine is falsely convicted of having murdered her husband. Since she suffers from amnesia she is at a loss to contest the charge. After a brief sojourn in prison (not shown), she rejoins her devoted friends. She suffers none of the isolation of a falsely suspected hero. Presently she marries a fine man and eventually recovers her memory and discovers she was not a murderess. But there is no urgency about avoiding imminent danger to motivate this discovery. In *Nocturne,* the falsely suspected heroine disports herself in swimming pools and on movie sets, while the detective hero, who is falling in love with her, appears off and on to ask some questions which she parries with wisecracks.

The exclusive application of the persecutory pattern to men in the film melodramas illustrates the well-known finding that persecutory ideas are usually related to homosexual wishes. The unacknowledged wish is attributed to the loved man who appears as a dangerous attacker.

The major mode of handling hostilities between men, as we have noted, is to present the hero as free from bad impulses, the object of unprovoked attacks, and as never having had any positive relation with his enemy so that he can dispose of him in an impersonal way, rather as if he were dismantling an undetonated bomb. In other words, there is a projection of hostile impulses, which are unacknowledged by the hero and seen as concentrated in his attacker, and a repression of the positive component of mixed feelings in the relation between the two men. However, there are occasional striking modifications of these devices. The hero, while not the manifest initiator or the direct agent of violent attacks against another, may be associated with less scrupulous characters who carry out such actions. He may be unable to oppose them when they undertake to carry out violent acts which are in keeping with his unexpressed wishes. The hero's bad impulses are thus less fully projected, less completely dissociated from himself. They remain embodied in others, but these others cease to be strangers and demand recognition for what is elsewhere an unacknowledged relationship. Also, the dissociation of the hero from his enemy is occasionally not complete. He may have a pseudo-friendly relation with the enemy, as he joins the enemy's gang or carouses with him in order later to betray him to the police. The hero and his enemy may even be ex-buddies.

In *Act of Violence,* the hero is being pursued by an ex-buddy who believes, apparently with some justification, that the hero betrayed other members of their outfit to the Nazis. The hero, in a panic because he knows the buddy is out to murder him, gets drunk and, in a low bar, falls in with some underworld characters. They draw from him an account of his troubles and offer for a fee to dispose of this enemy for him. The hero is too drunk and demoralized to oppose the scheme. Similarly in *Sorry, Wrong Number,* crudely destructive intentions appear in characters around the hero rather than in him. However, he is involved with these others, and their aims have a recognizable relation to his wishes. He has many reasons for hating his wife and wishes she would die, but would not himself murder her. Some gangsters, with whom he has had previous unlawful dealings, prevail on him to let them do the job. The gangsters have demanded a large sum of money which he can only hope to get from his wife's life insurance. Believing his wife to be very ill, he has promised the gangsters that he will be able to pay them from this source in a short time. He is then shocked to learn from a new doctor whom his wife has consulted that her disabilities are psychosomatic. When he reports back to the gangsters that there may be some delay in obtaining the money they demand, they tell him that he has no choice but to assist them in arranging for the wife's murder.

Where the hero assumes a temporarily friendly relation with the man whom he will face eventually in deadly hostilities, it is usually a pretense on the hero's side. He feigns friendship for a former jail mate about whose crimes he must get evidence for the police (*Kiss of Death*), or joins a criminal gang as an undercover government agent (*T-Men, The Street with No Name*). We see a show of comradeship between the men, but we know that the hero is only acting a part whatever his opponent may feel at the moment. The possibility of an ambivalent rather than a simply hostile relation between the opponents is thus only incompletely suggested. The danger of any mitigation of hostilities is pointed up as the man who experiences however briefly a comradely feeling for his opponent is made a sucker. Where the two opponents have once been real friends, we do not see them in their early friendly phase but are only told about it later when they have become enemies (*Act of Violence*). As is often the case with emotionally dangerous material, its impact is reduced by its not being visually presented.

In dealing with any important theme, American films present a major plot line built on the denial of dangers. A less frequent plot construction on the same theme is apt to reveal clues to the dangers which are usually warded off. Thus in the usual treatment of hostilities between men, one of the most frequent devices is, as we have seen, to make the relation impersonal and to eliminate any bad motives on the side of the hero. This would seem to conceal homosexual impulses which are felt as dangerous. The less frequent plots in which the hero is more nearly associated with immoral characters, and especially where there is some admission of positive feelings between him and his opponent, give us glimpses of this danger. Where the hero is pursued by the murderous ex-buddy we get the clearest picture of an intense friendship between men giving rise to the persecutory pattern. The latent positive feelings between the two opponents, usually unadmitted, here come to the surface.

The prescribed behavior of the hero in American film melodramas seems related to a fear of homosexual tendencies and the need to deny them. The hero must demonstrate his toughness, his ability to take a beating without for a moment relaxing his militant aggressiveness. There are times, as we have noted, when the hero is tempted to yield to his attacker, to become passive and let the other have his way. This danger is guarded against by the helping woman, whose relation to the hero, among other things, serves to combat any passive tendencies. Geoffrey Gorer has remarked on what appears to be a distinctively high degree of fear of passive homosexuality in American men. The film melodramas which we are discussing seem to confirm this point in their concentration on warding off this danger. While persecutory fantasies represent a common human potentiality, they do not everywhere contribute so significantly to the formation of dramatic plots. Neither French nor British films show a like preoccupation with the predicament of a hero fighting off false accusations and physical attacks.

§ THE PRIVATE EYE

THE nature of crime investigations is related to the nature of the police. In American films the police tend to be ineffectual. They suspect the wrong man; they are taken in by false appearances; they are apt to be satisfied with a hasty and incomplete investigation because they are under pressure to arrest and convict. Hence the major task of investigation is carried on by private individuals, sometimes professional private detectives, more often untrained persons whom circumstances force into the role of investigator. (The private investigator is sometimes called a "peeper" or a "private eye.") Since the police cannot be resorted to for help or safety, and must even be avoided since they mistakenly suspect the investigator, the atmosphere of the big city becomes that of the unpoliced frontier. The self-appointed investigator must take the law into his own hands.

The most frequent motive for crime investigation, as we have already seen, is to clear oneself from a false charge. A less frequent motive is to clear someone else who is falsely suspected. In some cases the hero or heroine is subjected to an unintelligible attack, or feels threatened and undertakes an investigation in order to locate and ward off the danger. In *The Strange Love of Martha Ivers,* the hero has been beaten up by hired thugs. He understands that someone wants to scare him into leaving town, and starts looking through old newspaper files to find out why. In *The Two Mrs. Carrolls,* the heroine begins to suspect from chance observations that her husband is trying to poison her and she starts a systematic investigation. Sometimes an investigation is undertaken on behalf of someone else who is in danger, as when the heroine's brother in *The Stranger* aids the detective who is pursuing the heroine's husband, a Nazi murderer. In all of these cases investigation is a defense against attack or threat. Occasionally the investigator may take as his starting point a completed act of violence against someone close to him, the murder of his father (*Johnny Angel*), of his wife (*Cornered*), of his friend (*Dead Reckoning, Ride the Pink Horse*), where for some reason the crime is out of the jurisdiction of the official police, or they do not recognize that a crime has been committed.

In the majority of cases the investigator is personally involved; or someone he cares about is suspected or in danger, or someone close to him has been murdered. In some instances, however, he is simply doing a job, for example, when he is called in as a private detective. Regardless of whether he is personally implicated or pursuing his profession, he is always in danger. One of the most frequent reasons why people get murdered is, as we shall see below, that they know too much.

The police, then, are usually only hasty and incompetent. The superiors of the policeman-hero in *Nocturne* are so convinced that his line of investigation is mistaken that they suspend him from the force; he solves the crime as a private investigator. In *Lady in the Lake,* a policeman, exceptionally, turns out to be himself involved with the murderer; in *The Fallen Angel* a former policeman is the murderer. Occasionally the police, recognizing their inability to capture the murderer, induce an outsider to help them. The man who is thus reluctantly impressed into the service of the police finds himself charged with the repugnant duty of betraying someone who regards him as a pal (*Crossfire, Kiss of Death*). While inclined to be mistaken, the police are not obstinate or malign. When the hero has brought his independent investigation to a successful conclusion, they are ready to acknowledge his point and to drop the case against him.

In British crime films the investigators are almost without exception from the police; they are almost always right; and they are rarely in danger. One type of official investigator is self-effacing, sober, unhurried, sure, soft-spoken, gentle and polite. He questions the criminal more in sorrow than in anger and, though he may have strong suspicions, lets his man go free until he is sure. (*Wanted for Murder, Dear Murderer, Bedelia.*) Another type indulges a prankish humor and cultivates his eccentricities. In *Clouds Over Europe* the official investigator interrupts his hectic pursuits with recurrent phone calls to "Daphne, my darling"—with whom he has a perpetual, and perpetually broken, dinner engagement; or drops everything to plunge into the concoction of an elaborate stew. This whimsical investigator illustrates a distinctive feature of certain British crime films; the use of comic relief to break the tension. In *Hotel Reserve,* the hero vacationing on the French coast has just been confronted with the news that the local authorities believe him to be a spy; he seems to be in a solitary and threatened position. At this point (where in an American film the tension would be steadily mounting), he tries a ruse which he thinks will produce information: he tells the greatest gossip at the hotel, in strictest confidence, that his room has been robbed. Then he gleefully watches the gossip wend his way among the guests, telling each, in strictest confidence, the story of the robbery, which assumes increasingly fantastic proportions. In place of this whimsical comic relief, American crime films present hard-bitten, somberly joking, concise dialogue which does not interrupt the action or break the tension. There is, however, a type of British crime plot which is unrelieved by comedy. This is where there is an intimate relation between the murderer and his victim. There, a continuous oppressive atmosphere attends the progress of the murderer towards his crime and his punishment. For these crimes the more-in-sorrow-than-in-anger investigator is employed.

In the less numerous British films where the hero seems falsely suspected, the authorities may know the truth all along and pretend to suspect him to stimulate him to useful researches or to lull the criminals into a false security. In *I Became a Criminal,* the falsely convicted hero breaks jail and comes back to settle the score with the criminal gang that framed him. A friendly police inspector catches up with him, intimates that he believes in his innocence (the hero, incidentally, has a distinguished war record), and informally commissions him to get the incriminating evidence on the gang. The inspector politely looks the other way while his man "escapes." The falsely accused heroes of *Hotel Reserve* and *They Met in the Dark* similarly learn that the authorities have known all along that they were innocent and intended to use them as unofficial investigators. American films have almost no counterpart to this pattern. (However, British films sometimes include the common American theme of the isolated false suspect, for instance, in earlier Hitchcock films like *The Girl Was Young* and *The Thirty-Nine Steps.*)

The authorities presented in British and American films embody the contrasting images of the father-figure. The still

preserved British father-image shows him all-knowing and
always right, while maintaining a hesitant, gentle, and un-
pretentious manner. He knows if you are good and, of course,
will have to punish you if you are bad. It could hardly be
dangerous for him to find out about your crimes (the police
inspector in *Wanted for Murder* gets the final clue by entering the murderer's bedroom and reading his diary)—he is
the father and you a child.

American films express the feeling that "Father is always
wrong" (Geoffrey Gorer). He is not a bad guy, but he is incompetent, and a younger man (someone not in authority, a
son-figure), will have to take over. But investigation pursued
by a son-figure may carry a wealth of other meanings. It is
apt to have the latent significance of the child's investigations into the mysteries of the night-time world. Then investigation is forbidden and subject to punishment. The
independent investigator of the films, like the curious child,
must be careful that the authorities do not catch him; he is
continually in danger. He is led to uncover an act of violence
(from the child's point of view, it is sex misunderstood as
destructive), and encounters a dangerous criminal (the father
in his night-time role, so discrepant with the harmless day-
time father as pal). The hero is threatened by this criminal
(as the feared but wished-for beloved man, as the embodiment of the hero's projected destructive wishes, and as the
punisher of forbidden investigations). Thus the unauthor-
ized investigator, the private eye of American films, has a
prototype in the secretly inquisitive child. The film melodramas are related to fantasies derived from earlier nocturnal
investigations.

The young hero investigating the crime in *The Naked City,*
is, by exception, a member of the police. His investigations and
those of the other young men in his department are encouraged by their superior, a genial little old man (Barry Fitz-
gerald), a clear case of the harmless, friendly manifest father
type. The young men have all the ideas and run all the risks;

the old man encourages them to follow their hunches even when they seem far-fetched to him, and is always ready to give them credit when the hunches turn out to be correct. The wife of the old man is dead; he occasionally quotes her in affectionate reminiscence. There is another dead woman who figures more prominently in the plot: a beautiful blonde whom we see at the beginning of the film being murdered in bed at night. In contrast to the hero's boss, the harmless little man (about half the hero's size), there is somewhere out in the city the murderer, a big, dangerous man (an ex-wrestler), whom the hero must pursue and capture. (Meanwhile another young man is falsely suspected of the murder.) The hero has a son, a little boy who is being introduced into the image of the world shown in the main plot. He is learning that father is sweet and harmless, but in the world outside there are possibly fatal dangers. His mother is perturbed because he has crossed a dangerous thoroughfare all alone and tries to persuade the extremely reluctant father to spank the boy so he won't do it again. The father is really pleased at the boy's enterprise: an urgent message recalling him to his own investigations exempts him from administering the punishment.

In *The Street with No Name,* another film in which a successful investigation is carried on by official agencies, the hero, a young FBI man, assumes a disguise and gains admission to the criminal gang. An older man who brought the hero into the FBI is assigned to watch over him. While the hero has the more active and dangerous job of dealing with the gangsters, the older man, disguised as a bum, haunts the low neighborhood where the gang hangs out, observes the hero with anxious looks, and transmits messages.

While British and American films differ in their image of the agents of criminal investigation, they agree in this: that in the end, with few exceptions, the truth is made plain, the guilty caught and the falsely suspect exonerated. While American films express on the whole the opposite of British confidence in the constituted authorities, they maintain the faith that, if the authorities are incompetent, someone else will come along to see that justice is done. French films differ from both American and British in this respect. They are sceptical about the likelihood of right being triumphant in human affairs. The authorities are generally incompetent, as in American films. But no one else appears to set things straight. While a falsely suspected hero in American films struggles and eventually clears himself, a French movie criminal may strive in vain to persuade the authorities of his guilt. In *Non Coupable,* the hero, who is otherwise a failure, discovers that he has a talent for crime. He then murders his mistress's lover in such a way that the mistress is implicated, and engineers her death so that it appears to be an accident. He confesses to these perfect crimes to gain acknowledgment for his genius. The police, however, interpret his confession as an effort to clear his mistress's name; he is unable to transform his reputation for being a good-natured incompetent. He then writes an account of the crimes and shoots himself. His cat, frightened by the shot, jumps onto the mantel where the confession has been carefully propped up in front of the clock. The confession falls into the fireplace and is burned.

In American films the authorities err through a hasty interpretation of the evidence. The complaint which French films make against the authorities is that they are too casual in reading men's souls. They accept what appears on the surface and do not probe into the depths. Where the American hero wants to be cleared so that he can go on his way, the French hero is more anxious to be understood. Thus for him there is an equal irony in being falsely accused and mistakenly exonerated. In *La Passionelle,* the heroine, a beautiful, pure-looking young girl fails to get anyone to believe she has murdered her lover. The hero, a gloomy, solitary young man who has always been misunderstood, allows himself to be arrested for her crime. The American movies' distaste for such ironical conclusions appears in the film version of the play, *Uncle Harry,* where the theme of a criminal whose confession no one believes is transformed into a dream from which the hero escapes by awakening. As we have remarked, both French and British films tend to be preoccupied with a known rather than an unknown murderer. In British films, however, he is usually known to the authorities; in French films, he is more apt to be known to someone who is not in authority, and who is unable to make the truth prevail over the false account with which the authorities are satisfied.

In *Panique,* an innocent man dies because he is falsely suspected of a murder. Suspicion falls on him largely because no one recognizes the noble character he conceals behind an eccentric façade. In the end, pursued by the police and an excited mob, he flees over a roof, slips, hangs by his hands from the gutter, and falls, just as the police ladder is about to reach him. A few minutes after his death, a police inspector discovers the evidence which identifies the murderer. Missing by a narrow margin is a recurrent theme in French films. In respect to justice, if the truth is discovered at all, it is a matter of chance whether the discovery will be made before it is too late. In *Quai des Orfèvres,* a favorable chance allows the falsely suspected character to go free. Imprisoned and hopeless he cuts his wrists, but the prisoner in the next cell happens to see the trickle of blood and raises an alarm in time for him to be revived. At the same time, the police inspector on the case happens on a clue which links another man who is being questioned on a different charge with the murder of which the hero is suspected. The attempted suicide expresses the characteristic helplessness of the falsely accused in French films. Unlike their counterparts in American and British films, they rarely show any tendency to undertake independent investigations to clear themselves, but feel at the mercy of capricious agencies.

In *Copie Conforme,* two men look exactly alike. One is a

meticulous clerk, the other an ingenious confidence man and gang leader. The clerk is arrested and charged with the other's crimes, but is allowed to go free after an inconclusive investigation. Feeling that his reputation has been tarnished, he is wading out into the river to drown himself when he is stopped by the crook who offers him employment: he is to double for the crook who needs an alibi when out on a job. The involved life together of the two doubles ends with the violent death of the crook. The authorities insist on confusing their identities—the dead man is misidentified as the clerk. The clerk is credited with having concealed an amazing career of crime behind a harmless façade (the credit refused to the hero of *Non Coupable*); the real clerk survives with another man's identity and possessions, including a beautiful girl friend.

In part such French films express the difficulty of disentangling good from bad. Everyone has capacities for wickedness; the need of American films to impute one's bad impulses to an alien outsider, to segregate the good and the bad, is less predominant. *Copie Conforme* seems to be a spoof of such an attempt. In *Quai des Orfèvres,* the suspect and his wife, both moderately sympathetic characters, might each have killed the man who happened to be murdered by a third person. The heroine was having dinner with the victim-to-be. Staving off his unwelcome advances, she knocked him out with a champagne bottle and fled, believing she had killed him. Her husband, enraged at the man's attentions to his wife, went to his house with the intention of murdering him only to find him already dead. The readiness to admit that one might have committed the crime and a greater emphasis on intentions presumably contribute to prevent the French hero from putting up the American style of fierce fight against false charges.

The agencies pursuing a criminal investigation in French films also display an admixture of baser impulses. In *Panique* the enraged mob which closes in on the innocent hero is interspersed with gendarmes who do nothing to restrain it. In *Le Corbeau,* a mob enraged by a series of anonymous letters take the pursuit of the criminal out of the hands of the ineffectual authorities and almost lynch an innocent man. *Circonstances Atténuantes* expresses in comedy form the intimate connection between crime and prosecution. An aging retired prosecutor finds himself by chance vacationing in a den of thieves. Their company turns out to have a rejuvenating effect and in return the prosecutor offers them instruction in dodging punishment. Soon he is playing the role of leader of the gang and hugely enjoys the careful plotting of a robbery of his own house, removing the knick-knacks with which his wife had encumbered it and to which he had always objected.

§ KILLING WITH A PURPOSE

AS TO the who-whom of killing in American films, murders of men by men are a little less than half of the total; murders of women by men and of men by women are about a fourth each; the remaining few murders are of women by women. Approximately the same ratios obtain in British and French films. Thus, hostilities between the sexes are fatal about as frequently as those between man and man; and the women seem to be giving as good as they get. Hostilities between women are rarely fatal. They are negligible as a theme for melodrama; in the few American films where woman-woman murders occur, there are usually man-man or cross-sex murders as well.

The one form of violent death which differentiates among the three groups of films is suicide. The ratio of suicide to murder in American films is about 1 to 20; in British films about 1 to 5; in French films about 1 to 2.

The most frequent motive for man-man murder in American films is to conceal some previously committed crime (usually murder or theft). The victim is killed because he knows too much. In *The Dark Corner*, the villain disposes of the hired killer whom he has employed to eliminate his wife's lover, and who alone knows of the villain's connection with the crime. In *The Killers*, the ex-gang-leader sends his thugs to murder the hero, a former member of his gang and the only one who could reveal to the rest of the gang how the leader cheated them out of a major haul. In *The Web*, the hero's boss, who tries to saddle the hero with his crimes, murders the two employees who shared the secret of his grand larceny. This fatality of knowing too much underscores the already noted dangerousness of crime investigation. It demonstrates the fate that threatens the hero investigator unless he exposes the concealed criminal in time. In British and French films this motive for murder is practically non-existent. We may relate this to our hypothesis about the models for crime investigation in American films on the one hand and British and French on the other. In the British and French films the investigation of crimes is an occupation of the authorities, whose responsibility it is to uncover and punish misdemeanors, as parents do with children. Investigation, then, is not dangerous for the investigator who can hardly know too much, or more than is good for him; it is his duty and his prerogative to know everything about his charges. In American films the model for crime investigation is the forbidden curiosity of the child towards the adults. The parents' sexual secret which is uncovered is frequently misunderstood as a destructive act; and there is fear of punishment for having found out. In the films, the victim who knew too much was usually an employee of his attacker, someone in a junior position, a son-figure.

Women, however, are rarely murdered for knowing too much. Occasionally a man attempts unsuccessfully to kill a woman who has uncovered his guilty secret (e.g., *Notorious,*

The Stranger). Women criminals may kill men in order to conceal their crimes (*The Big Sleep, Dead Reckoning, Dark Passage*), but do not kill other women for this reason. That curiosity is less dangerous for women than for men is shown by the fact that the male investigator's woman companion usually comes through without getting her hair disarranged, while he is apt to undergo severe beatings.

Frustration in love accounts for the greatest number of murders if we consider murderers of both sexes. There is an equal likelihood that a man frustrated in love will kill the woman he can't get or the man who stands in the way of his getting her. A woman similarly frustrated will almost always kill the man. In French films, a man tends to direct his attack against his male rival, not against the woman; or he may commit suicide. Women, correspondingly, tend to turn against the woman who stands in their way, or to kill themselves. Thus the French pattern for both sexes, when frustrated in love, is to attack the rival of the same sex or to commit suicide. In British films, love frustration for the man tends to produce rage against the woman. She may have withdrawn without there being any male rival. Similarly, frustrated women turn against the man, and occasionally attempt suicide. Here, too, there is not always a triangle. It is the person of the opposite sex who is frustrating. The American movie pattern thus contrasts with the concentrated sexual jealousy of the French hero, challenging the male rival, and the equally specific, violent reproach of the British hero against the depriving woman. The American reaction seems to be more one of sheer rage at being frustrated, striking out against one of the objects connected with the frustration. (There is, however, probably a greater complexity and pointedness about the murder of women.) This fits with the previously noted impression that murder in American films tends to be more impersonal, growing less out of an intimate relationship with the victim than in French or in British films. (The concealment motive previously cited is particularly impersonal: anyone who happens to know too much may become a victim.) Women murderers in American films rage specifically against men, in agreement with their English counterparts, while differing from the French. Neither men nor women in American films are inclined to commit suicide when confronted with difficulties in love; their fury is turned outwards.

Let us consider in more detail the man-man murders in American films motivated by frustration in love. In *The Postman Always Rings Twice,* the hero helps the woman he loves to murder her husband. The husband is an aging and unattractive man, obtuse, unenterprising, and stingy, whom the heroine married for his money, and who dully works over the account books of his small business while his wife flirts with his hired man. He is hardly a love rival, not an object of sexual jealousy, but just an obstruction. The woman is addicted to a certain degree of comfort and cannot be happy unless she adds her husband's money to the amorous satisfactions the hero provides. An attempt on the part of the hero to get her to run away with him fails. The husband, despite his friendly behavior towards the hero, is made unsympathetic and unregrettable. He precipitates his murder by his intention to take his wife away to some forsaken place to nurse his bedridden old sister. The heroine threatens to kill herself with a carving knife if the hero won't help her dispose of the husband. The husband thus increasingly becomes an obstacle to happiness, a frustrating object to be removed, rather than a person who is a focus of conflicting love and hate.

In *Suspense,* the hero has fallen in love with his boss's wife. The boss discovers this, shoots at the hero from a distance, accidentally falls off a mountain while doing so, and disappears. As he is presumed dead, the hero takes over his business and is about to marry the wife. Here, too, the woman never loved her husband, but was grateful to him for rescuing her from penury and promoting her career. The hero has an uneasy feeling that the boss is still around. This is not guilty conscience but a sound perception, as the boss, not dead, comes prowling around at night. He confronts the hero, who shoots him and burns him up in the furnace. This killing of the husband of a beloved woman springs from a mixture of motives. Retaliation for the previous attack and considerations of gain enter in. Before the murder is committed, the victim has been impersonalized by being reduced to an unseen presence, a *poltergeist* that makes unlivable the luxurious surroundings to which the hero has succeeded.

The tendency of British films to intensify, rather than to reduce, the intimacy between a prospective murderer and his victim is illustrated in *Dear Murderer*. (While characteristic in the quality of the relation between murderer and victim, this film is atypical in that it shows a man murdering his male rival in love.) The hero, who has been out of the country on business, learns that his flirtatious wife, with whom he is desperately in love, has been having an affair in his absence. He conceives a plan which he proceeds to carry out on his return. He pays a visit to the other man, introduces himself and persuades the man to write a letter breaking off all relations with the wife. There is an interlude of gentlemanly talk between the two men; they have a drink together, and there is the expressed feeling that, under different circumstances, they might have been friends. The husband then interrupts the writing of the farewell letter (which the other is writing at his dictation) at a point where it will sound like a suicide note, produces a gun, orders his victim to lie down on the couch, ties his hands and feet, climbs on top of him, tells him ragingly how much he has suffered from his wife's infidelity, and announces that he is going to murder him. The victim, with whom a moment ago he had been talking in a friendly way, the live young man who will so soon be dead, protests and is gagged. The murderer then proceeds to carry out the carefully planned murder which will look like suicide. The scene presents a contrast to the characteristic murder in American films. Here the victim is purposely humanized, instead of being dehumanized, before he is murdered; a positive relation, at least as a potentiality, between murderer and victim is evoked. Both physical and emotional contact between the two is heightened as the murderer climbs on his victim who lies bound and helpless on the couch, as he confides to him his sufferings and announces his murder intent. The scene is thus weighted with intense emotions of suffering and destroying. American films tend to drain murder of such emotion. The murderer becomes an impersonal, dangerous force or the victim an impersonal, obstructive being, or both, while physical and emotional contact between the two is reduced to a minimum. Another impersonalizing device frequent in American films is to have killings occur in a context of rapid and confusing action, which excludes an awareness of emotional relations.

As the previous discussions show, the murderer in American films usually murders because he has something to gain or protect, the murderer in British films because he has lost something. The hero in *Dear Murderer* has suffered from the infidelity of his wife. The hero in *The Upturned Glass* has lost the woman he loved because of the malicious interference of another woman, whom he proceeds to kill. In *Wanted for Murder*, the hero tries to kill the young woman who has refused his love. Less fatal violence against women is apt to be similarly motivated. In *The Seventh Veil* the hero beats with his cane the beloved woman who is about to leave him. These films illustrate not only the incidence of British male rage against a depriving woman (especially the woman who goes away), but also the more general point that violence is motivated by loss. This vindictive violence has a gloomy tone, while it may conceal an obscure hope of bringing the woman back by revealing to her how desperate she makes the man by her going away. Manifestly, however, there is nothing to be gained by this violence of reproach and revenge. Even if the hero were not apprehended for his crime, he would only have satisfied an irresistible impulse. In American films, murder is more frequently a means to an end. The victim stands between the murderer and things he wants, women and wealth; or he endangers the continued possession of them. If the murderer could get away with murder, he would profit by it. Desire for gain is one of the major motives for murder in American films, and only slightly operative in British or French film murders. It is the position of the falsely accused in American films which corresponds to that of the murderer in British films. It is the falsely accused whose wife has been unfaithful (*The Blue Dahlia, The High Wall*) or who has otherwise been cheated (*The Dark Corner*). Thus the falsely accused has the motive to commit a vindictive murder, a murder out of rage at being deprived; it is he who might kill out of passion and grief with nothing to gain. But he does not kill. A strenuous denial is advanced against the suspicion that he might kill from these motives.

The tendency of American films to make man-man murders in a love triangle impersonal, in the senses described above, has a further significance. Male friendship in American films is impervious to disruption by a woman. Where two friends fall in love with the same woman, they either abandon or share her (not sexually). The first alternative provided the Quirt-Flagg formula of some years back. In a series of films, a pair of First World War buddies perpetually scrapped and recurrently made up. They would regularly fall in love with the same girl, quarrel over her, and end by going off together like a cowboy and his horse, leaving the girl behind. The same pattern appeared recently in *Wild Harvest*. The second alternative, fairly frequent in comedy, is illustrated in *Two Guys from Milwaukee* where the friends competing for the girl tell her, "We want to marry you." Earlier, the friendly rivals exchanged a few blows. To the girl's disappointment, they were unable to maintain this level of hostility. At the last minute the girl decides whom to marry, whom to keep as the perpetual friend of the family. In the sentimental *Daisy Kenyon,* the two men who love the heroine conceive a lively friendship for each other and are not inclined to violence. At one point the heroine, distracted by the dilemma of choosing between them, goes out driving alone to think things through and crashes into a tree. At the same time, the two men are amicably drinking and chatting.

Thus man-man relations in American films tend to be either so stably friendly that nothing can disturb them, or so completely negative that they can kill each other without a qualm. Friendship turning to hate through rivalry for a woman, or some other fatal difference, rarely occurs. This is a special case of the general intolerance of American films for mixed feelings involving inner conflict.

While the effort to keep relations between men clear and simple, to avoid dubious and complicated involvements, usually predominates, it occasionally gives way before the opposite tendency to explore these murky emotional regions. When relations between men become complicated it is usually not through rivalry for a woman. On the contrary, where intense and mixed feelings develop between the hero and the other man, the hero is drawn by the strength of this relation away from the woman he loves. We see the hero apparently happily settled with his wife and kiddies in a little house in the suburbs. But he cannot rest; he must leave them behind and go out into the night for a violent encounter with an ex-buddy or a former prison mate from whom he cannot free himself. He sits alone in a restaurant or impatiently paces a deserted railway platform waiting for the other man, with whom he has once been on intimate terms, who now wants to kill him, and with whom he must have this last encounter. The final scene is a love-death in which the hero and the other man shoot each other and one or both are killed (*Act of Violence, Kiss of Death.*)

The hero in such a film is apt to be drawn in two conflicting directions. On the one hand there is the seductive influence of the dangerous man friend tending to involve him in illicit acts, on the other, an inducement to betray the man who so lures him, to consolidate his relation with saving authorities. In *Kiss of Death,* the hero has refused to betray his partners in crime. The district attorney, trying to wean him away from this misguided attachment, appeals to the hero as a family man, shows him photographs of his own children and asks the hero to see a picture of his little girls. Thus he tries to establish for the hero a different identification, an alliance with men who love women as against the involvement with the male gang. Later the district attorney persuades the hero to work as a stool-pigeon, to betray a former jail mate. The hero joins this criminal buddy in a night-club. The buddy, overjoyed to see the hero, immediately dismisses the girl friend who is with him: me and my pal want to be alone. The scheme for the hero to rid himself of his involvement with his criminal associate by his betrayal miscarries. His evidence is insufficient; the criminal remains at large and seeks revenge against his betrayer. The hero, so far from being able to settle down with his wife and children in the little house in the suburbs, is forced to send them away and to remain alone awaiting the attack of his former friend. As this waiting becomes too nerve-wracking, he goes out to look for the other man—overriding the district attorney who tries to prevent this reunion. In the final scene the hero provokes the criminal to shoot him (the justification is that the criminal can only be arrested if he is caught with a gun in his hand), and the police close in to shoot down the criminal.

In French films men's friendships are more subject to disruption by love rivalry. In *Les Visiteurs du Soir,* a beautiful woman, sent by the devil, precipitates a duel between a father and his prospective son-in-law. The older man kills the younger, to whom he had been attached, and then mourns by his bier. In *Falbalas,* the hero falls in love with the fiancée of his best friend; unable to attack the friend, he commits suicide. In *Le Corbeau,* an aging doctor turns against a younger colleague with whom his young wife has fallen in love. While outwardly continuing a friendly relationship, the older man launches a poison pen attack against the younger one. In other cases of love rivalry there may have been no antecedent friendship between the two men. But in contrast to the American pattern the man who is attacked arouses intense sexual jealousy and is never a mere external obstacle. In *Non Coupable,* the hero kills the man with whom his mistress has betrayed him. In *Quai des Orfèvres,* the hero is only prevented by an accident from murdering the man who has been pursuing his wife.

While the murder of a rather impersonally regarded victim as a means to an end predominates in American films, there are, as we have noted, exceptions. Where a man murders a woman who has been holding out on him, we get probably the least calculating murder in American films. In these cases, a middle-aged man stands between two women, an older one who has been in his life for some time and a younger one who is a more recent acquaintance. One or both of these women repulse the man's advances (or show contempt for him, or otherwise deprive him) until he is goaded into murdering one of them.

Scarlet Street presents a gentle middle-aged man, a bank clerk who has worked twenty-five years on the same job, a henpecked husband who washes the dishes and puts up with his wife's spiteful nagging and consoles himself with painting in his spare time. The latent discontent of this mode of life becomes apparent to him when he meets a beautiful young woman for whom he conceives a worshipful affection. The young woman plays him for a sucker, extracts a good deal of money from him by a skillful use of tears and scruples and, maintaining a pretense of shy innocence, holds him at arm's length. She has a lover to whom she is held by an intense physical bond and who directs her exploitation of the older man. The latter arrives unexpectedly one night at the apartment with which he provided the girl and sees the lovers in each other's arms. He waits for the young man to leave, confronts the girl and pleads with her to tell him that she was an unwilling victim. The girl laughs in his face. In a rage he stabs her with an ice-pick which he snatches from a champagne bucket.

In *A Double Life* a more glamorous middle-aged man, a successful actor, lives in continual professional and personal contact with his divorced wife, a beautiful actress. She behaves very charmingly towards him except that she keeps her bedroom barred. In his loneliness, he picks up a young waitress with whom he has a transient affair. His resentment against his wife is aggravated by the fact that a young stage designer pays her devoted suit and by the circumstance that they are playing *Othello,* the plot of which he comes to confuse with his life. After a scene in which he tries unsuccessfully to make love to his wife, who runs upstairs and locks the bedroom door, he goes out in a fugue state and murders the waitress, reciting "Put out the light and then—put out the light."

In *Three Strangers* an aging man stands between an older and a younger woman, who hold out on him financially. The man is a lawyer who has been embezzling trust funds and faces exposure if he cannot find the money to make it up. He first proposes marriage to a repulsive rich widow who laughs at him. He then turns to a beautiful young woman with whom he is joint owner of a sweepstakes ticket. The ticket, having been drawn, has an immediate market value, and the man pleads with the woman to sell it at once. She, however, is pursuing an all-or-nothing gamble. She, too, laughs at his distress and he brains her with a statuette of the goddess of fortune.

The rage against the withholding woman thus comes out in the middle-aged hero whose chances are narrowing down. The younger hero, faced with a withholding woman, can always bring her around by withdrawing or courting another girl (*She Wouldn't Say Yes, Without Reservations*). These films with their sense of life slipping away, and their expression of male rage against women who have withheld pleasure, represent a minority report. They insert a small but significant note of doubt into the more pervasive effect of American films with their image of perpetual youth and inexhaustible satisfactions. These murders of a woman by an older man also recall that a frequent crime of the bad father-figure is the murder of the mother-figure. This reflects the childhood fantasy that parental relations are destructive of the mother. Correspondingly, one of the most frequently warded-off false accusations of the young hero is the murder of a woman. In the films where the older man murders the woman because she frustrates his wishes, the son's disappointment with the mother is projected onto the father-figure.

There are other films in which men murder women out of frustration in love, but in a more optimistic spirit: they intend to remove a woman who has become an obstacle to their happiness. The hero in *The Two Mrs. Carrolls* poisons his wife when he falls in love with the heroine. Later he is barely prevented from murdering the heroine after he has fallen in love with another woman. In *Conflict* and *The Suspect*, of a few years back, middle-aged men murdered unattractive wives who refused to divorce them, hoping to marry younger women with whom they had fallen in love.

Cases where women kill men because of amorous difficulties are also of two types: either the woman wants the man and he enrages her by a refusal or she does not want the man and has to get rid of him so that she can be happy with someone else. The woman who murders out of baffled rage a man who refuses to love her is generally presented unsympathetically. The enterprising girl who removes an unwanted man who stands between her and happiness appears generally as sympathetic. This is particularly the case where the man with whom she wants to be happy also loves her. Thus sympathy is accorded to those who have an embarrassment of riches rather than to the deprived, to those whose ruthlessness is calculated to get them somewhere, not to those overpowered by an unavailing fury. There seems to be a sex difference on this point, since a man who murders because he feels deprived tends to be a more sympathetic figure (*Scarlet Street*). Where the deprived man is middle-aged, the deprived woman is young and attractive. The picture of an unwanted woman who is aging and no longer attractive is for the most part too unpleasant to contemplate.

The girls who murder men who reject them (and usually aggravate things by preferring another woman) have defective characters. The heroine's sister in *The Big Sleep*, who murders her father's secretary because he repulses her advances, is a nymphomaniac. The murderous twin of the heroine in *The Dark Mirror* is a psychotic. Men repeatedly discern that there is something wrong with her, and divert their affections to the normal twin. Enraged by this recurrent frustration, the mad girl is driven to murder her latest defecting man friend. These films express the American conviction (discussed by Geoffrey Gorer) that if you are unloved there must be something wrong with you. The second also conveys the point that, however little women may love each other, their major rage is against men. The discarded girlfriend of the hero in *Suspense* is only slightly less deviant than the girls just mentioned. She continues to throw herself at a man who has made it bluntly clear that he is through. As he persists in his attachment to a new love, she shoots him. The daughter of the heroine in *Mildred Pierce* is a spoilt, ungrateful, vindictive brat. She carries on an affair with her step-father and shoots him when he gets tired of her and tells her that her mother is the better woman.

Turning to the cases where a man has to be removed because he is in the way, the heroine of *Unfaithful* has been driven by loneliness into a brief affair with a disreputable artist while her husband was overseas. She is deeply in love with her adoring husband and they live happily together when he comes home. But the artist pursues her and she kills him. At first she tries to make out that the murdered man was a burglar. As the artist's wife spitefully threatens to expose her, she tells her husband all. He is more annoyed at her infidelity than at her having committed a murder. They are reconciled through their lawyer and family confidant. *The Postman Always Rings Twice,* in which the heroine removes her uncongenial husband so that she can be happy with her young lover, has already been cited. This heroine is a victim of circumstances. Her marriage has seemed the only possible escape from a disagreeable life as a waitress. The murder, no less than the marriage, is a step in her pursuit of happiness. In *Johnny Angel* a beautiful and insatiably acquisitive woman has married a repulsive rich man whom she drives to murder and grand larceny. As she loves the hero and wants to share her riches with him, she stabs her husband with a paper cutter. In *Deception,* the heroine believes that her lover, a European cellist, has been lost in the war. She has been having an affair with a famous composer when the cellist turns up again and she marries him. Convinced that the cellist will be shattered if he learns of her affair, she lives in anxiety that the composer will give her away. As he malignly threatens to do so, she shoots him. Her motivation is complicated by a fear that her two men may become friends. As they become absorbed in a collaboration from which she is excluded, she shows great distress. Instead of fearing that her two men will fight over her, she seems afraid that they won't. The man she murders seems to threaten her marriage not only as her past lover, but also as her husband's present friend.

In *The Macomber Affair,* more clearly, manly friendship stimulates the destructive impulses of a woman. On a big game hunt, the woman's husband, who is already the butt of her contempt, runs away from a wounded lion. She then openly transfers her affections to the virile guide, the hero of the occasion. But the husband shows an unexpected capacity for recuperation. He loses his fear in the next day's hunt and wins the approval of the guide. He is no longer afraid of his wife and assumes a dominant attitude towards her which she finds even more repellent than his previous weakness. The two men walk off together, talking in a warm tone; the guide expresses his changed opinion of the husband and confirms it with a cordial handclasp. The wife, left behind, shoulders a hunting rifle and, allegedly aiming at an oncoming beast, shoots her husband through the head. This is a woman with whom it is impossible for a man to win. She is the disturbing element in what would otherwise be the clean bright world of manly friendship and sport.

British films, as already mentioned, show a tendency for women frustrated in love to attack the man. In *Dear Murderer* the husband has killed his wife's second last lover and implicated the current one. The wife knows this. Anxious to recover her young man (who has been jailed on suspicion), she pretends to be reconciled to her husband and after a brief amorous interlude, gives him an overdose of sleeping pills. Just as he is overpowered by a paralyzing drowsiness, she tells him what she has done and how she will make his death appear a guilt-motivated suicide thus clearing the man she loves. Here, as in the earlier murder of the lover by the husband, the relation between murderer and victim is given an intimate quality just before the deed, while in the act itself the murderer makes the victim agonizingly aware of his imminent death. *Blithe Spirit* presents a comic version of the British love-suffused murder. The spirit of the hero's deceased first wife wants to kill him so that they may be reunited. As her first attempt accidentally carries off the second wife instead, the two ghostly women join forces and successfully translate their joint husband into the spirit world.

As mentioned above, French films show a contrasting tendency for women unhappy in love to turn against the woman who has frustrated them. In *L'Amour Autour de la Maison* an older sister jealously drives away her younger sister's suitors. Eventually the younger one finds out and murders her sister. In *Torrents,* the hero has been engaged to his cousin, but breaks with her because of her flirtatiousness and marries a woman he does not love. Later the cousins meet again and are overwhelmed by an unexpected revival of their love. The woman cousin follows the couple to the desert outpost where the hero is a doctor, persuades the wife to go for a drive in the desert and leaves her in the middle of the wilderness to die. However, the wife is rescued by a caravan. The cousin goes home and throws herself over a waterfall.

The prevailing intention to get something out of murder, to use it as a means to an end, is common to mad and sane murderers in American films. The mad ones are usually differentiated by the greater disproportion between means and end. By contrast there seems to be a tendency in both British and French films to depict the mad murderer as an artist in crime, which is rare in American movies. He becomes absorbed in murder because he cannot help himself or because he becomes fascinated with his technique as a perfect criminal. His criminal methods are intricate; he tends to take much pride in his work, to boast of it indirectly or to challenge the authorities by announcing his crimes in advance (*The Upturned Glass, Wanted For Murder, Non Coupable.*) The heroes in these films arrogate to themselves power over life and death. In *The Upturned Glass* and *Non Coupable* there are incidents in which the hero (in both cases a doctor) saves the life of a child. Their murders are invested with vengeful justice. In *The Upturned Glass,* the victim had driven another woman to suicide. In *Non Coupable* the hero punishes his unfaithful mistress and the man with whom she betrayed him. He is also convinced that the physician he murders follows mistaken ideas of medical practice by means of which he has undermined confidence in the hero's correct ideas. These heroes are involved in a complex struggle with the authorities. In part they challenge the sole right of the authorities over life and death. In *Wanted for Murder* the hero cannot understand why his father, the public hangman, had the right to kill people and he has not. At the same time, they are anxious to win the admiration of the authorities by the brilliance of their crimes. They wish to demonstrate the fallibility of the authorities by eluding their justice. And by the announcement of their crimes they offer themselves for punishment. In the end they demonstrate the superiority of their own justice by killing themselves. While the similarities between the British and French versions of the mad murderer are substantial, we may perhaps discern a difference in this: the French seem to show a greater scepticism about the authorities. While the hero who arrogates to himself the power over life and death ends by destroying himself, the authorities remain stupid and blind throughout. In the British films, they are more discerning and more likely to be right in the end.

Thus the mad murderer in these French and British films is a hero who tries to usurp the role of an authority conceived as omnipotent and acting in the name of justice. Alternately he imagines that such an authority exists outside himself, and fiercely struggles against it. In American films the image of a powerful and moral authority has less plausibility. There is only the dangerous older man who attacks the hero and tries to saddle him with his crimes; and the police who, it is taken for granted, will suspect the wrong man. (In French films the police may appear as similarly stupid, but there are other father-figures who are more admirable.) In American films the hero is the only one who is in the right. His struggle to establish this point is waged against physical attackers and false accusers without moral authority. Thus it does not involve the arrogation by the hero of an authority not rightly his. It is more a struggle for self-preservation in an amoral world, or like bringing law and order to a previously unpoliced border area.

Where, by exception, American films present an approximation to the crime artist, his role is apt to be different from that of the heroes of the British and French films we have just discussed. *Rope,* notably exceptional among American films, pictures a murderer whose express purpose in killing is to set himself above the law and above other men. A college undergraduate, he has been overly impressed by the "Nietzschean" philosophy of an idolized prep-schoolmaster, and he prevails on a weak friend whom he dominates to collaborate in murdering one of their chums in order to prove their superiority. The related French and British films follow a murderer who finds killing uncannily easy, and create suspense about the accomplishment of the seemingly inevitable killing in which we identify with the murderer and hope and fear that he will succeed. In *Rope,* the murder is committed in the first minute of play, before we have had a chance to identify with the characters. As we watch them and suffer with them thereafter, what we experience is the situation of two jittery schoolboys who have done something very wicked and dread being found out. These boys are not masters of life and death. It is clear from the first that they are only kidding themselves. Their overly wordy ideology is labeled as being the same as Hitler's, completely unsympathizable. Where the comparable French and British heroes are driven in spite of themselves to contend with justice, these killers derive their action from bogus theorizing. In their assumption of power they do not save (contrast *Non Coupable* and *The Upturned Glass*) but only kill; hence, again, they are made unsympathizable. They are not led to condemn themselves in the end, but are caught. In place of inner conflict there is a split between the two boys: the dominant one has no regrets, the weak one goes into a complete funk from the moment the murder is done. The authority figure towards whom this crime is directed is the schoolmaster. The dominant murderer is anxious to present the crime to his teacher and win his admiration. When he finally does so, he receives a shock as the teacher refuses to accept

any credit, renounces his former views and disowns his pupil.
The teacher here approximates the usual falsely accused hero
who dissociates himself from crimes with which he seems
connected. The dependence of the murderer on this external
authority figure, and his collapse when he fails to get approval, contrasts with the independence of the British and
French counterparts. In the end, this murderer appears as a
sucker for having taken his teacher's spouting too seriously,
just as his weaker boy friend is a sucker for having let himself
be led into crime.

§ MURDER BY SUICIDE

SUICIDES in American films tend, to a considerable extent,
to express an attack against someone else, in so far as it is
possible to discern a tendency in the rare instances. In *Leave
Her to Heaven,* a woman commits suicide in such a way that
her half-sister, of whom she is jealous, will be suspected of
having murdered her. In *Out of the Past,* the hero goes into
a death trap which he has arranged, taking with him the
woman who has ruined his life and from whom he has been
unable to escape. In *The Strange Love of Martha Ivers,* a
husband, who has committed crimes for a wife who despises
him, kills her and himself. In *Uncle Harry,* the hero's sister
allows herself to be executed as a revenge against her brother
who has falsely implicated her for his crime, but later wants
to clear her. (In the film this is a dream.) In *This Love of
Ours* the heroine has long been separated from her husband
because of his unfounded suspicions of her fidelity. When
she sees him again for the first time in years, she registers a
reproach against him by a suicide attempt.

The prominence of the attack against someone else in

American film suicides is in keeping with the American tendency to turn aggression outward. Even if one kills oneself, one is attacking someone else. While this intent is apt to be present in every suicide, it may be expressed with greater or less overtness; American movies make it rather overt on the part of both men and women.

Another active form of suicide occurs occasionally where a character kills himself, or attempts to do so, to avoid capture and punishment for his crimes. He is warding off an attack by others, even though it be through his own execution. The murderer in *The Red House* commits suicide just as his pursuers are closing in on him. A man in high position, whose crimes have just been uncovered, attempts to kill himself in *The Naked City*. The suicide of the hero at the climax of his trial for murder in *They Won't Believe Me,* admits, at least in part, of a similar interpretation. While these suicides, especially the last, may seem to be motivated by self-accusations, none of the characters showed any inclination to suicide before the law closed in. A more clear-cut case of suicide motivated by guilt occurs in *All My Sons*. The father kills himself after his son has uncovered the father's war-time swindles and revealed that they caused the death of his other son. However, the father has long been aware that he was responsible for the death of American fliers through his delivery of defective airplane parts. As long as he was able to get away with it (his partner had taken the rap), his conscience did not seem to trouble him. In the end the intention of his son to expose him coincides with the revelation of his responsibility for the death of his other son. If he did not commit suicide at this point, he would face prison and financial ruin. His suicide forestalls this punitive onslaught.

An exceptional case of a passively suicidal character, one who is unable to ward off the attacks of others against him, appears in *The Killers*. The hero ends his career lying on his bed in a darkened room waiting, defenseless, for the fatal attack which he knows is coming. Earlier, when he had been deserted, deceived, and robbed by the woman he loved, he had attempted suicide. Previous to this he had gone to jail for a theft committed by the woman. This film presents a cautionary image of passivity against which most of our film characters react. We may recall that murder is preferred to suicide by a much wider margin in American than in British or French films.

Male suicides in British films show the same active motivation as the American ones which ward off capture. The hero in *Wanted for Murder,* swimming away from his pursuers in a lake at night, shouts that they shall never hang him, submerges himself and drowns. The warding off of passivity is particularly neatly expressed here in that the hero's father had been a public hangman. In *The Upturned Glass* the hero's plan of a perfect murder has miscarried and he has been led to suspect he is going insane. His suicide wards off capture by the police and the more subtle attack of madness. In *I Met a Murderer,* the hero, on whom the police are closing in, swims out to sea and drowns. There is also in these cases a component of executing justice on oneself. This relation between self-condemnation and suicide is brought out most clearly in the repeated suicide attempts of the hero in *October Man.* He blames himself for the death of a friend's little girl who had been killed in an accident while riding with him on a bus. He himself received a severe head injury, and attempted suicide several times while in the hospital. Later, after he has been released and has returned to ordinary life, he is falsely suspected of having murdered a young woman who lived next door to him. While he tries to discover the murderer, he is oppressed by the feeling that his presence brings fatality to those around him. In this mood he is again tempted towards suicide. However, the effort to free himself from blame by finding the murderer eventually wins out.

Women in British films express a more passive tendency in their suicide attempts (which seem to be more frequent than those of men). They try to kill themselves when they are being mistreated by their men, thus in effect complying with the man's destructiveness. In *The Seventh Veil* the heroine's jealous guardian beats her when she announces she is leaving him. She runs away with her intended lover who, however, smashes her up in an auto accident. Afterwards, disoriented, she rises from her hospital bed at night, wanders out into the moonlight and jumps off a bridge. (She is, however, pulled out of the water and later receives successful psychiatric treatment.) The heroine in *Frieda,* a German girl married to an Englishman, similarly jumps off a moonlit bridge after her husband has turned against her. (She also is rescued.) *They Were Sisters* makes the point explicitly that the destructive man is responsible for the woman's suicide. The heroine has suffered through seventeen years of marriage with a man who alternately terrorizes her and imposes on her sympathy. After a particularly violent scene, she rushes out of the house and into the path of an oncoming automobile. At the inquest a case is made out by the righteously indignant sister of the deceased that this apparent accident was suicide, that this seeming suicide was murder. *The Upturned Glass* makes the impact of the destructive man more indirect. The hero has pursued a tender relationship with a married woman who, when threatened with a scandal on his account, jumps out the window.

British films, in the tradition of *Clarissa Harlowe,* tend to dwell lovingly on the image of a suffering woman, whether she is bullied, beaten, raped, murdered, or driven to suicide. By contrast, American films tend to avoid placing characters of either sex in a passive position. This is illustrated in the difference between a British film about a serial murderer and his female victim (*Wanted for Murder*) and an American treatment of the same theme (*Lured*). In the British film, the audience knows the identity of the murderer who feels compelled repeatedly to kill young girls to whom he first makes love. The police also have strong suspicions. But the delicate

heroine whom the murderer has selected to be his next victim knows nothing. We see her go to her rendezvous with
him, we see him take her to a lonely island in the park. Male
destructiveness descending on a helpless woman is elaborated. The American-made *Lured* is explicitly based on a
British pattern, as the scene is laid in London, and the two
main male roles are played by English actors. However, an
American actress appears as the heroine. She is an energetic,
worldly, wise-cracking girl who knows all the answers and is
working with the police to get the repetitive killer. When she
has her scene alone with him, it is with full knowledge of his
identity and presenting herself as a decoy so that the police
can catch him in the act. British films may show a woman as
suffering in her attachment to a man who treats her badly;
she nevertheless remains bound to him (*They Were Sisters,
The Seventh Veil*). Women in American films show little inclination for such relationships. In a rare case where a
woman is bound to a brutal man, she derives ecstatic pleasure rather than suffering from his treatment of her (*Scarlet
Street*).

In French films suicide is the most likely recourse of both
men and women if they are driven to violence by frustration
in love. This contrasts with the American tendency to commit murder under such circumstances and the British tendency to have men destroy women though women may destroy
themselves. The self-destructive reaction to frustration in love
accounts largely for the high suicide rate in French films. In
Sirocco, the hero, whose wife had disappeared supposing him
dead, carries on an unwearying quest for her. He finds her
married to another man and shoots himself. His suicide is
preceded by ineffectual destructive gestures towards both his
wife and his successor. He invites the wife, who still loves
him, to meet him in a low hotel room, and brings in a crowd
of his comrades to whom he exposes her as a whore. He visits
the second husband, waves a gun at him, makes a high-flown
speech and withdraws. French movie love suicides tend to be

associated with such ineffectual gestures of aggression against the rival or the disappointing loved one. In *Falbalas,* the hero jumps from a window clasping in his arms a dress dummy in a bridal gown; he hallucinates the dummy to be the girl he loves. In *Le Revenant,* the young man who has been dismissed by his dancer sweetheart throws himself down from the overhead cat-walk onto the stage where she is dancing. He does not hit anyone and does not kill himself either. In *Torrents,* as previously mentioned, the woman disappointed in love makes an unsuccessful attempt to eliminate her rival before committing suicide. In American films, in the context of a much higher murder rate, the murderous intentions associated with suicide suggest a constant turning of aggression outwards. Also, the American murderous suicide tends to get his man. In French films, with a much lower ratio of love murders to love suicides, the ineffectiveness of the suicide's last aggressive gesture seems to show that his victim can only be himself.

Women who succeed in committing murder in French films are almost always sympathetic. This contrasts with the British preference for women victims and with aggressive American women who do not have to be pistol-packing mamas to prove it. The woman who uses violence in French films expresses perhaps less female destructiveness (there is no counterpart to Mrs. Macomber) than repressed male aggression. In American films, violence which men are unable to express directly is attributed to an unsympathetic man. In French films, in the tradition of the symbolism of Joan of Arc and Marianne, the same impulses may be embodied in a sympathetic woman. In *La Passionelle,* the aristocratic heroine murders a servant who has been her lover and who is trying to blackmail her. The humble hero, who has worshipped her from afar, is disillusioned when he learns her story and gloomily assumes responsibility for her crime. He had detested the heroine's lover long before he knew of the relationship. This man had been a robust, vulgar character, popular in the town, who had always mocked the dreamy, solitary hero. Once the hero had knocked him down, protecting a poor match-girl from his unwanted attentions. But it is the heroine who murders him. The image of the woman defending herself supplants the image of the man defending her. In *Boule de Suïf* a woman has a better chance than the men to strike at the invader. A good-natured and patriotic prostitute murders a misbehaving Prussian officer. In *Le Corbeau,* it is a woman who, at the end, murders the author of a poison pen campaign who has been terrorizing the whole town.

Curbed aggression in French films is also shown in the already mentioned tendency for a falsely accused hero to attempt suicide. False accusation, as we have seen, spurs American heroes to the most strenuous and violent activity. British heroes are apt to react with righteous retaliatory rage. In *Murder in Reverse* the hero, who has unjustly served a long prison term for murder, seeks and finds the wicked man he was supposed to have killed and presents him to his former prosecutor. When he is denied a rectification of the record, he kills the man for whose murder he has already paid. In *I Became a Criminal* the hero, victim of a frame-up, breaks out of jail to get evidence to clear himself and in the course of this causes the death of the person who framed him. In *October Man,* the self-accusing hero more nearly approximates the French attitude as he considers suicide when he is the victim of false suspicions. The suspicions in this case chime in with previous feelings of responsibility for an accidental death. His suicidal tendency is also referrable to incomplete recovery from a head injury. However, even here the suicidal tendency gives way to a stronger impulse to expose the real murderer.

In French films, the striving to clear oneself is almost completely lacking. In *Quai des Orfèvres* the innocent character who is jailed on suspicion of murder, cuts his wrists. His inability to struggle against the false charge seems related to the fact that he wanted to commit the murder but found his man already dead; and that he suspects his wife did it. Thus his situation coincides with that of the hero of *La Passionelle* who allows himself to be apprehended for the murder of the man he hated by the women he loved. The acknowledgment of guilty wishes seems to deprive French heroes of strength to oppose false accusation. Making the woman the agent of destruction does not produce a clear conscience for the man. He acknowledges the act which was his in intent, under the guise of protecting the woman from punishment. *Non Coupable* presents this pattern in reverse. The hero makes his mistress appear guilty of his crime, then tries to take the blame himself. Unable to convince the authorities, he commits suicide.

§ THE DENIAL OF DEATH

WITH all the killings that occur in American films, there is little acknowledgment of death. Death is denied by furious activity and grim humor. A film may be called *The Big Sleep* (a joking denial of death), but in the rapid and confused action there is hardly time to identify or count the corpses, much less mourn them. (We have already dealt with the denial of mourning.) For the most part those who meet a violent end are unsympathetic, not objects for identification or regret. Death in these films means exciting danger and the fulfilment of destructive impulses, not loss or the awareness that we, too, shall die. We may contrast the American movie melodramas with classical tragedy which takes its point of departure from the murder of a father and elaborates the suffering, mourning, and punishment for his death. The movie melodramas end with the unregrettable killing of a bad father-figure which has been paid for in advance. A murder victim is less apt to leave his survivors with a burden of guilt and regret than with the problem of how to dispose of the body. This problem is given comedy treatment in *A Slight Case of Murder* where a retired gangster finds the bodies of a half a dozen of his former colleagues in his summer home.

Where a murder victim is not immediately forgotten, we may have the bouncing Danny Kaye playing a lively ghost (*Wonderman*). Where the dead live on in this fashion, they stimulate the living to a fuller life, not by a *memento mori,* but because they (the ghosts) insist on it. (Similarly, mourning is supposed to go against the wishes of the dead.) The ghostly Danny Kaye drags his timid identical twin out of the library and forces him to assume the former role of the deceased as a night-club singer and play-boy. Thus activated, the live twin finds excitement, success and love. This is a comic reversal of mourning in which the survivor feels compelled to circumscribe his life activities. The influence of the ghost has to some extent a double aspect as he forces his brother into danger by charging him with the pursuit of his murderers. However, emergence from a sheltered life into the dangerous outside world is frequently equivalent to growing up. Being thrown into contact with danger has more an enlivening than a destructive significance. In the *Topper* series of a few years back, the ghosts of a frivolous young couple, killed in an auto accident, made life more exciting for a staid, aging man. The dead are more alive than the living. The dead are young, the living old.

A rare scene in *The Naked City* presents grief for a murder victim. A beautiful young girl from a small town, who became involved in a career of crime in New York, has been murdered. Her homely, hard-working parents are called in to identify the body. On the way to the morgue, the mother is full of bitter complaints about how the girl was no good, and a shame to her parents. But when she sees the face of the dead girl, she is wracked with sobs, cries, "My baby," and embraces the body. Later, seated by the river overlooking the city in twilight, the parents tell the sympathetic detective the girl's story: how she was always impatient to have fine things, how badly they felt when they heard she had changed her name (theirs is foreign-sounding), how pretty she had been and how she wasn't really a bad girl. When the attempt is made, by exception, to introduce grief for a murder victim, it is done by clichés. Also, the exponents of this grief are peripheral characters.

Funerals very rarely appear in American films. One may recall *Shadow of a Doubt,* where the heroine and her young man listen with mixed feelings to the eulogy of her uncle who, as they alone know, had died trying to murder her; *Little Caesar,* where the gangster sends huge funeral wreaths as tribute to the rival gang-leader whom he rubbed out. These funerals are occasions of false sentiment whether unwittingly or through hypocrisy.

British films propose a riddle: When is a funeral not a funeral? The opening scene in *I Became a Criminal* shows a hearse drawing up in front of a cheap undertaker's establishment. As the assistants carry in the coffin, an elderly, genteel woman who seems to be the proprietress exchanges appropriate remarks with them, reflecting how the deceased only yesterday seemed to be in the prime. The coffin is carried into an inner room, opened, and black market commodities unloaded. The gang gets down to business. In *The Adventuress* an impressive funeral procession moving along a mountain road turns out to be a device for smuggling guns over a border. As a counterpart to such deceptive uses of death ceremonials, the tendency of middle-class women to speak euphemistically about death is ridiculed in *This Happy Breed.* The more forthright husband keeps impatiently correcting his wife: Mother wasn't taken anywhere; she died. In *Love on the Dole* three lower-class gossips sit around drinking in a pawnshop like a debased image of the Three Fates. One of them is a professional layer-out and there are continual joking references to her profession. The hero, a socialist militant, is killed in a workingman's demonstration, and the heroine arranges to have him cremated according to his wishes. The heroine's grief is somewhat obscured by the voluble protests of the three old gossips who feel cremation is a funeral that isn't a funeral.

In other British films the return of the dead is a nuisance. The ghost in *Blithe Spirit* is as lively as the American comedy ghosts, but less benevolent towards the living. Where the American ghost urges survivors to a greater enjoyment of life, this British ghost jealously interferes with the pleasures of the living. The ghostly first wife of the hero, evoked by an inept spiritualist, competes with the second wife to win back the husband, upsets their lives, ends by killing them both. What has been elsewhere a theme for tragedy (*Rosmersholm* shows the joint suicide of the hero and his second wife with the closing line: The dead wife has taken them) is here given comic treatment. But then, as we have seen, British films do not on the whole take the destructive potentialities of women seriously. Especially, mutual hostilities of women are easily resolved in an *esprit de corps*. When the second wife in *Blithe Spirit* has been accidentally killed by a device intended for the husband, the two spirit women join forces to prevent their man from enjoying his freedom and arrange his prompt removal to the spirit world. Elsewhere in British films the hand of the dead rests more heavily upon the living (*Wanted for Murder, Notorious Gentleman*), but there it is the hand of a dead father.

Another demonstration of the inconvenience of having the dead return occurs in *The Years Between*. The heroine has received what we know to be an untrue announcement of her husband's death in the war; a funeral ceremony has been observed (a funeral that is not a funeral); the heroine has gone through a painful and protracted period of mourning: she is then ready to start life anew, having fallen in love with a devoted suitor of long standing. At this point the husband comes back. The announcement of his death had been necessary to enable him to change his identity for espionage work. Later he had been in a concentration camp. He returns moody, disagreeable, changed. Like the appearance of the first wife's ghost in *Blithe Spirit*, his return from the dead spoils things for the living.

In French films a funeral is a funeral. Even when it is joked about, its significance is confirmed rather than denied. In *Les Neuf Célibataires*, a motley group of indigent old men are recruiting members for an old bachelors' home when they come upon an old man who is walking as a solitary mourner behind a hearse. In response to their question he tells them that it is his wife who has died. The other old men consider that this makes him eligible for the bachelors' home and stop him to explain this while the hearse continues to move on. The bereaved husband, suddenly noticing this, exclaims: I've lost my wife! The others remark: You had already lost her. The husband says: I've lost her a second time— and hastens after the departing hearse. In *Circonstances Atténuantes*, a funeral procession appears unrelated to the plot but emotionally congruent as a *memento mori*. The film deals with the rediscovery of pleasures in life by an aging couple who had resigned themselves to a hypochondriacal decline. As the wife stands on a balcony in the embrace of a newly acquired young lover, a funeral procession passes opposite. The young man tips his cap without interrupting the kiss. In other French films a funeral may be a central event. In *Farrebique*, the funeral of the grandfather culminates the protracted tracing of his decline and reluctant transfer of the family property to his son. In *L'Amour Autour de la Maison* a highborn woman falls in love, for the first time in her life, with a rather wild-looking recluse. After some hesitation, she arranges a rendezvous with him, but she waits for him in vain; he has been killed in a shooting accident. In a despair which she cannot show she sees his body carried home and later watches the simple funeral march. In *Le Corbeau*, as a climax to a poison-pen campaign which has been disrupting the life of a small town, the recipient of one of the letters commits suicide. The whole town turns out for his funeral. As the procession moves down the main street, a letter with the mark of the crow on it (the signature of the poison pen) suddenly drops as if from nowhere, falls to the ground and is stepped over by row after row of the funeral marchers, all eying it, none stooping to pick it up. Finally, some little boys take it. The unknown assailant seems to be gloating over his victim.

Other French films evoke a painful awareness of the imminence of death. In *Jericho* a group of hostages, during the Occupation, spend the night in a church awaiting execution at dawn. The collaborationist among them mounts the pulpit and delivers a sermon: Let us try to purchase life at any price. If we die, a monument in our honor will in due time be unveiled one sunny afternoon on the main square of the town. Who will drink the beer, flirt with the girls, walk in the sun that afternoon? Not we! We will have ceased to be. What will it matter to us?—The hostages are at the last moment rescued by an Allied air attack. This ending does not, however, cancel the impression of facing unavoidable death. It does not have the same effect as the hero's escape from danger at the end of an American film melodrama. The American hero has been carrying on a vigorous fight against attackers whom it is possible to eliminate. In the French film, the characters are helplessly awaiting their death which the last-minute rescue only postpones. In *Vertiges,* the hero, a physician, becomes aware that he is suffering from an almost certainly fatal disease. He takes an X-ray photograph of his brain and discovers a tumor (a pictorial transcription of the Existentialist saying that if man examines himself he discovers that he is going to die). He devotes what he believes will be his last months to alienating his wife, so that she will suffer less from losing him, and to earning as much money as possible, to leave his family well provided for. In the commercial laboratory job which he takes, he succeeds in making a great discovery and is just receiving the congratulations of his staff when he collapses. (This achievement of success at a moment when one is too sick physically or emotionally to appreciate it occurs also in *Falbalas*. The hero, in a psychotic state, walks blindly through the enthusiastic crowd who have just viewed the opening of his collection.) While it turns out not to be too late for the hero to be saved by an operation, the impression of confronting death remains.

The tendency of American films to deny death is an instance of pervasive denial of unpleasant experiences. Various denials of this kind may be related to each other. We have observed the numerous devices which exempt the movie melodrama hero from guilt. Feelings of guilt and expectation of death are often connected, and this connection has frequently provided the basis for dramatic tragedy. French films avoid making anyone guilty, in contrast to the American concentration of blame on a bad character; but the French hero is often unable to deny his guilt, even where he is technically innocent. Possibly the greater readiness in French films to acknowledge the prospect of death is related to such unexpressed feelings of guilt. This acknowledgment seems also related to the tendency in French films to inure oneself to the disappointing aspects of life by facing them. In American films, the denial of mixed feelings further reduces the impact of death. The acknowledgment of death wishes towards a beloved person, for whose loss one would feel painful regret, is another source of tragic plots. Where such acknowledgment is avoided, it is possible for characters to be killed off without evoking a sense of loss. The tendency to make dangers external also contributes to the denial of death. The dangers that appear in American films can usually be mastered by strenuous activity. Just as bad impulses are not in us, so the sources of decay are not in us. The threat of death is not expressed as in *Vertiges* by a photograph of the hero's brain with a malignant spot, but by a gangster with a gun in his hand who can be disarmed and wiped out.

The theme of the triumph of love over death has recently appeared in the American *Portrait of Jenny,* in the British *Stairway to Heaven,* and in the French *Les Jeux sont Faits.* In each of these films death is temporarily set aside in favor of a pair of predestined lovers.

The American film conveys characteristically that death cannot frustrate human wishes. A young girl who has died without having found love lives a portion of her life over again so that she can meet and love the right man for her who happened to be born at a later date. (This easy juggling with time contrasts with the recurrent French theme that even slight discrepancies of timing are apt to cause irreparable loss.) Though she must then die again she feels, and succeeds in convincing her young man, that once you have had the great love which is your due your life is complete and you need have no regrets. In the course of their acquaintance she teaches him that mourning is unnecessary. Her parents are both killed in an accident. In consoling her, the young man points out that the parents now feel no pain. The girl then recalls that they had told her that if anything happened to them, they would not want her to be unhappy. She discovers that she is not weeping for them but for herself. Since the emotion is selfish she is exempted from feeling that she ought to feel it; she starts at once to be more cheerful. The hero learns this lesson so well that after her death he is also able not to mourn: I haven't lost her; everything is all right. The absence of mourning here as elsewhere in American films is related to the absence of guilt. The film deals with a recurrent theme of folk-lore and literature, that art requires a human sacrifice; the artist may destroy his human model for the sake of the work of art. In the film, the hero is an artist whose masterpiece is inspired by the girl; once the painting is finished, the girl dies. In this version of the legend, the artist does everything he can to save the beloved girl. (Incidentally, the American feeling of the tough-

ness and near invulnerability of the human organism is conveyed by the fact that a huge tidal wave—to contain which
the screen must be enlarged to twice its usual size—is necessary to carry off this slip of a girl.) Since the fatality has been
produced by forces beyond his control, the hero is free from
self-reproach.

In the British film a grandiose trial is held in heaven to
decide whether the lovers should be separated by death. If
they can prove that they are good enough to deserve it, the
just paternal powers which rule the next world as well as this
(with only slight interference from America—represented by
a captious prosecutor) will set death aside so that they can
be together. After prolonged juridical proceedings, the case
is won by the girl's willingness to die for the man, and the
couple are happily united. Since from the British point of
view happiness in love is constituted by a long life together
rather than the youthful realization that one has experienced
a great love, a more long-term postponement of the interruption of death is required. However, there is no doubt in
either the British or the American version that if untimely
death could be set aside, complete happiness could be achieved.

In *Les Jeux sont Faits,* the hero and heroine discover only
after they are both dead that they were made for each other.
The bureau in charge of these matters recognizes that a mistake has been made and restores them to life. They then find
that, distracted by all sorts of conflicting motives, they are
unable to achieve the ideal love which seemed so certain
when they were dead. Under the shadow of death it seems
that life could be beautiful, but this is an illusion. When
death is set aside, we see in life itself innumerable causes of
frustration and disappointment. Thus the American film on
the theme of love and death denies the deprivational impact
of death. The corresponding British film acknowledges that
untimely separation by death would be painful, but advances
the reassurance that the good will be vouchsafed a long and

happy life. The French film, while admitting the painful reality of death, is more sceptical about whether we could find happiness in life even if we were insured against its untimely interruption.

4

PERFORMERS AND ONLOOKERS

AMERICAN FILMS are preoccupied with showing events from a variety of viewpoints. We have seen what importance is attached to discrepancies between appearance and reality; the hero and heroine in melodramas frequently appear different from what they really are. We are shown how the hero appears to the police, as a criminal, how the heroine appears to the hero, as a wicked woman. The plot is less one of action than of proof or rather disproof. The incriminating false appearance must be dispelled. It must be proved that what was supposed to have happened did not happen. The potentialities of the hero and heroine for serious action are realized only in a false appearance, which indicates what they might have done if they had been carried away by dangerous impulses. This is what we have called the eat-your-cake-and-have-it aspect of American films. We can see the hero and heroine carrying out forbidden wishes and in the end see them escape penalties since these acts are shown to be merely a false appearance. Hence the character who sees things mistakenly has a special importance in American films. It is from his point of view that we can see the fulfilment of forbidden wishes, while at the same time we get the assurance that nothing has happened.

In comedies we find an onlooker who habitually sees illicit implications in the innocent behavior of hero and heroine. From his point of view we can see a young couple carrying on a secret affair, the heroine being untrue to her husband, or two men friends sharing a woman, all of which we know does not really happen. The comic onlooker is the counterpart to the blundering police in the melodramas, who are also taken in by misleading appearances. In the melodramas these appearances have to do with a crime of violence, in comedies, with sexual misbehavior. The situation in the melodramas is more serious because a crime has been committed, though not by the hero. In the comedies nothing has happened at all except in the imagination of the misguided onlooker. The false appearances in either case represent the fulfilment of wishes that remain unacknowledged or are not acted out. The melodrama hero, as we have noted, usually has a motive for the crime of which he is falsely suspected. The innocent characters in the comedies may be supposed to have unadmitted wishes corresponding to the forbidden pleasures which they are suspected of enjoying. The contention throughout is that mere wishes are harmless and that one should not feel guilty for them. The belief in the wickedness of forbidden wishes and in the likelihood of their being acted out is projected onto the onlooker who is shown to be foolish and mistaken.

The importance of proving to the onlooker that nothing

happens also has other sources. In the archetypal situation of looking, that of the child who investigates the activities of the parents, the onlooker discovers that something happens from which he is excluded and of which he feels envious. American film fantasies playing on this theme transform the original situation in order to deny envy or disappointment. Thus the onlooker who, busily piecing together fragmentary clues, infers that something has happened just beyond the range of his vision is mistaken. We in the audience, to whom the film shows everything, can see that nothing happens at all. Similarly the melodrama hero to whom the heroine appears to be involved with other men learns in the end that this was not so. French films treat this theme in an opposite way. The onlooker who falls in love with a beautiful woman thinks that she is pure and innocent, but later sees that she is involved with another man. The French films re-evoke the disappointment of the childhood experience; the American films deny it.

The theme of looking and being looked at leads us to an examination of plots dealing with professional performers. The career of the performer, particularly for a man, is fraught with danger. The actor, prizefighter, or magician finds himself carried away by destructive impulses which he cannot control. The professional performer thus tends to merge with the performer of crimes. We may recall that the preferred role of the hero in melodramas is that of the investigator, the private eye, one who looks rather than acts. In the less frequent case where the hero becomes a performer with catastrophic results we get confirmation of how much to be preferred is his usual role as an investigator.

It is a function of drama generally to give the audience a feeling of release and exoneration in relation to the acts of violence and forbidden love which they see the characters in the drama perform. The audience can feel: they did it, we only watched. In the case of American films the advantage of the onlooker's position is reaffirmed within the drama as well.

The hero, as long as he confines himself to the role of investigator, triumphs; when he assumes the role of performer he is likely to suffer for it. Thus we are confirmed in the belief that in being spectators we have chosen the better part.

There remains, however, a way in which the performer's role may be exempted from penalties. To the extent to which the performer resembles a child, he is able to succeed. This is illustrated in the comic hero, who is innocent of dangerous impulses and whose performance is marked by ridiculous blunders, alternating between unexpected demonstrations of skill and sudden collapse. He embodies the legend of the child as harmless and as the amusing exponent of incompletely acquired skill. By assuming this appearance of innocence and ineptitude, the performer may safeguard himself against the hazards of his career.

§ THERE IS LESS THAN MEETS THE EYE

THE husband is out of town on business. The wife is spending the night with friends. The three boys are being taken care of by a man who stays at the house. In the middle of the night one of the boys is sick and calls for his mother. The mother, summoned by phone, throws a coat over her bathrobe and rushes home. After the boy has been soothed and put back to bed, the man and woman are talking, both in their bathrobes. The man is holding a bottle labeled Gin, which happens to be the family water bottle. At this point a neighbor, a spinsterish elderly man, curious at seeing the lights on so late at night, bursts in. We see at once how the situation looks to him, and how difficult it would be to persuade him of the true state of affairs.

This scene from *Sitting Pretty* presents a recurrent comedy situation. American film comedies are haunted by a character whom we may call the comic onlooker, whose function it is to see a naughty meaning in an ambiguous but actually harmless situation. The young couple and their friends are almost without exception well-behaved, as we in the audience, who see everything, can testify. However, they repeatedly get into predicaments that are hard to explain and then, one may be sure, the comic onlooker will turn up with his mistaken interpretations. In a way he performs a useful service for us as he conjures up a pleasurable aura of illicit possibilities around harmless acts. We can enjoy the suggested infidelity of the faithful wife, or the possibility of two men friends sharing the same woman, while assuring ourselves that these things do not happen. Thus we have the same sort of eat-your-cake-and-have-it solution to the alternatives of sexual goodness and badness which we found in the case of the good-bad girl. In the comedy situation, we know the true state of affairs all along, and laughingly repudiate the mistaken interpretations of the comic onlooker without acknowledging the satisfaction he provides.

In *The Sailor Takes a Wife*, the newly married heroine is moving into a new apartment while her husband is away in the navy. She gets a long-standing suitor to help her move her belongings and explains to the superintendent that her sailor husband will be back soon. The superintendent, watching the domesticated boy-friend going in and out, gets the impression that he is moving in for the interim. Later the husband, who has been unexpectedly discharged from the navy, appears in civilian clothes and makes himself at home. To the superintendent, who is still expecting the sailor, he appears to be another lover.

The comic onlooker is apt to be ineffectual; no serious penalties ensue from his mistaken suspicions. Where he is not so easily discounted, he can be fooled again, so that one mistaken impression counteracts the other. In *Janie Gets Married*, a little bald-headed man keeps popping up to catch the heroine in dubious situations. As this man is a visiting executive of the newspaper syndicate for which her husband works, his misunderstandings may involve difficulties. The newly married heroine, who has become jealous of her husband and wants to make him jealous in turn, is just throwing her arms around a reluctant former suitor when the little man appears. He assumes that the young man is the girl's husband, is unfavorably impressed to learn he is not. Later, a girl-friend asks the heroine to put up for the night a boyfriend from out of town. This young man, a somnolent character, retires to the bedroom and is about to go to sleep. At this point, the little man arrives for dinner, by mistake opens the bedroom door and is confronted by a young man in pajamas, still not the heroine's husband. It is characteristic of the treatment of the comic onlooker that he never learns the truth, but is in the end taken in by still another hoax, this time one that sets everything right. After a dinner-party marked by family quarrels, during which the little man's unfavorable impression is intensified, he leaves in a rage. The heroine's mischievous little sister runs after him and confides to him that her sister is going to have a baby (which is not the case). This so fills him with benevolence that he returns to reward the heroine's husband with a fat contract.

In *Guest Wife*, the heroine is harmlessly, and on her husband's urging, posing as the wife of her husband's best friend. Various onlookers evoke through their mistaken interpretations the stimulating potentialities of the situation. The loyal wife appears to be unfaithful; the two friends seem to be sharing the woman; the husband appears as his wife's lover and must elude the suspicious detective in the hotel where she is registered as the wife of the friend. Thus the relationship of an impeccable married couple gets spiced up through its fantasied transformation into an illicit love affair. The possibility of a relation between the wife and the husband's friend remains one of the unused sexual opportunities which, as we have noted, occasion such euphoria in American film comedies. The comic onlooker contributes to this effect by underscoring the imminence of the possibility. The escape from the temptations and hazards of the opportunity is celebrated as we see the onlooker unable to prove his point. As the wife and the friend are dining in New York, they are spied by a suspicious little bald-headed man, a shoe-salesman from her home town. He recognizes the wife and officiously bustles over to her table. She veils her face and pretends that she only talks Turkish while her escort assures the man he must be mistaken. The shoe-salesman is unconvinced, and as he never forgets a foot, resolves to settle the matter by inspecting her feet. He starts crawling under tables, loses direction and is caught by a surprised woman who, feeling something moving against her knee, reaches under the table, puzzledly explores the bald head, then screams. The suspected couple escape in the confusion.

The deceptive appearances are never explained away in *Guest Wife,* but are resolved through a final deception. The most important of the comic onlookers in the film is the boss of the hero's friend, for whose benefit it was necessary for the friend to produce the bogus wife. The problem arises of how the friend will ever be able to return the wife to her proper husband without revealing to the boss the deception which has been played upon him. In the end the husband punches the friend and runs off with his wife. The boss, who has suspected the husband of being an interloper, consoles the friend for his misfortune. In *The Miracle of Morgan's Creek,* by a similar development, a final false appearance rectifies the difficulties created by a previous series of false appearances. The innocent hero seems hopelessly incriminated, charged with abduction, corrupting the morals of a minor, impersonating a soldier, resisting arrest, perjury and bank robbery. In the end he is pardoned for everything without having to explain, because he is mistakenly given credit for being the father of sextuplets.

This resolution of the comedy of false appearances corresponds in part to the conclusion of the melodrama in which the hero is falsely suspected. There, too, as we have seen, the suspicious circumstances are rarely reinterpreted; instead the criminal is produced so that it becomes unnecessary for the hero to explain himself. Truth does in effect triumph. But the movies seem to express scepticism about the possibility of communicating the truth to people who have got things wrong. Truth triumphs in spite of the difficulty of communication. In the melodramas the demonstration that someone else is guilty relieves the hero of trying to get people to believe his story. In the comedies a final mistaken impression may cancel the negative consequences of previous false impressions, and so make everything turn out well for the victims of misleading appearances. The onlooker, who caused all the trouble, is paid off by remaining deceived.

The comic onlooker makes us feel effortlessly omniscient. We in the audience know the true state of affairs; we know that what we see is all there is. The comic onlooker does not see everything as we do. Thus he fails to realize that he does not miss anything. If he could only believe that less goes on behind the bedroom door than he sees when the couple emerge (*Because of Him*)! We who see what happens on both sides know this. But the comic onlooker mistakenly believes that what he sees is only a fragment of a larger whole, the rest of which he attempts to reconstruct. We are able to laugh at his superfluous mental exertions. Without making any such efforts we know everything since the film obligingly shows us everything there is. The onlooker is prevented by his mistaken suspiciousness from enjoying an approximation to the same omniscience. Though he does not see everything, he does not miss anything that matters. The significant events which he imagines are happening just out of sight exist only in his imagination.

It is a characteristic point of American film comedies to prove the non-occurrence of sexual happenings. Thus these comedies repeatedly show us that nothing happens between the couple whom the comic onlooker suspects. The central characters are even innocent of forbidden sexual wishes. The onlooker cannot believe in the harmlessness of apparently risky situations, which makes his vigilance superfluous. It is because of his suspiciousness that the couple may be forced to fabricate false appearances which they think he will find more plausible than the truth, but which then make them liable to further misunderstandings. Thus the young couple who for non-sexual reasons must share the same tourist cabin or hotel room pretend to be married because of course no one would believe that they will virtuously divide the room in two, or that the young man will sleep on two chairs. (*It Happened One Night, Pillow to Post, Runaround.*) They now incur the risk of further difficulties if the onlooker discovers that they are not married. He will find it yet more difficult to believe that they have put up a false pretense to cover innocent behavior.

These films seem to demonstrate that social sanctions to enforce good behavior are superfluous. People are good anyhow, and if left to themselves would behave impeccably. The onlooker fails to understand this and is continually alarmed about possibilities which never materialize. Contrary to his belief the world would run quite serenely without him. Similarly, in the melodramas, as we have seen, the police usually cause more problems than they solve. They also falsely suspect the innocent and are ready to apply inappropriate penalties. The world in the films would run just as well without the interference of these official and unofficial authorities. The police, with their mistaken suspicions in connection with crimes of violence, and the comic onlooker, the self-constituted and misguided censor of sexual morals, are equally unnecessary.

In comedies the central characters frequently produce the false appearances which get them into trouble, by the pretense that the hero's wife is married to his friend, or that the unmarried young couple are married. They may also produce the false appearance which placates the onlooker in the end. Thus they are more in control than the hero and heroine in melodramas who are apt to be the victims of false appearances constructed around them by a malign opponent. The central characters in the comedies have the advantage that they can playfully manipulate appearances, and also that the situation is much less dangerous.

False appearances, whether they occur by chance, or through pretenses, or by a frame-up, whether they have to do with violence or forbidden sexual behavior, have a common meaning: they stand for wishes that are not acted out and which often remain unacknowledged. It is a major theme of American films that mere wishes should not be the occasion for guilt feelings or blame or punishment. Thus they are represented by a mere appearance which for the most part only incompetent characters—the police in the melodramas, the onlooker in the comedies—take seriously. The progress of the drama, which is equivalent, as we have said, to a process of proof, succeeds in disqualifying any condemnatory views based on false appearances.

In comedies, in contrast to melodramas, false appearances are more gratifying and less anxiety-provoking; they correspond to wishes phrased in less disturbing terms, and at the same time taken less seriously. Prominent among such wishes is that of sharing a woman between two friends. A man will ask his wife or fiancée to pose as the wife of his admired friend. (*Guest Wife, Easy to Wed.*) This is always to serve some non-sexual purpose, which we are made to see as perfectly reasonable, such as providing the basis for a bogus law suit, or making a boss believe a bachelor employee has a wife. The idea of woman-sharing gets projected into the thoughts of the comic onlooker. Thus the husband whose wife is posing as the wife of his friend meets the friend in a bar and asks jokingly: How is our wife? The bar-tender gives them a look of deep distrust. It is he who brings out the latent meaning of the pretense in which the two men are participating, the wish to share the woman. By being expressed in the thoughts of the foolishly suspicious onlooker the wish is repudiated and denied, at the same time that it is, on a make-believe level, indulged.

The playful and pleasurable manipulation of false appearances in comedies is illustrated in the recurrent marriage pretense. The pretense of being married acts like a good luck charm for the young couple. It helps them to obtain a wide range of benefits and immunities, from getting a seat on a crowded train to escaping the pursuit of traffic police. The marriage pretense may be advantageously supplemented by a pregnancy pretense—the young man on the train gets a seat for the young woman he has just met by telling a sympathetic older man that she is expecting a baby (*She Wouldn't Say Yes*); the young couple stopped by the traffic policeman claim that they are rushing to the maternity hospital (*Young Widow*). The couple posing as married are frequently forced by onlookers to give demonstrations of affection, or are propelled into situations where they can prove their adherence to premarital abstinence. The hero who is pretending, in connection with a detective job, to be married to the heroine slips out of the hotel room that they are supposed to share. An onlooker who thinks he is a shy bridegroom compels him to go back (*Runaround*). The onlooker in such cases unwittingly and unsuccessfully encourages illicit acts. Just as elsewhere the onlooker is the only one who thinks such things happen, here he is the only one who wants to make them happen. For the young couple who pose as married without taking any improper advantage of the situation, the pretense is is a good omen of their eventual happy and licit union.

The marriage pretense of the young couple corresponds to wishes as yet unacknowledged by them and is manifestly motivated by some other, also harmless purpose, for instance, the need to obtain a tourist cabin (*It Happened One Night*, *Pillow to Post*). The pretense creates the test situation in which the couple demonstrate the impeccable behavior for which the onlooker does not give them credit. Also in the end the pretense will become reality, the couple will marry. Thus the marriage pretense is an elaborate retort to the mistakenly suspicious onlooker. It is an arranged false appearance which is on the surface virtuous, which conceals only virtuous behavior, and which in the end ceases to be false. It is a specially contrived proof that none of the naughty intentions or actions which the comic onlooker suspects exist outside his imagination.

The virtuous pretense to cover virtuous behavior, where the only suggestion of wickedness is conveyed by the mistaken impressions of the onlooker, seems to be a distinctively American comedy device. Pretenses in French films tend to reveal a discrepancy between the façade and what is concealed behind it. A harmless façade may conceal bad intentions, or, conversely, a wicked façade may cloak good intentions. The prostitute in *Macadam* arranges for her bed to break down in the middle of the night in order to lure to her room the naive young sailor in the room next door. In *Circonstances Atténuantes*, a retired prosecutor who has fallen in with a gang of thieves poses as a master crook in order to reform them.

While American film comedies provide a considerable range of comic onlookers, who may appear as a crowd as well as in individual embodiments, there is one type of character who most frequently assumes this role. He is an elderly man, usually short and bald-headed, who appears slightly worried, fussy, and ineffectual. He belongs to the gallery of devalued father-figures. He is the father to whom nobody tells anything, and who, in his blundering efforts to find out what is going on, invariably gets things wrong. A counterpart to the police in the melodramas, who mistakenly suspect the hero, the comic onlooker is more harmless and easier to handle. As we have seen, it is not necessary to prove to him how things really are; he can easily be deceived and thus diverted by yet another false impression. The comic onlooker is the reverse of an older image of the father as an omniscient moral authority. This older father-image was the counterpart of a belief in sexual dangers. The father stood as a warning against such temptations, and a judge of wrong-doing. The old preacher in *Flesh and the Devil* always happens to be sitting on the next park bench when the lovers have a secret rendezvous. In his pulpit, looking down on his congregation, he sees the signs of a developing affair and launches on a sermon against adultery which makes the woman against whom it was addressed faint. This watchful and righteously censorious father-figure has disappeared with the belief in the dangerousness of sex. Where the young people are unlikely to be carried away by wayward impulses, the suspicious watcher becomes a ridiculous character.

In a recent appearance of the omniscient onlooker, he, too, becomes a comic character. His purpose is not censorious; on the contrary it is he who mock-heroically defeats the usual misguided onlooker, and who demonstrates that nothing wicked was going on. The mistaken onlooker in *Sitting Pretty* is a prim elderly man who lives alone with his old mother. He is not merely a chance passer-by who blunders in at the moment when things happen to look suspicious. Rather, urged on by his mother, he habitually pries into and gossips about the affairs of the neighborhood. Circumstances, however, collaborate with his curiosity and suspiciousness, revealing to him ambiguous fragments of events which are especially suited to confirming his and his mother's image of the world as scandalous. The omniscient counterpart of this misguided onlooker is a writer who eventually writes a best-selling novel about the life of the suburban neighborhood. Before this he becomes a major object of the other onlooker's suspicions as he seems to be carrying on with the attractive young matron at whose house he is staying. The novel exonerates him in the usual way of dispelling any doubts by a sensational success (like the sextuplets in *The Miracle of Morgan's Creek*), but also by demonstrating that his purpose was only to look, not to do anything. This omniscient on-looker is not a moral authority but a detached observer who only participates in the action in order to free himself and others from the discomfiting attentions of the usual comic onlooker. The one who sees things truly testifies that no censorship is required since everyone was behaving circumspectly all along.

Another derivative of paternal omniscience appears in the persecutory bad father-figure of the melodramas. He knows the real event underlying the false appearances which he may have arranged, and in which the hero is enmeshed. Where the hero and heroine want to deceive him, they may fear, and with good reason, that he will find out about them (*Criss-Cross*). Thus omniscience together with any other attribute of strength tends to attach mainly to the dangerous fantasied father, while father-figures who approximate somewhat more closely the manifest father tend to appear ineffectual, foolish, and mistaken.

We may ask why the mistaken onlooker of the comedies is almost never a woman, in view of the widely alleged curious, moralizing, gossiping, and interfering tendencies of women. One reason would appear to be a very general one having to do with the greater comic potentialities of the male sex. A more specific reason would be the strongly marked tendency of American films to avoid putting women in any situation where they would appear ridiculous. We have already spoken of the way in which the films endow women with superior skills and capacities for achievement. In a rare film where a woman appears as a comic snooper, she may play a crucial role in the capture of a criminal (*Bungalow 13*). It is difficult in American films to reduce a woman to the level of comic male ineptitude. Also, a woman in the role of the onlooker who falsely suspects young people of sexual irregularities would seem more clearly a deprived character. Again, American films hesitate to show women

in any such disadvantageous position. The male comic onlooker is almost always a character without any sex life, but
we are not aware of this as a deprivation in his case.

The situation of the elderly onlooker and the young couple who are the objects of his attention reverses the situation
of the curious child in relation to the parents. Any fantasy
about looking will have this original situation as one of its
sources. One of the major reactions to childhood investigations reflected in American films is to deny that anything
happened. The usual painful discovery of the child that
something happens between the parents from which he is
excluded is negated. Thus in the melodramas the woman
whom the hero loves is so often shown to be, contrary to appearances, entirely virtuous and to love only him; her relation to the other man, the father-figure, is explained away as
merely apparent. In the comedies, where the young couple
are the objects of investigation of an older person, they prove
by their sexual abstinence the plausibility of the view that
nothing happened between the parent couple. One might say
that the young couple by doing nothing exercise a retroac-
tive magic gesture to render the parent couple equally innocent. The comic onlooker embodies the suspicions of the
child about things which he does not see. We in the audience are encouraged to laugh at him and to enjoy the fantasy
that if we could see everything we would see that nothing
happens. The peculiar elation in American film comedies in
demonstrating that nothing happens would seem to derive
in part from this source. The comic onlooker frequently
combines with his characteristics of an elderly man certain
traits of the child, as well as selected features common to
both. Like a child he is unabashed about crawling under
tables or listening in on private conversations. He is also
typically small, bald (as infants often are), sexless (as children
are supposed to be), likely to misunderstand things in comical ways, and a nuisance. The position of the American father

as surpassable makes him an eligible object for the projection of supposedly foolish childish mistakes no less than for repressed dangerous impulses.

In French films, the father as the watchful observer of the young couple appears, as we would expect, in a different light. He usually sees things quite accurately, judges authoritatively, and exercises the characteristic function of the father in French films of separating or uniting. In *Fanny*, the father, correctly anticipating a hazardous meeting between the former lovers, arrives on the scene, witnesses their love avowals, and prevents them from renewing the affair in order to safeguard the marriage which the girl has made while the hero was away. In the sequel, *César*, when the heroine's elderly husband died, and the formerly young couple, now middle-aged, might finally come together, they find themselves estranged despite their continued love and have difficulty finding the right words to seal their reunion. The father, watching this scene from behind a bush, comes out to say what must be said and to join their hands. In *Le Père Tranquille*, the father of the girl correctly observes the incipient relation between her and an appropriate young man. He suggests to the young couple, as a maneuver in connection with some Resistance activity (their neighborhood is to be bombed and everyone must be got to another part of town without knowing the reason) that they should celebrate a pretended betrothal party to which they will invite all the neighbors. He teasingly pretends not to know that this coincides with their wishes, but does not show too much surprise when, at the celebration, they shyly tell him that they would like the pretense to become real.

Where mistaken onlookers appear in French films they may assume the sinister form of a lynching mob. The object of their attack is not suspected of ordinary sexual misbehavior; on the contrary, their victim is a person who, through lack of any apparent normal pleasures, becomes suspected of perverse and criminal tendencies. The solitary man with no woman in his life and no taste for the convivality of the café is suspected by his neighbors of living on raw and bloody meat and of trying to seduce little girls. When a murder is committed, they are convinced he did it and come out in a crowd to pursue and torment him, and drive him to his death (*Panique*). Similarly, in *Le Corbeau*, the suspicions of a whole town turn against a middle-aged spinster nurse and she is mercilessly chased by an angry mob. False impressions in French films are thus apt to have dangerous consequences, for the person who looks worse than he is as well as for the one who sees others as better than they are (the man who idealizes the bad woman).

The possibility that the hero may be the jealous and envious onlooker of the relation between the woman he loves and the other man is suggested, as we have seen, in American melodramas, but almost always with strong mitigating factors. The usual development, as we have noted, is that the appearance of bad behavior on the part of the woman is eventually explained away and the hero gets the assurance that she has never loved anyone but him. Frequently the woman has become involved in the seemingly dubious connections in which the hero sees her for quite virtuous reasons which she is later able to explain (*The Big Sleep, Cornered*). Occasionally she may produce a false appearance of wickedness out of love for the hero, to make him jealous and keep him interested (*Gilda*). In a less usual case, the hero may have the painful experience of watching a girl who is incapable of real love going with men who can give her more than he can, but he still gets the assurance that next to herself she loves him best (*Criss-Cross*). The melodramas usually put the audience in the same position as the hero. We are not in the situation of omniscience which we enjoy in comedies. Thus we share the hero's suspicions, and like him do not know until the end that the suspected goings-on have not really happened. Our relation to the onlooker in the comedies is quite different since there we know the truth from the beginning. However, comedies and melodramas both converge in demonstrating that the suspicions of the on-looker are false. The melodramas further tend to exempt the hero from jealousy and envy by making him either temporarily or permanently detached from the disputed woman. The hero in *The Strange Love of Martha Ivers* tells the powerful couple who rule his home-town that he pities them —the reverse of envy. He leaves them, witnesses their love-death through the lighted window, and, forgetting them, goes off with his girl.

Where an exceptional film shows a seriously deprived on-looker witnessing the embrace of an envied couple, it is an older man. The despised aging man, who has been deceived and robbed by a beautiful and vicious young woman, returns to her apartment unexpectedly to find her in the arms of her young lover. He remains in the shadow of the vestibule to listen to their amorous words, and is forever after haunted by their voices (*Scarlet Street*). Thus his fate is very different from that of the young man who so easily forgets an unenviable scene of love. Bitter and lasting disappointments, like foolish errors and dangerous impulses, are projected onto the older man.

French films treat the situation of seeing a beloved woman with another man according to their usual rule of evoking the disappointing aspects of life in the presumable hope of mastering painful feelings and inuring oneself to inevitable frustrations. Thus the hero first sees a beautiful woman alone, becomes preoccupied with watching her through her window, and dreams of a future relation between them. Later he suffers disillusionment as he sees her with another man. He has committed his feelings without anticipating this possibility, and may be unable to detach them. The childhood experience of disappointment with the mother, and the difficulty of breaking away from her, is re-evoked. In tragic instances the hero does not survive this unhappy love and the woman's betrayal.

In *Panique,* the lonely hero, looking from his bedroom window, sees through the window across the way a beautiful girl undressing. The girl becomes aware of his interest and finds him distasteful. Later she spitefully leaves her curtain open to allow the hero, now always watching, to see her being embraced by her lover. This disillusionment is not all that the hero suffers. The girl and her lover plan to inculpate him for a murder which the lover has committed. For this purpose the girl proceeds to encourage the hero, tells him that her lover beats her, that she yields to him only out of fear, and appeals to the hero to rescue her. She finally visits the hero's room, the lonely room where he had so often wished her to be, but only to plant incriminating evidence. Making the excuse that she fears her lover may come, she leaves hastily, postponing the fulfilment of the hero's desires. Shortly afterwards he is pursued by a mob who have broken into his room and found the planted evidence, and he is killed.

In *La Passionelle* the bedroom window of a poor, lonely young man faces that of a beautiful young countess. He watches her nightly through the torn piece of burlap which serves as his window curtain. When one night she, who has long been aware of his attention, beckons to him, he goes to her overwhelmed with happy expectations. But she has called him only because she can use him. She has just, on the eve of her wedding to a foppish aristocrat, murdered a blackmailing servant who had been her lover. She appeals to the hero to dispose of the body, and offers herself to him as payment when he shall have completed this task. She hides him behind the curtains of her bed—the bed on which the murdered lover lies—and from there he watches while her maid helps her dress for the ball which her parents are giving. When she goes out, he picks up the body which he carries down the corridor, dodging from the view of an amorous pair of party guests escaping from the crowd. He carries the body through the town to the river into which he throws it.

Returning to the girl's bedroom late at night, he demands
to hear her story, bitterly reproaches her for having shattered
his dream, and leaves without claiming his reward. Afterwards the girl, who does not want to marry the aristocrat,
confesses to the murder, but does not succeed in convincing
anyone. In the end the hero is arrested for the crime. He
has come out of hiding to see the girl as a beautiful and unhappy bride. The police pick him up at the church door.

In these films the major complaint for the onlooker's disappointment seems to be leveled against the woman. Her
hidden life has a criminal aspect and she sacrifices the onlooker in order to guard her secret. It is the woman who embodies the punitive threat for his forbidden, though, as he
thought at first, harmless looking. The fatality which he undergoes is equally motivated on his side by the irrevocable
emotional attachment precipitated by his observations. The
development in these films is the reverse of the American.
Instead of the dispelling of false suspicions, we see the disastrous revelation of hidden evil to the unsuspecting. The
hero first sees things as he would wish them to be, later
learns that they are different. In American films, the hero
first sees things as he fears they may be, in the end gets the
assurance that they are just as he would wish.

§ PROMOTERS OF LOVE

WHILE the mistakenly suspicious onlooker is a nuisance,
American films abound in other onlookers whose attention
is welcome to the hero and heroine. The distinguishing feature of these other onlookers is that they are permissive.
They may sanction or promote the relation of the young
couple or at least accept it with an amused tolerance. Fre-

quently they are father-figures: the priest, the old training analyst, or, in a more demoted position, the old servitor. These characters closely approximate the manifest father, especially the father of the heroine who, as we previously observed, is frequently concerned about her marriage and is an ally of her young man. In these instances the hero is assured that the older man is neither grudging nor censorious about his happiness in love.

Buddies of the hero may also be onlookers of his happy union with the heroine. These buddies rarely have girls of their own, but are quite unenvious of the hero. They seem like over-age schoolboys who have not yet developed to the point of wanting a girl. The defense against the dangers of envy is double in this case. The hero is in the position of the lover whom others watch; thus he is not liable to be feeling envy, but is, rather, enviable. However, since it is also undesirable to be the object of envy, the assurance is given that the onlookers are insusceptible to this emotion. At the same time, there is a mild atmosphere of woman-sharing in the recurrent situation of the hero and his girl being watched over by one or more of his friends. Their tolerance for his relation to the girl further assures him that he has not lost their friendship by this new involvement. Heroes and heroines generally enjoy having witnesses to their happiness. It is only an occasional wicked character who resents having these bystanders around and wants to be alone with the loved one.

The old family retainer may anticipate the hero's incipient feelings towards the girl, and, by demonstrating a favorable attitude, sanction them. In contrast to an older father type whose permission had to be asked, he encourages the hero to follow his feelings; there need be no anxiety about getting his approval. Thus in *Love Letters*, the old caretaker of the hero's country house expresses his accord with the hero's shift of allegiance from his fiancée to a new girl. When the financée, whom the hero no longer loves, comes for a visit, the caretaker is taciturn and unobliging. As soon as the heroine appears, he shows a beaming alacrity. This benevolent onlooker, who sympathetically fosters the hero's wishes, contrasts with the censorious comic onlooker who tries to interfere with wishes that he mistakenly ascribes.

The frequently homeless hero is apt to find instead of the family retainer a more transient, and also more buddy-like servitor as an aid to his romance: the taxi-driver, check-room attendant, or railway ticket seller. While the hero and heroine are usually free from family interference, it seems preferable not to leave them alone. The various functions of supervision over marriage choice, match-making, and betrothal ceremonies, no longer performed by institutionalized agencies, are taken over by casual bystanders. But the functions are still performed; the young couple are given the assurance that their love is approved. In *The Lost Weekend,* the hero and heroine are introduced through a check-room attendant who has got their coats mixed up. The attendant nods smilingly as he sees the hero take advantage of the opportunity to accompany the heroine when they leave the theater. The attendant through whose agency an apparent accident has occurred which will change two lives resembles not only an earthly but a divine match-maker. We have previously mentioned the more prescient ticket-agent in *She Wouldn't Say Yes* who intentionally sells the hero and heroine tickets to the same upper berth in order to insure their meeting again. In *Adventure,* a taxi-driver acts more as a witness than an arranger of the hero's romance. He first offers the hero forecasts as to his eventual success after seeing the heroine slam the door in his face. Later it is the same driver who sees the hero enter as the heroine's husband.

The onlooker is moved to unite the young couple. Even the comic onlooker, as we have seen, may force together an unmarried pair whom he mistakenly supposes to be married. The benevolent onlooker regularly assumes the function of bringing the young people together. This activity of the onlooker again serves to deny envy in the outsider looking on at the happiness of the couple. This is most obvious where the onlooker has been attached to one member of the couple. In *The Sailor Takes a Wife,* the vamp, who has made an unsuccessful play for the young husband, observes the incipient breakup of his marriage, and does her best to arrange for its reconsolidation. In *Because of Him,* the aging actor who has been rejected by the young actress discerns her love for a younger man and brings them together. The various efforts of onlookers to unite the hero and heroine also relieve the young people of sole responsibility for carrying their wishes into action. In this respect the uniting onlooker acts like the jolting train or overturning automobile that accomplishes the wishes of the couple for precipitate contact without their having to initiate the move themselves.

The onlooker may also afford reassurance against fears of possible sexual dangers. In *Spellbound,* the psychoanalyst heroine takes the hero, her patient and pretended bridegroom, to stay at the house of her old training analyst. The fatherly analyst watches at night while the disoriented hero wanders about the house with a razor in his hand. While more usually the onlooker facilitates the carrying out of harmless wishes, he provides in this case insurance against the fulfilment of dangerous ones.

In *The Bells of St. Mary's,* a sympathetic priest arranges the reunion of a long-separated couple. He is not only the witness of their meeting, but is urged by them to stay and sing for them a song which had been an old favorite of theirs, "The Land of Beginning Again." As the rather tongue-tied couple sit by, the onlooker voices the emotions which they presumably feel. The feelings of the couple thus obtain a double sanction as the onlooker puts them into action and also into words. The song which expresses their feelings and unites them resembles the words of a marriage ceremony which are also spoken by a priest and to which the couple give assent. The vows of the ceremony are replaced by an expression of feeling rather than resolve and the prescribed ritual gives way to the informal song. In *Canyon Passage,* as the hero and heroine ride off together into the sunset, the hero's friend rides along behind them, strumming a guitar and singing a song which contains the line, "I'm going to pop that question." A famous singer (Bing Crosby) and a famous composer of popular songs (Hoagy Carmichael) play in these two films the role of the onlooker who unites the couple. Thus they enact in the films a role similar to that which they exercise in real life. Young people who sing the songs provided them by such composers and singers gain the assurance that their feelings are not strange and secret but have the sanction of being shared by millions. The priest as a singer of popular songs supplies a link between the constituted authority who sanctions the love of the young couple and the chance onlookers who more often give this sanction to the movie hero and heroine.

The hero's buddy, a frequent attendant of the happy young couple, usually lacks any amorous aims of his own. Thus he appears as free from envy, and the woman-sharing aspect of the situation is veiled. In *Pardon My Past,* the final sequence shows the enamoured hero and heroine and the hero's buddy together in a taxi. As the hero and heroine kiss and exchange affectionate remarks, the buddy grumbles: Do I have to listen to all this mush? This impatient, humorously detached attitude is similar to that of the little brother in *Kiss and Tell,* who continually remarks about the amorous problems of the teen-agers: I think it's all very dumb. In *The Blue Dahlia,* the final shot shows a group of the hero's buddies witnessing the embrace of the hero and heroine (which we do not see). As the most naive of the buddies suggests that they should wait for the hero before going off to have a beer, the others inform him jokingly that they cannot wait that long.

Films with a happy romantic ending frequently close with a shot of the onlooker rather than of the happy couple. This may have the function of shifting the audience back to a recognition of their own position as onlookers, easing them out of their identification with the hero and heroine. The comic aspect of the onlooker last seen in the film may have the further effect of relieving the audience of anything unsatisfactory in their onlooker status. The negative associations of being an onlooker become attached to the onlooker in the film from whom we differentiate ourselves. In *Spellbound,* the hero and heroine are at one point in a railroad station; they puzzle an onlooking ticket-collector by kissing each other, like other couples around them who are saying goodbye, but then both boarding the train. At the end of the film they are again about to take a train. As they find themselves faced by the same ticket-collector they repeat their previous performance. The film ends with a closeup of the still more puzzled ticket-collector. As the end of the film introduces a break in our identification with the hero and heroine, and the possibility of an awareness that we have only been onlookers at the triumph and happiness of others, we are distracted by the final view of the onlooker in the film whom we can laugh at because of his incomprehension of what he sees, and over whom we have the advantage.

The hero and heroine are apt to be much less alone together than the advertisements often suggest. The advertisements present the names of the co-stars joined in isolation, and their faces in absorbed proximity looking as if no one else existed. In the film, the hero may have a ship-mate and the heroine a girl-friend in almost constant attendance (*Adventure*). The image of the couple alone together which the advertisement suggests may be what the audience think they want, while the situation in the film, where the couple are hardly ever alone, may please them better. When a hero and heroine get off on an island, there is apt to be a sage old light-house keeper not far off, who befriends and approves of them (*Stolen Life*).

It is only a bad character who does not welcome onlookers

and may try to eliminate them to be all alone with the loved one. The heroine in *Leave Her to Heaven* is indifferent to display; rather than exhibit to the world a husband who is a successful writer, she would prefer to have him stop writing so that he can spend all his time with her. She is displeased that he has taken his crippled younger brother along with them on their honeymoon, and impatient with the old caretaker who is always around the house. When she slips into her husband's bed in the morning, they are interrupted by the boy who knocks on the wall from the next bedroom and calls some cheery morning greeting. Shortly after this, she takes the boy out swimming and drowns him. She attempts to persuade her husband to fire the caretaker. Later she produces a miscarriage because she feels a child would be an intruder. This is the image that American films present of the woman who only wants a private lover and can dispense with onlookers. It indicates yet another service which onlookers perform for the man, that of saving him from possible envelopment by an exclusively amorous woman.

§ SUFFERING STARS

TURNING from the role of the onlooker to that of the performer, we find that professional performers in American films are very often shown as unhappy. This unhappiness may derive from negative feelings about their professional activities or from failure to find happiness outside these activities, or both. There is a tendency to make the performer who finds his work congenial suffer unhappiness in love or some other penalty. Conversely, the performer for whom things turn out well in life is likely to experience negative feelings about his work. The combination of happiness in both public performance and private life is exceptional. The picture of the public performer as unhappy, or incompletely happy, serves to mitigate the envy of the audience. In the treatment of the onlooker a major tendency, as we have seen, is the denial of envy. The portrayal of the performer contributes to the same end: the performer, the object of jealousy and envy, is revealed as not really happy.

The successful performer's unhappiness in love is not related to a possible limitation in the capacity for love on the part of individuals who are absorbed in self-exhibition. American films show little recognition of disturbances in the capacity for love. The problem is rather that of being able to win love. The successful performer who is unhappy in love simply suffers the misfortune of not being loved in return by his or her chosen loved one. The singer is in love with the composer while he loves someone else (*Night and Day*). That the misfortunes of the successful performer are an external penalty is further suggested by the fact that they may take the form of illness or death. The successful and happily married actress has a heart disease to which she succumbs (*Sentimental Journey*). The happily adept singer and dancer in *Wonderman* is killed by some gangsters whose crime he accidentally witnessed. The ghost of the performer then forces his timid twin brother to take his place. The twin is overcome by stage fright and commits numerous blunders. For this unwilling and embarrassed performer everything turns out well in the end; there is no exhibition enjoyment to be penalized. In an instance where the tendency to show off manifestly interferes with a love relation, the show-off's loss is quite temporary. In *The Well-Groomed Bride,* the heroine becomes disaffected from her bridegroom, an ex-football hero, when she finds him posing for newspaper photos instead of coming to the wedding. The football player promptly revives a relationship with a former girl-friend whom he decides he has loved all along.

The public performance of a woman frequently occurs in

a negatively toned context. A love conflict or some other disaster has forced her to become a singer in a nightclub. Her appearance carries associations of a vaguely degraded sort. The man who watches her may have doubts about her virtue or suspect her of involvement in crime. It is stressed that as a result of these negative circumstances the woman does not enjoy her performance. This serves to ward off jealousy on the part of the onlooking man who loves her: the woman who is performing for another man or other men does not enjoy the act. In *Gilda,* when the heroine sings and dances at the hero's nightclub, it is only because he has driven her to desperation by his coldness. She does not enjoy the performance by which she excites other men, and is not interested in them. In *This Love of Ours,* the heroine becomes a nightclub performer when she is driven from home by her husband's mistaken doubts about her fidelity. She finds her performer's life, in which she is teamed with a man who loves her but whom she does not love, so dreary that she is ready to commit suicide. The heroine in *The Bribe* has been forced to become a nightclub singer in a Central American town where she has been stranded with her unemployed alcoholic husband. The hero who first sees her at one of her performances is investigating her possible relation with a criminal gang. The skating star in *The Countess of Monte Cristo* gives her major performance in an atmosphere of anxious tension as she believes there are detectives in the audience who mean to arrest her as soon as the show is over. These performances under negative auspices may appear quite pleasurable while the performance is going on, as the girl throws herself into her work with verve. Thus the pleasure in the performance, denied by the negative setting, tends to break through. The effort to deny on the part of the onlooking man that there are any grounds for jealousy of the performing woman must work against the same counterindications which generally complicate the case of the goodbad girl.

In French films, as we have noted, there is no such attempt to relieve the onlooker of disappointment, jealousy, or envy. In the depiction of women performers, accordingly, there is little tendency to show them as suffering displeasure in their performance. Women performers typically arouse intense disturbances in the men who see them, without being affected themselves. In *Les Enfants du Paradis,* the heroine appears first at a fair as a naked Venus in a bath. Later, the hero has her play a goddess in a pantomime which he produces. He plays a sad clown who loves her and is deceived by her. When he is asleep she descends from her pedestal to join her lover, played by the hero's friend with whom the heroine is having an affair. This play within a play epitomizes the French tendency to preserve in dramatic treatment the love disappointment of the excluded member of the triangle. Nor is there an attempt to attribute to the beautiful woman any distaste for the display by which she attracts so many men. One of these men kills another for her sake, and the hero is made permanently unhappy by his love for her. But she moves through the film with invulnerable beauty, unaffected by the disturbances which her appearance arouses. Similarly, in *Les Visiteurs du Soir,* the beautiful woman, who appears disguised as a troubadour, rides away as she had come after having provoked a fatal duel between two rivals for her favor. In *Le Revenant,* a ballerina plays with the affections of a naive provincial youth and drives him to attempt suicide by coolly throwing him aside when her lover joins her. The woman who appears as a public performer has the same disastrous impact as the woman who is revealed to the hero in private glimpses. She arouses love and illusions in the man who sees her; but he later becomes painfully aware of her involvement with another man or other men. The woman is the indestructible cause of destruction for her beholders.

The role of a public performer involves much more serious dangers for men than for women in American films.

Where the hero is an actor, prizefighter, or magician, we frequently get a cautionary tale of the disastrous risks involved in a performer's career. We may recall that the favored role for the hero in the melodramas is that of an investigator, an onlooker rather than an actor. While the role of investigator is also dangerous, it is not likely to be as disastrous as that of a performer. The plot in which the hero is a performer resembles that of the sorcerer's apprentice; he gets started on something which he discovers he cannot control. Once the hero has assumed the position of a performer, he suffers from the unleashing of unanticipated destructive impulses in himself or finds that his acts have unforeseen destructive consequences. He then becomes subject to punitive counterattacks.

In *Nightmare Alley,* the hero, ambitious to become a performer, steals the secret of a mind-reading act from a couple of aging, shabby carnival actors. In the process of doing so, he seduces the wife, and accidentally kills the husband. He then goes off on his own and achieves a sensational success. However, he goes too far; he undertakes to do spiritualistic evocations and is exposed as a fraud. Further threatened by a woman to whom he has confessed his accidental killing, he becomes an alcoholic tramp like the derelict performer whose secret he had been so anxious to steal.

In *A Double Life,* an aging famous actor is prevailed on, against misgivings on his part, to play *Othello.* Increasingly the role takes possession of him. As he thinks he has reason to be jealous of his wife, he begins to confuse play and reality. Eventually he reënacts in life, towards another woman, the murder which he has played on the stage. In *Body and Soul,* the hero's successful prize-fighting career involves him in unforeseen catastrophes. Under the tutelage of a vicious manager, he almost kills in the ring an opponent with an old head injury; the manager had agreed that the hero would treat the opponent gently, but had not communicated this to the hero. Later the hero's friend is killed by the manager's gang after a dispute with the manager. Led into a dissipated life by the manager, the hero alienates the girl he loves. To conclude his career, he agrees with the manager to throw his last fight. All his money as well as the manager's is bet on the contender. Moved at the last minute not to betray those who have faith in him (he is a Jew, and the Jewish community regards him as their champion), he wins the fight, saving his soul and losing his money.

The hero as performer is led to commit the crimes of which more often the hero as investigator is falsely suspected and of which he succeeds in exonerating himself: the murder of an envied man or of a jealousy-provoking woman. In the relatively infrequent case where the hero is a performer, he thus becomes the bearer of the dangerous and uncontrollable impulses which are usually projected onto other characters. That the role of the public performer tends to merge with that of the performer of crimes confirms that the archetypal performance, the one at which the child is a nocturnal spectator, is understood as a crime of violence. It also suggests that conversely the envied career of the public performer tends to be invested with destructive connotations.

Comedies present a solution to the problem of the performer. The comic hero is able to perform and yet escape the penalties of more serious performers. He is usually lacking in any ambitious drive of the sort which might threaten rivals. He may be thrust into his career by chance, and succeed by a series of accidents. His performance is mitigated by childlike ineptitude; he is scared or embarrassed or sometimes unable to perform what is expected. Like the previously discussed performers, he is a sorcerer's apprentice, getting into something that is beyond his capacities. Unlike them he damages no one, but is rather exposed himself to apprehensions and embarrassments.

Danny Kaye is the stock comic performer who habitually gets caught in situations which are beyond his capacities. In *The Kid from Brooklyn* he is, as a result of accidental circumstances, promoted as a prizefighter. His performance alternates between abject terror, as aware of his incompetence he runs away from his opponents, and an equally comic false confidence as he is fooled into believing in a competence which he lacks. Gradually he becomes convinced that he is a veritable tiger. He begins to revel in the publicity stunts which his manager arranges for him. His sweetheart becomes alienated, offended both by his apparent brutality and by his unabashed showing-off. Just before the championship bout he learns that he is not strong, that all his previous fights were fixed and that he now faces his first real fight. His terror revives and he almost collapses before he wins by a fluke. This film is a comic counterpart to *Body and Soul* which, as we have seen, elaborates the dangerousness of the competent performer and the punishment that entails. By contrast to the intensely ambitious serious performer, the comic one is precipitated into his career unwillingly and by accident, just as he wins by an accident in the end. The comic performer is thus free from either motive or competence that could be a threat.

In *Wonderman* Danny Kaye, a shy bookworm, is forced to take the place of his murdered twin brother as a night-club performer. He is again petrified at finding himself in a position where he is expected to perform while lacking the relevant skills. After embarrassed and desperate stalling before an increasingly impatient audience, he is able to go on with the act because the ghost of his brother, whom he invokes, takes possession of him. This is a comic parallel to *Nightmare Alley* in which the hero takes over the act of a murdered performer. Only in the comic version the hero does not have anything to do with the murder and is innocent of any ambition to take the performer's place.

In *The Secret Life of Walter Mitty* Danny Kaye is a meek, self-effacing editor of thrilling fiction magazines who intersperses his drab ineffectual everyday life with day-dreams modeled on the magazine stories. Through a series of accidents he is confronted with an outfit of real gangsters. He then demonstrates his usual alternation between flight and over-assertiveness. He tries to use the tricks of fictional heroes, at times unmasking by mistake his own pretenses. Pointing a finger in his pocket as if he has a gun, he makes a gangster back away from him. He then shakes his "gun" in the gangster's face, giving away the fact that he does not have one. His difficulties are complicated by the fact that no one believes his story about the gangsters; everyone supposes that he is confusing thrilling fiction with reality. In the end, by the usual accidents, he is shown to be right and triumphs over his opponents. This comedy is a parallel to the tragic *A Double Life,* in which fiction passes over into reality. The dramatic role which takes possession of the serious hero, and which he acts out, is one of passion and destructiveness. The fictional theme which the comic hero succeeds in realizing corresponds to the harmless school-boyish dream of being the good man who defeats the bad men. Again, the comic hero is less responsible for what happens as circumstances drag him into the action where, through improbable luck, he becomes a hero in spite of his ineptitude.

The triumph of the comic hero, whose performance is exempted from penalties because it is accompanied by a display of weakness and ineptitude, has certain counterparts in American life. American public speakers tend, to a distinctive degree, to tell stories at their own expense. In these stories, the speaker presents himself as the comic hero, subject to all sorts of embarrassments, revealing blunders and ineptitudes, and suffering a variety of minor misfortunes. In this way he negates, both for himself and for his audience, the destructive connotations of his public position and performance. He demonstrates his harmlessness by allowing himself to be laughed at and disarms the latent envy of the audience. It is then permissible for him to triumph like the comic hero and he may intersperse the stories at his own expense with accounts of achievements and successes. He may permit himself a fair amount of boasting as long as he mitigates it with stories of blunders and embarrassments. Political figures may present themselves in buffoonish postures, dressed up as Indians or cavemen or strumming a guitar, thus complementing their more serious public appearances and the efforts they make on their own behalf.

The song-and-dance performances which Danny Kaye gives, after his reluctance, embarrassment and ineptitude have been established, combine skill with apparent lack of skill, control with apparent loss of control. The songs with their rapid verbalization seem to demonstrate linguistic mastery. But the sounds resemble the gibberish of the infant who has not yet learned to talk or the older child who pretends to be talking a foreign language. A second surprise reveals that the seeming nonsense shapes up into sixty-four-dollar words. Similarly, the hyperactivity of the dancing suggests an infantile lack of control; but then the frantic movements convey both a rhythmic and expressive pattern. This combination of control with apparent absence of control is illustrated in numerous details. For instance, in a dance sequence in *Wonderman*, the comedian appears to be frightened by his own hand which, as if impelled by an independent movement, wriggles towards his face like a snake.

The model for this comic hero is the child, conceived as harmless (free from sexual and destructive impulses) and still in the process of acquiring adult skills. American children are much encouraged to show off. Gregory Bateson has pointed to the contrast between American and English child-training in this respect. At the dinner table, for instance, American parents are apt to be the audience while the children do the talking. In Britain the reverse is apt to be the case. Margaret Mead has suggested that, as a result of this, Americans, when they speak, tend to retain the clamorous and boasting tone of the young child trying to hold the attention of the parents. The English, who learn to talk by listening to the father, tend to assume a quietly reserved but authoritative tone.

Adults applaud the child's performances, but also laugh at them. The child with his stream of talk interspersed with verbal and factual mistakes wins the flattering attention of the adults and also frequently their unexpected laughter. Dramatic performances, exhibition speeches and recitations by children are traditionally enlivened by endearing comical blunders, which may be painful to the child at the time, but which he learns to turn into a funny story at his own expense as he grows older. The model for permitted self-exhibition is the child, whose performance supposedly expresses no dangerous impulses (sexual or destructive) and evokes laughter rather than envy because of the child's incomplete mastery of skills. The comic hero (and to some extent the public speaker) reproduces these aspects of the child's performance, maintaining a perpetual disclaimer of complete skill acquisition in demonstrations of (or stories about) his ineptitude.

The comic hero, corresponding to the image of the harmless child, is the counterpart to the manifest father, whom the films also present as harmless. We have remarked that this image of the father serves as a defense against the dangers of hostility and rivalry between fathers and sons. The presentation of the father as non-competitive, ungrudging, non-authoritarian, and a pal tends to disarm any combative tendencies in the son (although, as we have tried to show, an opposed image of a strong and dangerous father persists). In the role of the comic hero, the son is invested with a similar disarming façade. Apprehensions of counterattack for an aggressive performance are warded off by this presentation of the performer as comically weak, fearful, and inept. The dangerous impulses which are here denied break through in the hero who appears as a serious performer.

Another aspect of the contrast between the serious and comic performer is that, while the serious performer is carried away by uncontrollable destructive impulses, the comic performer embodies immature sexual impulses. His incomplete body control, alarmed surprise at his own move-

ments, and recurrent comical collapse in attempted feats
which exceed his capacities are a legend of childish sexuality.
This sexuality is harmless not only because of its incompetence but because it is unmixed with destructiveness. Sex
which is free from destructive admixture tends to appear as
harmless and without behavioral consequences, as we have
also seen in the case of the young couple in comedies who
never do anything no matter what others may suspect.

§ LOOKING IS ENOUGH

ANOTHER dramatic possibility emerging from the per-
former-onlooker complex presents the man as professionally
occupied with the woman's exhibition before others. He
may be a designer of women's clothes, a discoverer and pro-
moter of a woman's talent, a producer of shows in which a
woman stars. Implicit in his exhibition of the woman is his
wish to see other men attracted to her, and, on a deeper level,
an overture to other men, mediated by the woman. The
woman's success in attracting other men may have unforeseen repercussions. The man may react against the fulfilment
of his latent wishes, which become unacceptable to him as
they are brought closer to the surface. This reaction may
take the form of an increased attachment to the woman of
whom he now becomes desperately jealous. This plot occurs,
with some variations, in both French and British films. In
American films, the situation tends to develop differently.
The woman's success with other men is accepted as more
gratifying and also more harmless. Under favorable circumstances, especially in comedy, the satisfaction afforded by the
woman's success with another man need not be warded off.
The threat of serious rivalry is reduced by the circumstance

that the man who is attracted by the woman's appearance may be satisfied with just looking. Moreover the man who promotes the woman feels less responsibility for having attracted the other man. The woman is less an extension of himself, since American film heroines are too active in their own right to assume such an instrumental role.

In *Falbalas,* the hero is a successful Parisian dress designer. He is a Don Juan, without any feeling for women; he regards them merely as stimuli for his invention of designs and as mannequins for the exhibition of his creations. He excludes from awareness the function of the dresses he designs in implementing the exhibition of the woman to another man whom she will marry. This is symbolized by the traditional conclusion of a Paris opening, the display of a bridal gown. This latent meaning of his work is brought to the surface when he undertakes to design a trousseau for his friend's fiancée. He finds himself for the first time jealously and desperately in love with a woman. Unable to resolve the emotional conflict thus aroused, he suffers a psychotic breakdown and commits suicide. In *Le Silence est d'Or,* a film producer and director makes a young girl whom he discovers the leading actress in his productions. He becomes jealous and begins to fall in love with her when the men around the studio look at her admiringly, and his feelings are intensified when she attracts, and falls in love with, a young actor with whom he has had an affectionately friendly relation. In the end, he directs the young couple in a happy love scene together. Thus he resorts to the stock French solution to a love disappointment, to inure oneself to it by repeated exposure, and in addition gains control of the situation by becoming the director of his own tragedy. In the present context, a further satisfaction appears to result from viewing the couple, that of obtaining an indirect contact with the man friend in his role as lover.

Another variation on this theme occurs in *Le Revenant.* The hero is a successful ballet impresario who returns after

many years to the city where, in his youth, he suffered a
nearly fatal love disappointment. The nephew of his former
sweetheart comes to see him, and he takes the young man
behind the scenes and introduces him to his beautiful pre-
mière ballerina. In this case the man who exhibits the beautiful woman, and who was himself previously the loser in a
love triangle, obtains the satisfaction of seeing another man
disappointed. The ballerina, after leading the young man
on, reveals that she is not serious and that she has another
lover. The youth attempts suicide but not fatally. In the end
he goes away with the impresario. The impresario, having
been disillusioned with women, is not susceptible to jealousy.
His use of the woman to establish contact with the young
man aims at evoking love only as a means to achieving a like
disillusionment on the basis of which the two men can become comrades.

In the British *The Seventh Veil,* the hero makes the
heroine into a successful public performer with the indirect
result that she attracts another man. The hero is a handsome
and embittered man who would have liked to be a musician
but was somehow unable; his handicap for public appearances is underscored by his having a club foot. His orphaned
young ward shows a talent for music, and he undertakes to
fashion her into his tool for achieving vicarious success. By
intensive and tyrannical training he makes her into a successful concert pianist. He enjoys the tours and acclaim, while
she carries out his wishes like a weary captive. This woman
is more under the domination of the man (the Trilby tradition) than in the related French films. The relationship becomes disturbed when he begins to fall in love with her. He
is impelled to substitute for her public exhibitions to a large
audience a private exhibition to another man, a painter
whom he hires to paint her portrait. The painter and the
girl fall in love. When the girl informs the hero of this, he
flies into a rage and beats her over the hands. As the sig-

nificance of her performances as exhibitions before other men has now become more apparent, he wishes to stop them. While this violent demonstration of his monopolistic demands at first drives the girl away, it brings her back to him in the end.

The theme of the man's exhibiting the woman to other men is less likely to involve serious conflicts in American films. The man's estimate of the woman's attractiveness remains unsettled until he gets the confirmation of other men. He needs the demonstration of other men's interest in her before his own feelings can become definite. His reaction corresponds to that of the reader of advertisements who becomes convinced of the merits of a product when he is assured that many prefer it. The possibility of serious rivalry is further mitigated by the fact that admiring onlookers can get pleasure from looking at the pretty girl without being impelled to go further. The hero can get the confirmation of other men's positive reactions without the risk of their becoming amorously involved.

In *Easter Parade,* the hero is in love with his glamorous dancing partner, with whom his best friend is also involved. Piqued when the partner leaves him, he undertakes to promote the career of an obscure entertainer whom he finds in a nightclub show. He wants to demonstrate how easy it is to replace the lost partner, but he is uncertain about the attractiveness of the new girl. He asks her to walk ahead of him on the street so that he can observe whether other men look back at her. The girl, who is sweet and wholesome rather than glamorous, tries without success to interest passing men with an over-bright encouraging smile. We then see, however, that every man who passes turns to look back at her, and the hero is tremendously pleased. As we see her face again, we find that she has achieved this effect by making a grotesque grimace. While the film thus rebukes the hero for demanding the obvious glamor which attracts every

man at first sight, he is nevertheless given the needed
assurance of the girl's attractiveness when his friend, who
had not been serious about the previous partner, falls in
love with this one. The hero's interest in her develops after
his friend has become attached to her. As the girl prefers
the hero, the friend generously becomes her ally in bringing
the hero to a recognition of his true feelings.

That there is slight possibility of a man's using a woman
as an instrument of his self-display, or molding her for his
own purposes, is also demonstrated in this film. The hero
thinks that the heroine is untrained and that in promoting
her he will be creating something out of nothing. After
struggling unsuccessfully to teach her a style of dancing
which is uncongenial, he discovers by chance her already per-
fected talent in a different style of song and dance. Generally
the Pygmalion theme has little viability in American films.
Rather women tend to use men—producers, promoters, night-
club owners—as means towards advancing their careers as
performers.

The American tendency to share a woman without osten-
sible rivalry is illustrated in the pin-up girl. Her many admirers tolerate each other without rivalry or wish for ex-
clusiveness. The enjoyment of the pin-up girl also illustrates
another tendency. Looking at the picture of a beautiful girl
under conditions where girls may be unavailable (in various
Army situations, for instance) can presumably be pleasurable
only if it does not evoke too strongly the impulses which re-
quire more than looking for their satisfaction. Americans
cultivate to a high degree the capacity for the enjoyment of
looking, without the evocation of longings which would
end in feelings of frustration and resentment against the
tantalizing stimulus. This dissociation of looking from longing and disappointment is, as we have seen, also a major
aspect of the movie treatment of looking. Looking becomes,
on the surface at least, free from tension and is accompanied
by the feeling that one only wants to look. (This may also

apply to the presumably pleasurable looking at ads for luxury products which the person looking cannot at the moment afford.) In the case of the many men who share the pin-up girl, their pleasurable impressions of her are presumably also related to their comradely feelings of sharing her with each other, a sharing which remains free from too much conflict as long as it remains imaginary. The image of a girl may even serve to moderate the intensity of their feelings for each other.

In *Brute Force* a group of convicts with a strong esprit de corps share a cell and a dreamy-eyed pin-up girl. (This is a post-war equivalent of Army life; some of the convicts are veterans.) An insurance against rivalry is provided by the explanation that to each of them she is a different girl. As each man looks at the pictured face it changes to the image of a girl whom he remembers and about whom he tells his cellmates in a flash-back. These reminiscences, nostalgic in tone, deal mainly with women who cheated their men or forced them to steal. Thus an implicit cynicism about women contributes to the men's feelings of alliance and makes it easier to share the woman whose destructive potentialities mitigate her attractiveness.

In comedies, as we have noted, woman-sharing frequently occurs under the guise of a harmless pretense. A man will promote a piece of private play-acting in asking his wife or fiancée to pose as the wife of his friend. While the husband may, after sufficient urging from his wife, produce a mild outburst of jealousy as he suspects the other man of trying to turn the pretense into reality (*Guest Wife*), he may also punch his friend for assuring him that nothing has happened, that the girl was not his type (*Easy to Wed*). On the whole there is little danger of pretense passing over into reality. The pleasure in the harmless pretense, in the mere appearance, is another aspect of the pleasure in looking which need not develop into action.

§ THE MAGIC CONTACT

A CHARACTERISTIC American plot about a performer's career shows a young girl successfully pursuing a prominent man whose sponsorship will assure her success. The legend of an obscure talented youth being accidentally discovered by a great personage is here revised. The active heroine does not wait for chance to bring the needed patron her way; she selects the person who is to discover her. Her dependence on others in order to succeed is minimized since she is able to manipulate the one whose sponsorship she needs.

The girl is a would-be singer or actress who has not yet begun her career. All her thoughts are concentrated on a prominent older man, a famous conductor or actor, or perhaps the owner of a major nightclub, who must be made to see or hear her, and who will then immediately open to her the performer's career to which she aspires. The crucial man, however, is busy, uninterested, inaccessible. The problem is to get him to look or listen and this is usually achieved by a trick. The audition then proceeds in an atmosphere of tension: will the important person delay his displeasure about the trick long enough to get an impression of the performance? His approval becomes doubly welcome since it implies not only acceptance of the performance but exemption of the performer from any penalty for the trick she has played. The envy of the audience is also disarmed by this device, since we see the imminently successful performer in a position of potential disadvantage, risking at least a severe scolding, which we are anxious to see warded off. But it can be warded off only by the performer's success. Thus we scan the face of the important person whose gradually appearing smile conveys not only recognition but also forgiveness.

In *One Hundred Men and a Girl,* the heroine, a juvenile soprano, tries unsuccessfully to get a hearing with a famous conductor. Her envy-evoking ambition is mitigated by the fact that she hopes through the same contact to promote the fortunes of a band of unemployed musicians. She finally slips into the empty concert hall where the conductor is rehearsing and conceals herself in a stage box; at an appropriate point she begins to sing. Any impulse to resent her intrusion is overcome by the beauty of her voice; the conductor and orchestra continue their performance as an accompaniment to hers. She is then accepted as soloist with the orchestra and also wins the patronage of the famous conductor for the unemployed musicians. In *Stork Club,* the heroine, a hat-check girl in the nightclub and an aspiring singer, tries unsuccessfully to get a chance to demonstrate her singing to her boss. One one occasion when she is singing at a canteen and hopes he will hear her, he leaves before she comes on. Like the previous heroine she is not exclusively concerned with her own success, but is also trying to get an opening for a band with which she is associated. Eventually she phones the boss, mimicking Walter Winchell, and gives herself and the band a glowing recommendation. The boss rushes over to her house to hear them. There is the usual audition in which everyone fears he will be enraged, but where he is delighted and promptly offers the girl and the band the desired contract. In *Because of Him,* a young waitress who wants to become an actress concentrates her efforts on a famous aging actor. She fakes a letter of recommendation for herself purporting to have been written by the actor. As a result of this she comes to his rather annoyed attention, but manages to convince him of her talent, and in the end appears with great success as his leading lady.

The dangers associated with being a performer, which we have already noted, appear again, although in relatively mild form, in the magic contact situation. The performance is associated with something slightly illicit, the trick which is played in order to gain the attention of the important person. The risk which the performer runs is that of being rebuked for having obtruded herself when the person whom she wants to attract is busy with other things. A situation of early life which this plot reflects is that of the child who wants to interrupt the parents when they are otherwise preoccupied. In this wish-fulfilment fantasy, the girl attracts the attention of the father and exhibits herself so dazzlingly that he not only forgives the interruption but is ready to suspend his own activity in order to admire her, and subsequently accepts her as his partner. What is notably omitted or denied in the movie fantasy is any rivalry of the aspiring girl performer with a mother-figure. The situation in which the girl interrupts the older man is desexualized, and her aim is confined to that of successful exhibition.

In *One Hundred Men and a Girl,* the girl who charms the famous conductor and wins the chance to appear with him is the only girl in the life of all the musicians (as the title suggests), and is besides too young to think about love. In *Because of Him,* the heroine is the only woman in the life of the aging actor. She is suspected of being his mistress, but this is one of those false appearances by which, as we have seen, forbidden wishes are denied. Eventually he falls in love with her; she rejects him, having satisfied her one real wish to appear on the stage with him. The public appearance together is substituted for, and explicitly excludes, the fulfilment of amorous wishes. Moreover, the girl's aims manifestly extend beyond the older man who, by giving her access to a performer's career, becomes no longer necessary to her. In *Stork Club,* the heroine's struggles to become a performer are complicated by the suspicion that she is involved both with her boss and with an elderly millionaire. However, these are comic misunderstandings; the wife of the millionaire suspects the girl only very briefly before becoming convinced of her innocence.

In a French film dealing with a similar theme, the young

girl's attempt to achieve a performer's career is fatally complicated by rivalry with an already established woman star. This star is the mistress of the famous producer who discovers the girl's talent. The star stands in the way of the girl's ascent and in the end defeats her. Thus as is typical in French films dealing with looking and exhibition, the envy, jealousy, rivalry and disappointment associated with the archetypal childhood situation are preserved, while in the corresponding American films they are eliminated.

The heroine in *Étoile sans Lumière* is a maid in a provincial inn, who happens to be endowed with a wonderful voice. A film producer and his mistress, a beautiful film star, are staying at the inn. The star is depressed as sound films have just been introduced and she fears she will no longer be a success in them. The director, struck by the maid's singing, conceives the idea of using her voice, dubbing it in for that of the star. He persuades the maid to come and work for them in Paris, and she is tricked into recording her voice without understanding the procedure. At the opening of the film, which she attends in her shabby maid's dress, she finally understands; she sees the star receiving everyone's acclaim for the beautiful voice which she has stolen from her maid. The maid now wants to reclaim her voice, but the star tells her contemptuously that she is too homely ever to be a success herself. The producer, who can always win her over if he is friendly and sits down with her to drink a bottle of wine, also persuades her not to make an issue of it. The star is killed in an auto accident, after which the grieving producer intensifies his persuasions to the girl; she must not destroy the image of the star in her last success. The girl nevertheless tries to make a debut as a singer. On the stage, she is haunted by the discouraging and protesting voices of the star and the producer, is unable to sing, and is hooted from the stage. She returns to her provincial town and the humble boy-friend who is still waiting for her. Where the corresponding American heroine could have the important older man if she wanted him, but prefers the young man (*Because of Him*), the French heroine disappointedly has this alternative forced upon her. Where the American heroine succeeds by dissociating her performance ambitions from Oedipal rivalry and jealousy, the French heroine fails because of the inextricable involvement of the two sets of motives. Also where the American girl controls and manipulates the situation, the French girl is caught unknowingly. She is precipitated into a performer's career which will lead to disappointment just as the heroes in French films are caught by a chance glimpse through a window, become involved with what they see and are led on to disappointment.

The American film heroine who becomes a successful performer through the magic contact is the counterpart of the comic hero who also achieves success as a performer without serious risks. Both resemble children who are the models for permitted self-exhibition. They are children conceived as free from any dangerous impulses. In the case of the comic hero, his harmlessness is assured by his lack of aggressive motivation and his ineptitude. The girl performer, more ambitious and more skilful (following the usual pattern of feminine superiority in achievements) is nevertheless harmless in her lack of Oedipal strivings. Deanna Durbin has been the main bearer of the girl-performer legend, repeatedly charming with her voice a prestigious father-figure who then facilitates her career (*One Hundred Men and a Girl, Because of Him,* etc.). As she has grown older the vocalizations by which she has successfully obtruded herself on the attention of a busy father have sometimes become increasingly infantile. In *For the Love of Mary,* she appears as a White House switchboard operator who wins the solicitous attention of the President by hiccoughing over the phone.

§ PLAYING THEMSELVES

BEFORE the movies it was not possible to see nearly so much of the lives of fictional characters. What novels could tell, movies can show. Walls drop away before the advancing camera. No character need disappear by going off-stage. The face of the heroine and the kiss of lovers are magnified for close inspection. The primal situation of excited and terrified looking, that of the child trying to see what happens at night, is re-created in the theater; the related wish to see everything is more nearly granted by the movies than by the stage. The movie audience is moreover insured against reaction or reproof from those whom they watch because the actors are incapable of seeing them. The onlooker becomes invisible. The possibility thus suggested of peering with impunity into other people's lives probably facilitates the wish to break through the fictional façade, to see the actors as they really are. This wish is to some extent offered satisfaction outside the films in the fan magazines which purport to reveal the private lives of the stars. It would also seem that the members of the audience tend to fuse the identity of the actor with that of his film role. In re-telling film plots, they are likely to use the names of the actors rather than the names of the characters they portray.

The ultimate fulfilment of the films' promise to reveal everything would be achieved if the actors were to play themselves. American films play with this possibility; actors do sometimes play themselves. This tendency to dispense with aesthetic illusion, and to promise satisfaction to simple looking impulses, seems peculiar to American films. In British films it is a rarity and in French films still more so. In an exceptional British film, *Holiday Camp,* Patricia Roc plays the movie star Patricia Roc judging a bathing beauty contest. This self-portrayal occurs in a film expressing the breakdown of the traditional British value of privacy. The scene is a crowded vacation camp whose inmates are organized into mass dancing and kissing games approximating Huxley's orgy-porgy forecasts. British films on the whole suggest considerable reticence about looking and exhibition; they seem to be much less occupied with these themes than either American or French films.

In French films we have noted the tendency to resolve the disappointments of the onlooker through a dramatic repetition of his experience. The audience, by watching the unhappy onlooker in the film, can put their own corresponding experiences at a distance. The onlooker in the film may in turn produce a play within the play repeating his tragedy. The French treatment of the looking theme thus tends towards an indefinitely receding series of aesthetic illusions, of plays within plays. The American enjoyment of looking, which is successfully dissociated from risks or painful feelings, works in the other direction. The possibility which the films afford to show the real thing is more likely to be pursued.

In half teasing side glimpses stars appear as themselves. In *Without Reservations,* the heroine's best-selling novel is about to be made into a movie and Cary Grant is mentioned as the probable male lead. When the heroine gets to Hollywood, we see her dancing with Cary Grant, played by Cary Grant. In *Two Guys from Milwaukee,* a young man who has frequently mentioned that Lauren Bacall is his favorite actress is stunned to find her in the seat next to his on an airplane. Humphrey Bogart immediately appears to oust the young man from his favorable position. In *Night and Day,* Monty Woolley plays Monty Woolley, enacting a version of his life which is said to resemble his life in part; while Mary Martin plays Mary Martin. Professional performers imported into films from other media are most likely to play themselves

(José Iturbi, Leopold Stokowski), but then they are themselves in their aspect as performers, and the promise of revealing something beyond the performer's role is unfulfilled. Occasionally also, actors portray, although in a fictional guise, the same relations to each other that they have in life. In *The Major and the Minor,* the mother of the girl played by Ginger Rogers is played by Ginger Rogers' mother. In *Adventure in Baltimore,* Shirley Temple and her husband play a couple of young lovers.

The temptation to break through the aesthetic illusion is generally countered by a tendency to build it up again. Where stars play themselves they are apt to produce an unsettling double image, an uncertainty about what is real, rather than a simple voyeuristic gratification. We may feel that Cary Grant playing himself, or Shirley Temple and her husband as young lovers, are playing fictionalized versions of themselves. The same perhaps applies to the revelations of fan magazines which present a set of plots different from, but just as stylized as those within the films. The process is a kind of strip tease in which as much is put on as is taken off.

The tendency to create uncertainty as to what is real by having actors play themselves is illustrated in a scene in *My Favorite Brunette.* The star, Bob Hope, is suddenly recalled to an awareness of his real life identity. He is rushing down a street where he passes Bing Crosby, who does not otherwise appear in the film, leaning against a wall. After passing Crosby, the hero has a startled reaction, as if suddenly surprised out of his play-acting to a realization: that's Bing Crosby, I'm Bob Hope. He goes back, stares for a moment at the unresponsive Crosby, then shrugs his shoulders with the remark, "It couldn't be," and goes on. Thus there is a reversal in the relative credibility of reality and make-believe. A similar unsettling effect is produced in a more implicit way by some of the instances just cited. When Cary Grant playing Cary Grant dances with Claudette Colbert who is playing a lady novelist, two realms of discourse suddenly interpenetrate. Cary Grant should recognize the equally famous star Claudette Colbert, but he accepts the convention that she is someone else. Since the real Cary Grant assures us that she is not Claudette Colbert, the impression of the reality of the fictional role is reënforced, and that of the reality of the actor playing himself reduced.

The opening of *Miss Tatlock's Millions* shows a violent fight in which a man is knocked down from a roof. The scene then widens, and we can see that this was part of a film that is being made. The fall from the roof has been doubly a pretense since it was enacted by a stunt-man, and the star, Ray Milland, now appears to continue with the less dangerous part of the action. The stunt-man, about to leave, is waylaid by an old man who wants to hire him for a job, and the two go out together to get a cup of coffee. We feel that now the real action begins, that is, the real fictional action of the private life of the stunt-man. The scene enacted in the studio was play-acting, a play within a play. But part of what we saw in the studio was also real; Ray Milland appeared as Ray Milland. However, we may suspect that this was not a real film that we saw being shot, but a pretense of film-making to provide the opening of the present film. Thus again, where an actor appears as himself, there is an unsettling of reality orientation.

In American films the tendency towards revealing everything is particularly marked. But just as it seems that the wishes of the insatiable onlookers are about to be gratified, a final defense is interposed in the suggestion that the real thing is not real at all. The onlooker, anticipating the final revelation as the star is called by his real name, is dazzled by an interplay between the real and make-believe, baffled in his wish to penetrate the mystery, and left uncertain as to what is the reality he wanted to see.

CONCLUSION

DRAMATIC PRODUCTIONS may show human fate in various ways. The story may be of love and we may see the happy lovers joined as in a dream while seeming obstacles melt away before them. Or love may contend with other powerful motives in the lover, or be opposed by strong antagonists. Love may overstep the bounds of licit choice. Lovers who defy the law to come together may be overwhelmed by punishers who overtake them or by their own conscience. Or conscience may run on ahead of longing, chastening their wishes and sending them apart without their ever having been together. Rivals in love may be brought into deadly conflict, or to renunciation. The lover may find he is not loved in return; his love may change to rage or self-destruction, or he may find someone else. And so again confusion may be sorted out and each one find a partner.

Thus wishes working their way through various hazards may win happy fulfilment, may be denied, or may by being fulfilled bring down hard penalties. The plot may be of violence, and we may see the hero carrying out acts we wish but dread to do. He commits the dreamed-of crime but also bears its awful recompense. Or injury may justify his deeds, or call for deeds he cannot bring himself to do. Battles may be won or lost; victory may be dimmed by regrets for the loser, or gladdened by assurance of a righteous cause. Justice may be done or may miscarry. We may feel both triumph and pain as we see the hero undergo inevitable punishment for his rash deeds. Or we may see the fallibility of human justice as misplaced penalties fall on the innocent.

The world may appear in various aspects, as beautiful or dangerous or sordid, ruled over by benign or punitive gods or none at all. The main point of the drama may be not to exhibit conflicts between protagonists who may win or lose but to show the opposition of human wishes to the nature of life itself. The contest becomes one in which we all lose in the end, and the aim of the drama may be to reconcile us to this eventuality.

The dramatic productions of a particular culture at a particular time, or even over a considerable period, tend to exhibit a distinctive plot configuration. This configuration gives the various individual dramas the distinctive atmosphere which we can recognize as pervading them all. Obviously a group of plots or even a single plot is exceedingly complex. Nevertheless a certain basic plan may be discerned; we can see that one pattern from among the range of dramatic alternatives has been chosen for major emphasis.

Looking back over the films which we have been discussing, we shall now indicate briefly the essential plot configuration which distinguishes each of the three groups of films with which we have been concerned, the British, the French, and the American.

The essential plot in British films is that of the conflict of forbidden impulses with conscience. Either one of the contending forces may win out and we may follow the guilt-ridden course of the wrong-doer or experience the regrets of the lost opportunity virtuously renounced. In the happy instance, wishes may coincide with the demands of virtue and a fatherly fate will reward the good children. The world is presided over by authorities who are wise and good and against whom the wilful and unlucky may contend. But the counterpart of these authorities is also implanted in the individual soul; the evil-doer will be self-condemned as well as pursued by the authorities.

British films evoke the feeling that danger lies in ourselves, especially in our impulses of destructiveness. In a cautionary way they show what happens if these impulses break through, particularly where the weak become the victims. Thus they afford a catharsis at the same time that they demonstrate the value of defenses by showing the consequences of their giving way. The character who embodies dangerous impulses is apt to be a superior person, one who should be able to control his own destructiveness, and in whom it is all the more terrible to see it get out of hand. Violence is not simply a destructive force but a breaking both of the pattern within the individual personality and of the order which prevails in his world. The complete murderer is one who disputes the rule of just authorities, in his pride setting himself up as an arbiter of life and death, and doomed by his own struggle. While violence is on one side related to a whole social framework, it has also another side of intimacy and isolation. The act of violence is slowly prepared and may be preceded by special closeness between murderer and victim. Violence is thus often pervaded by the tenderness which in ordinary circumstances serves to ward it off.

Self-accusation is prominent in British films and may be

evoked by wishes no less than by acts. Characters feel guilty when circumstances beyond their control produce fatalities coinciding with unconscious wishes. Lovers tempted to overstep lawful bounds draw back alarmed by guilty apprehensions. However, the pure in heart find that the authorities of this world and the next are their allies. The hero, temporarily distressed by a false charge, discovers that the police know all along that he is innocent and are quietly working side by side with him. The fine young couple who for the moment fear that fate has brought them together only to separate them learn that even death can be set aside so that they can be joined.

British films preserve, in a modern idiom (the peculiarities of which we shall not analyze here), many of the themes of Shakespearean drama. There are heroes who like Macbeth are carried away by criminal impulses and then punished; heroes who like Hamlet suffer pangs of conscience for crimes they did not commit. And there are young couples briefly and playfully threatened by the same fate which intended all along to wed them as Prospero did with his daughter and Ferdinand. The image of a perfect father, like Hamlet Sr., still presides over the scene, and constitutes the model for an exacting conscience.

In the major plot configuration of French films, human wishes are opposed by the nature of life itself. The main issue is not one of inner or outer conflicts in which we may win or lose, be virtuous or get penalized. It is a contest in which we all lose in the end and the problem is to learn to accept it. There are inevitable love disappointments, the world is not arranged to collaborate with our wishes, people grow older, lovers become fathers, the old must give way to the young, and eventually everyone dies. The desire for justice is ranged alongside other human wishes which are more likely than not to be frustrated. French films repeatedly present these aspects of life so that we may inure ourselves to them and master the pain they cause us. It is the Mithridates principle of taking a little poison every day so that by and by one becomes less vulnerable to it.

It is in keeping with this tendency that French films so often take as their central character an aging man. He is not the triumphant hero whom we wish to become nor the criminal hero whom we fear to become, but simply what we must become: old. In him we see concentrated disappointment, lost hopes, change, decline of physical powers, and imminent death. We can observe his sadly comic struggle against his fate as he refuses to realize that he is no longer eligible to be the lover of a young girl, or learn from him the compensations of later life as he renounces the role of lover for that of father. He helps to reconcile us both to our past and to our future. We see in him our own father no longer dominant and powerful but a sharer of our common human fate. He who was in possession of things which we as children were denied is now seen suffering disappointments more grievous than we suffered then. In making peace with him we also make peace with our own future.

The young hero no less than the aging one in French films is likely to be disappointed. We see him in his pursuit of a beloved woman about whom he gradually learns much that is contrary to his wishes. He is not spared the discovery that this woman is involved with another man, and we in following his fate may work through our own similar disillusionments. Knowledge which at first glance increases sorrow in the end mitigates the pain which, we see, could not be avoided.

We must learn that the world is not arranged to fulfil our demands for justice any more than to satisfy our longings for happiness. Human agencies of justice are obtuse and inefficient, and there are no divine ones. We are shown how the innocent are convicted, how the guilty are exonerated; they may even confess without being believed. Where justice is done, it is made clear that this is a happy accident. A clue uncovered by chance a moment earlier or later makes the difference between life and death for an innocent man. No one is watching over him, nor is he able to be the master of his own fate. Things may turn out happily. The suicidal bullet misses, the brain tumor may be operable, the hostages facing execution may be rescued at the last moment, the aging couple may find an unexpected revival of pleasure in life. The pleasure, no less sweet for that, is tinged with sadness; we know it is only a reprieve.

The major plot configuration in American films contrasts with both the British and the French. Winning is terrifically important and always possible though it may be a tough fight. The conflict is not an internal one; it is not our own impulses which endanger us nor our own scruples that stand in our way. The hazards are all external, but they are not rooted in the nature of life itself. They are the hazards of a particular situation with which we find ourselves confronted. The hero is typically in a strange town where there are apt to be dangerous men and women of ambiguous character and where the forces of law and order are not to be relied on. If he sizes up the situation correctly, if he does not go off half-cocked but is still able to beat the other fellow to the punch once he is sure who the enemy is, if he relies on no one but himself, if he demands sufficient evidence of virtue from the girl, he will emerge triumphant. He will defeat the dangerous men, get the right girl, and show the authorities what's what.

When he is a child, he is the comic hero, showing off, blundering, cocky, scared, called on to perform beyond his capacities, and pulling through by surprising spurts of activity and with the help of favorable circumstances. He is completely harmless, free from sexual or aggressive impulses, and the world around him reflects his own innocuous character. Its threats are playful and its reproaches ridiculous. When he is a man he is the melodrama hero and the world changes to reflect his changed potentialities; it becomes dangerous and seriously accusing, and launches him on his fighting career. The majority of the melodramas show him coming through successfully. A minority reveal various perils which lie off the main track; they are cautionary tales. The hero may succumb to his attacker; this is his bad dream. The men around him may be less dangerous than he suspects. Under the delusion that he attacks in self-defense, he may initiate hostilities; then he will lose. In this case he is crazy. Without being deluded to this extent, out of greed and overconfidence, he may try to get away with murder; he commits the crime of which he is usually only suspected and he has to pay for it. The girl may turn out to be worse than he believed. He will have to go off without her; then he is lonely. He may not be able to produce anyone on whom to pin the blame for the crimes of which he is falsely accused; then he is a victim of circumstances. If circumstances fail to collaborate with his need to blame someone else, he may even end by blaming himself. These are the various hazards which the usual melodrama hero safely passes on the way.

The fantasy which provides for defeating dangerous men, winning the right girl, and coming out in the clear, is produced under the auspices of two major mechanisms: projection and denial. Self-accusations are embodied in the blundering police and destructive impulses in the unprovoked attacker. The beloved woman seems to be involved with another man but investigation ends in the gratifying demonstration that she never loved anyone but the hero. The love disappointment to which the French movie hero is repeatedly exposed is here denied.

The external world may be dangerous but manageable, or, at other times, uncontrollable but gratifying. Where things seem to get out of control the results turn out to be wish-fulfilling. The overturning automobile throws the girl into the hero's arms, the rocking boat tosses the heroine's rival into the waves. The world that is uncontrollable but gratifying expresses an omnipotence fantasy while at the same time eliminating guilt. As soon as an internal problem is replaced by an external one, we can see the promise of success. The hero suffering from kleptomania becomes involved in investigating the activities of a gang of thieves; the amnesiac hero pursues his memories only long enough to unearth clues of someone else's crime before he rises impatiently from the psychiatrist's couch to embark on a successful detective job.

The world, which is not effectively policed, does not need to be policed at all. The hero, the self-appointed investigator and agent of justice, is able to set things right independently. The world thus appears as a kind of workable anarchic arrangement where, although hostilities are far from eliminated, life need not be nasty, brutish, and short, at any rate not for anyone we care about. The unofficial supervisors of private morals, the comic onlookers, are just as superfluous as the police. No one has any intention of doing anything naughty; only the mistakenly suspicious onlooker fails to recognize the natural goodness of the clean-cut young people.

American film plots are pervaded by false appearances. In this shadowy but temporarily vivid guise, the content of what is projected and denied tends to reappear. It is in false appearances that the forbidden wishes are realized which the hero and heroine so rarely carry into action. In a false appearance the heroine is promiscuous, the hero is a murderer, the young couple carry on an illicit affair, two men friends share the favors of a woman. This device makes it possible for us to eat our cake and have it, since we can enjoy the suggested wish-fulfilments without empathic guilt; we know that the characters with whom we identify have not done anything. The contention of American films is that we should not feel guilty for mere wishes. The hero and heroine are threatened with penalties for the incriminating appearance but in the end are absolved. The misguided police or the foolish onlooker in comedies convey a self-accusation from which the hero and heroine struggle to dissociate themselves, a vestige of archaic conscience which is to be dispensed with.

What the plot unfolds is a process of proof. Something is undone rather than done: the false appearance is negated. The hero and heroine do not become committed to any irretrievable act whose consequences they must bear. Nor do they usually undergo any character transformation, ennoblement or degradation, gain or loss of hope, acceptance of a new role or the diminution and regrets of age. They succeed in proving what they were all along. They emerge from the shadow of the false appearance. What has changed is other people's impressions of them. In so far as the hero and heroine may be unsure of who or what they are except as they see themselves mirrored in the eyes of others, they have succeeded in establishing for themselves a desirable identity. In so far as they struggle against a projected archaic conscience that persecutes the wish as if it were the act, they win a victory for a more tolerant and discriminating morality.

NOTE ON DATA AND INTERPRETATIONS

THE GENERALIZATIONS in this book are based on the American movies appearing since the latter part of 1945, which are listed in the index, and on a group of contemporary British and French films also listed there. We analyzed all the American A-films with a contemporary urban setting which were released in New York City for the year following September 1, 1945. Quantitative statements about American movies refer to this group. Since melodramas had proved to contain particularly significant material, we further analyzed all the American A melodramas released in New York City from September 1, 1946, to January 1, 1948. We have also attempted to take account of developments in American films generally in 1948–1949.

Our statements about films fall into three classes which should be distinguished since they represent different degrees of confirmation. First there are statements about the manifest themes in the films which we have studied. These are the most frequent and the best confirmed. We have looked for the recurrent or "typical" themes within each of the three groups of films, American, British, and French. Let us clarify briefly what is implied or not implied in calling a theme typical. To say that a particular theme or manner of treatment is typical for American films is not to say that it admits of no exceptions. There are, for example, certain relatively infrequent plot modes which deviate from the usual pattern, but which, as we try to show, are systematically related to it. When we say that a theme is typical for American films, we refer to the period of time on which our analysis has concentrated. We do not imply that it was typical of the past or that it will necessarily remain so in the future. Occasionally we have indicated by a retrospective comparison how certain current themes differ from those of earlier films. The contrasts which we draw between American films and British and French films do not preclude similarities. To say that a particular theme is typical for American films is thus not to deny that it may also occur in British, French, or other films. What is apt to be unique is the total configuration of themes. Comparing films of various cultures as we do here does not imply that films in these cultures occupy the same position between "low" and "high" art. It is possible that some of the discrepancies between films of different cultures are related to this factor. But then cultures presumably differ in the distance which separates high and low art within them. For example, it seems likely that this distance is greater in contemporary American than in contemporary French culture.

A second class of statements contains guesses about the psychological processes of movie makers and audiences to account for the emotional significance of recurrent themes. We have based these interpretations on psychoanalytic psychology. Let us take, for example, the frequent American melodrama plot in which the innocent hero is attacked and falsely accused. We have applied to this the psychoanalytic finding of a connection between delusions of persecution and the projection of one's own forbidden impulses and self-accusations. The tension of inner conflict is replaced by anxieties about external dangers as both the accusations of conscience and the threat of uncontrollable impulses are experienced as coming from outside. Assuming that movie makers and audiences identify with the melodrama hero, they may find relief from guilt about forbidden impulses through the fantasy that the hero is free from these impulses, which are attributed exclusively to those around him. Guilt feelings, also projected, assume the appearance of false accusations from which the hero eventually escapes by proving someone else to be the criminal. Of course these film plots differ from persecutory delusions, as movie makers and audiences understand them to be make-believe and do not confuse them with real life. When we say that the mechanism of projection is operative in the formation of this type of plot we are making the guess that certain emotions of the film makers and audiences are being handled by this mechanism in the construction of, and participation in the fantasy. Such statements are obviously less confirmed than our statements about manifest plot constellations. Research into the psychological processes of movie makers and audiences, on various levels of depth, would be required to validate them.

In a third class of statements we have, occasionally, made certain assumptions about real life patterns in American culture and attempted to connect them with some of the movie themes and their emotional bases. This class of statements, containing the greatest number of hypothetical connections, is the least confirmed. We have attempted in some places to trace themes back to childhood experiences. In so doing we assume that such experiences are relevant; we do not imply that they are exclusively so. In general, wherever we relate a theme to an emotional meaning or to a real life experience, we do not imply that the factors invoked are its sole determinants.

We should not expect the relation between movies and real life to be one of simple correspondence. Thus we would not, as foreigners occasionally do, infer from American films that gangster hostilities are the major preoccupation of urban life, or that life-and-death chases in high-powered cars constitute the main traffic on the highways. Nor would we, as American critics sometimes do, criticize the films for not presenting an accurate reproduction of manners and customs. Rather we expect to find in these ready-made day-dreams an interplay of real life experience with the hopes and fears it awakens, the wishes it encourages or rebukes. For instance, in American movie melodramas, we find as a recurrent theme that the hero is loved by the heroine, who has never loved anyone but him, while he remains in doubt about how good she is and holds his love in suspense. We would see in this movie theme, among other things, a rectification and reversal of the experience of American boys with their exacting mothers. The film hero, in relation to the woman he loves, gets the assurance of being loved unconditionally, while he withholds his love pending investigation of her merits. In this case the relation between a movie theme and one of its probable real life sources is a reversal rather than a reproduction. In some instances the resemblance between film and life may be closer, in others more remote.

The ways in which movies pattern the expression of impulses such as those of hostility which are strongly interfered with in real life can yield many clues to an understanding of the culture in which the movies are produced. There are many different ways of interfering with the all-out hostility which would make social life impossible. These ways of repressing or re-channeling hostility will depend on the image of what would happen if hostility were fully unleashed. Movies show us what some of these images are. British films, for instance, are repeatedly preoccupied with the victimization of the weak, particularly of women. This seems to be one of their major images of the form destructiveness would take if it were not blocked. In American films, nobody is weak, certainly not women. A major form of violence is that of hostilities between men in which the hero will be beaten if a sufficient number of his opponents gang up on him, but will recover to win whenever the odds are not overpoweringly against him. These differing images of the hazards of violence probably contribute to the different ways in which destructive impulses are controlled in real life. The British tendency to transmute destructiveness into its opposite, tenderness for the weak, as shown for instance in the prominent concern with the prevention of cruelty to animals, seems related to the image, as seen in the films, of destructiveness being aimed particularly at the weak. The different image of violence that we get in American films would find its counterpart in different real life attitudes. The cultivation of toughness rather than tenderness seems appropriate where the danger of violence is imagined as a possible attack which one must be ready to meet. The ready-made day-dreams of movies are thus related although in quite complicated ways to the larger pattern of the culture of which they form a part.

INDEX OF FILMS

INDEX OF FILMS

* American A-films released in New York City during the year following
September 1, 1945.

Br. British   *Fr.* French

MARTHA WOLFENSTEIN is Associate Clinical Professor of Psychiatry at Albert Einstein College of Medicine, New York. Her books include *Children's Humor* and *Childhood in Contemporary Cultures,* co-edited with Margaret Mead.

NATHAN LEITES is Professor of Political Science at the University of Chicago. He is the author of *A Study of Bolshevism* and *The Rules of the Game in Paris.*

Atheneum Paperbacks

Atheneum Paperbacks